Jennifer Lane is a green witch a[...] in wildlife communications. As a [...] the *Guardian* and the BBC, pron[...] [...]nts of nature, birdwatching and living in tune with the land. In 2018, she won a Northern Writers' Award. Jennifer is based near Manchester with her partner and a calico cat called Linnet. IG: @thegreenwitchwriter

Praise for *The Wheel*:

'In short – it's a book that has grabbed me by my very core and inspired me to make some long-awaited changes in my own life . . . More than a spiritual guide for modern-day witches, this book calls for all of us to pay more attention to the world around us . . . Jennifer's passion for this subject emanates from the page, pulling the reader in so that we begin to look at the trees around us through her eyes, with that child-like sense of wonder. It's a joyous and magickal experience.'

Carly Tremayne, *The Folklore Podcast*

'Jennifer Lane's writing is sincere, tender and rich with wonderment, empowering her readers to resist a conventional existence and look deeper into the heart of nature.'

Tiffany Francis, author of *Dark Skies*

'Skilfully written, remarkably honest and bravely open . . . I very much hope *The Wheel* finds its way into the hands of a wide range of readers, from naturalists to practitioners of modern witchcraft and modern Druidry, from those finding themselves stuck in occupations or even lives that don't particularly suit them to those who suffer from the often difficult-to-explain but all too real effects of anxiety and similar conditions that place very much unwanted limitations on their daily lives.' @WRNBookReview

'This fascinating and engaging read will satisfy the reading curiosity of anyone who has an interest in witchcraft, pagan paths, or those who miss nature in their stressful daily lives.' LoveReading.co.uk

'*The Wheel* is such a beautiful, tender book. It is a truly soul-soothing read which takes a reader on a journey of (self-) discovery through wild landscapes of the British Isles filled with wonderment, gentleness and magic . . . Highly recommended.' @the_exiled_soul_reads

'Engaging and thoughtful.' @halfmanhalfb00k

'Jennifer Lane casts a contrary nature spell over her readers, full of glitter and acorns, fire and firecrests.'

Derek Niemann, country diarist, *Guardian*

JENNIFER LANE

THE
WHEEL

A WITCH'S PATH TO
HEALING THROUGH NATURE

1 3 5 7 9 10 8 6 4 2

This massmarket paperback published in 2022 by September Publishing
First published in 2021 by September Publishing

Copyright © Jennifer Lane 2021

The right of Jennifer Lane to be identified as the author of this work has been asserted
by her in accordance with the Copyright Designs and Patents Act 1988.

All rights reserved. No part of this publication may be reproduced, stored in a retrieval
system, or transmitted in any form or by any means, electronic, mechanical, photocopying,
recording or otherwise, without the prior permission of the copyright holder

Wheel illustration on page xi by Leo Nickolls

Typeset by RefineCatch Limited. www.refinecatch.com

Printed in Denmark on paper from responsibly managed, sustainable sources by Nørhaven

ISBN 9781914613203
EPUB ISBN 9781912836925

September Publishing
www.septemberpublishing.org

To Em, Lottie and April – my witchy sisters

CONTENTS

'[Magic] is something built into the universe. Hence, there is nothing really supernatural or supernormal, in the strict sense of these words. All is part of nature; but much of the realm of nature is "occult", that is, hidden.'

Doreen Valiente, *Natural Magic*, 1975

'Though this is sometimes a lonely path, it leads to places of great beauty.'

Rae Beth, *Hedge Witch*, 1990

OPENING

31 October

'Yarrow for vision, mugwort for foresight. Cerridwen, I am ready; show me your wisdom, show me what I must do.'

My eyelids feel heavy with candle wax. The bathwater is up to my collarbones, spilling over the ridges to form soft, milky pools below my shoulders. In the low light, a drift of mist carries the scent of herbs and the bathroom tiles vibrate with the sound of my exhale until I am in an echo chamber of breath.

I really hope the cat doesn't come crashing in.

Trick or treaters muster in the darkened streets below me. In my mind's eye, I watch their painted faces squeal and cackle under the street lamps. Their parents have worked so hard on the Dracula make-up and bumpy warts – 'Hold still!' Now, mums and dads stand a few paces away in their slippers planning to swipe a few Haribo when the kids are in bed. Once their buckets are filled, the children trundle off down the street to the next house like a troop of eerie orphans.

This is the usual way of Samhain night, Halloween; the night when the veil between our world and the spirit realms is at its thinnest. We pull ghoulish faces with the torchlight under our chins. We tell ghost stories under the covers. Children will check under their beds more than once tonight. In Mexico, people are making their costumes for the *Día de los Muertos*, painting neon white skulls onto papier mâché, ready to dance for their passed loved ones in a colourful carnival. Across the world, bouquets sit in the hallway, soon to make their way to the graveyard. We might have turned Halloween away from its more macabre traditions and into an orange-and-black plastic parade, but there is still a darkness to this time of year; one that witches revere.

All the witches are celebrating tonight.

In my ritual bath, I slip in and out of a meditative state. The candles flash shadows on my skin like I am a spectral being myself.

Samhain (pronounced *'SOW-in'* or *'SOW-een'*, with *'sow'* as in *'how'*) is an ancient Celtic fire festival, a night when ghosts and goblins would roam the village in the flicker of the samhnagan or ceremonial bonfire. Quick, put a mirror in your window to ward off the demons; pile salt on your doorstep to keep the bogeys at bay! Fix a rowan branch across your latch to protect the house from evil witches. The shadowy things of this world and the next are out in their numbers, riding on a wave of power. On Samhain, the thrum of magick is in our fingertips.

But Samhain is more than just a chill down your spine.

This is the most important day of the Celtic calendar – the witches' New Year. It is the time when we all must turn inwards to face the darkness of the coming months, where we will stay throughout winter until the green world is reborn in spring. Just as the Earth is closer to the sun on the summer solstice, Midsummer's Day, so we are closest to the underworld on Halloween. Over many centuries, people have used this day to commune with spirits, goddesses and their ancestors, taking full advantage of the thin slip of fabric dividing the worlds to divine the future and get answers to life's most difficult questions.

Right this second, modern Pagans and witches are raising their arms to the sky or sitting in quiet meditation engulfed by the flickering of the candle flame. We welcome in the Goddess of the colder months, the wizened crone of darkening days; the one who stirs her cauldron in the deep wildwood and has a voice that rasps from her throat like a slowly drawn match. She is Cerridwen, the Keeper of the Gate to the underworld; she is Grandmother Time with her smile that knows our past, present and what will come to pass. Her wisdom will keep us safe as we bury ourselves in the dark womb of winter. Tonight we raise our energies to the moon, to the Goddess and to the dead. Tonight, the world is preparing to be reborn.

But, right now in my bathwater, I feel like I'm barely in this world. I'm floating. The steamy mist, like glowing moonstone, is thick around my head. Tonight, I ask the Goddess to guide me, to show me what I must do next.

'Cerridwen, the great Wheel turns and the year renews; show me your wisdom, show me what I must do.'

I close my eyes and my perception shifts, as though my eyes have sunk back into the shadow of my skull. In a rush, I dream of the woods. I'm soaring over the pine tops among an outcrop of startled crows, feeling the low cloud trail in my long hair. I dream of moss-heavy rocks, my feet skimming sticky ferns, and I see the grey-haired Goddess with her hand outstretched over her cauldron.

She is smiling at me.

YULE

Witchcraft, it's been a while.

Over the past few years, witchcraft and I have drifted apart, like two weird childhood friends that always promised to live two doors down from one another until one family decided to up sticks and move to Skegness. We didn't have a falling out, no fights or pinching under the table; but my life took a different path for a little while, so witchcraft and I had a break.

Thrust into the adult world where I found myself as a copywriter, sub-editor and sometime librarian, things got a little busy. Most of my time was spent in offices with pipes that creaked and air con systems that sometimes gave up the ghost on the hottest day of the year. I was an employee now, reliant on showing up to my day job to afford my little rooms in city-centre flat shares. Evenings weren't spent reading about ancient runes under the covers until after midnight as had been the case in my teenage years and early twenties; they were spent filling in job applications and scrubbing mysterious stains off the kitchen worktop. Things were a little less magical now.

But how could I ever forget the quiet coils of witchcraft?

Ever since childhood, I had found myself drawn to the slightly stranger things in life. At seven years old, whenever it was my turn to choose what game we played, it was always 'Witches'. If we weren't stirring imaginary cauldrons in the corner of the schoolyard and sending bats off to do our dirty work, I wasn't interested. At home, I dressed up with green plastic fingers covering my own and I would wear my mum's old black skirts as cloaks, straddling the big old broomstick from my grandma's garage. It was all a lot of silliness, a bit of fun, but as I grew older the idea of magic and being able to influence the world around you with the twitch of a nose or the flick of a finger became very appealing. Especially as I was a quiet girl who wouldn't put up her hand in class for fear of the teacher saying, 'No, anyone else?' I yearned for magic to be real with a longing that was slightly unhinged, and for a tawny owl to squeeze itself through the classroom window and tell me I was Hermione Granger 2.0.

When I hit my teens and discovered the mystical powers of the internet, I found that the other world I craved was very real. I *could* actually be a witch if I wanted to, minus the flying broomsticks.

For many years, I practised Wicca, a form of 'white' witchcraft, in secret in my room and in quiet places within nature. It was an invisible veil I wore over my skin; part of my identity that people could only guess at. But as I got older, there seemed to be fewer hours in the day; I was tired at the end of the working week and those dishes weren't going to do themselves. There were press releases to finish and trains to catch, conferences to attend and flats to view. People say you 'make time for the things you love', but I didn't know where these folk found the wormhole that could materialise extra minutes. I slowly found my time in nature decreasing and my hours in front of a screen engulfing most of my daylight hours – and there was nothing less witchy than a swivel chair.

In late autumn 2018, I realised that some things in my life just weren't working. I was always tired, my hair peeled away from my scalp in spidery tendrils that clogged up the shower drain, and my joints ached a lot more than I thought they would at twenty-eight years old. Maybe I'd missed the memo and everyone worked very hard to keep their limbs, hair and nails clamped to their body as they approached thirty. But it wasn't just the physical falling apart that bothered me. Staring out of the window of my then workplace – across the car park, over to the nearest fast-food joint and then on to the next grey expanse of concrete beyond that – I would stand and search for the nearest speck of green. Two hundred years ago, a bird would have flown over the same area to see a patchwork of fields and peat bog, home to species of butterfly and vole that have long since fled the urban sprawl of Manchester. Now, that same bird would have to fly quadruple the distance to find a tree to rest in; the perfectly planned symmetry of a tarmacked car park not offering much in terms of a hopeful meal. Maybe birds liked popcorn chicken, I wasn't sure. Up in my office, no natural air could enter the second-floor room unless the glass was smacked with an emergency escape mallet. To my horror, the police had recently visited the dual-carriageway bridge visible from this same window to haul a suicidal man back from plummeting thirty feet over the edge. We all watched it happen.

How had I ended up here, sandwiched violently between a drive-thru KFC and a local jumping spot?

Before I took the role just over a year earlier, I had been a full-time freelance environmental journalist and had been doing pretty well, but I took on the full-time job to get myself out of the flat and back into the realms of social interaction. Working at home was all well and good, but sometimes the overwhelming pull of the biscuit tin could be a bit too much and, as much of an introvert as I am, seeing another living, breathing human more than once a day was actually quite nice. So, I was back in the rat race. Commute. Nine to five-thirty. Commute. Sleep. Losing my vision in the fug of blue light and fluorescent glare, I soon realised that this new direction hadn't been what I needed. Not what I had needed at all.

I couldn't deny it by this point, I was depressed. Panic attacks rocked my nervous system, leaving me shaky for weeks on end, and seasonal affective disorder (SAD) made my mood dip lower each day as we got closer to winter. But there was much more to it than just the early sunsets and dark skies. I was sad with the nine-to-five-thirty structure of the day, the declarations of climate emergencies lighting up phones across the world and the streams of faces devoid of wonder pouring from the bus station each morning. Every evening on the way home, I blotted out my day with nuggets of sunshine I had stored up in my head from years' worth of summer hikes: the path down to the river bordered by red campion; a walk across the clifftops, where the clear sea air was so rich that I would sleep for eleven hours afterwards. I had always felt this draw to greenery and the small creatures within it. When my peers were at their ballet and tap classes, I was lying under the pear tree in my grandparents' garden, trying to spot their resident greenfinches through an ancient pair of binoculars. I would imagine fairies among their fuchsia patch and every touch of light breeze was that of some beautiful goddess trying to comb my hair. These small golden droplets of nature in my memory had been keeping me going for some time, fuelling my quickstep walks down city alleyways. But the splutter of cars and planes was drawing me away from the green core in my heart. In among the screen-glare headaches and sardine-crammed tram journeys through the city, I began to realise with horror how much I had fallen out of touch with my nature-loving roots and the Pagan path I had studied with so much joy and curiosity for almost fifteen years. I found that key festivals, such as Ostara and Samhain, would jump out at me from nowhere; my chaotic mind meaning I'd prepared nothing whatsoever. Solstices and equinoxes went by without so much as a second thought. There was no joy, no celebration. It was like Christmas with beans on toast and all the gifts still in their Amazon boxes. I wondered how I had let it get to this point.

My spiritual connection with the world in my late twenties was in tatters.

Witchcraft, something so closely bound up with my appreciation of the natural world, called to me. No nightmares or screaming cackles; witchcraft had always been a part of me, long before I learned how to articulate my attachment to nature and find the secret spots filled only with birdsong. But as my bond with the natural world had frayed, so did my love of all things magical. I had called myself a witch for a long time, but I had been out of the loop for about two years – almost twenty-six turns of the moon, eight seasons of wandering on this Earth without feeling the world vibrate under my bare feet, without once speaking to my Goddess, Mother Nature, who I loved so dearly.

*

'Your bloods all came back normal. You're really, really healthy.'

He gives a little chuckle of disbelief and I look at Dr Khalid blankly. I think he's misunderstanding here.

'Sorry, but all my symptoms would say otherwise.' I'm being tart and I know it.

'Jennifer, your ferritin is normal, your blood count is great, your B12 is excessively high; almost above a normal range. Potassium, sodium, blood pressure, haemoglobin. There's nothing here to explain your symptoms. On a physical level, you are, enviably, above averagely healthy.'

I look down at my hands, past the cannula sticking out of my left arm. There is a smear of translucent blood below it. 'So . . .'

'So, what does it mean?'

I nod, wearily. 'What's the matter with me?'

'It sounds to me like you have an anxiety disorder.' I open my mouth but Dr Khalid raises his head slightly and continues. 'It might seem like this is a very physical problem and if you had rung us beforehand and explained your symptoms, I would *absolutely* have said come straight to A&E as soon as possible. But these are all also very clear symptoms of anxiety.'

We're so deep in autumn right now that the bright colours have turned to pavement sludge outside North Manchester General. My hands are slack on my lap in the triage room. The doctors have been telling me this line for months – you're anxious, stressed, you need to *relax*. I've seen naturopaths, three different GPs and several thousand A&E doctors. But how can anxiety be causing my exhaustion, my thirteen-hour naps, the sore joints, the fainting, the bald patches on my scalp, the tingling through my hands and feet, the migraines, the blind patches in my left eye and the memory loss? Hadn't I just a few days previously woken from a nap and lain still for a further hour because I was too shattered to leave my bed? It. Didn't. Make. Sense. These all must be symptoms of a blood disorder, an extreme vitamin deficiency, a rare form of bone cancer; something wrong that I can fix with a lifelong course of drugs.

They must be.

It's not that I want to be ill; I just want an explanation. I think back to the other time in my life when I had symptoms similar to this. A few years ago when I started a job I hated, the very job that had triggered my transition into the full-time freelance world, I would walk into the building and feel the swell of nausea beating the bottom of my ribcage and the idea of taking off my headphones to talk to anyone made my eyes flare in panic. It wasn't that my office comrades were 'bad' in some way or that the work shredded my brain with its complexity; it was a feeling deep in my gut that had its own voice and that voice was screaming, 'Unsafe! Unsafe!' Anxiety or intuition? I'm unsure. But now, in another role that makes me feel physically sick with fear, is it any wonder that these symptoms are rearing their troublesome heads again?

The doctors are right.

I can't believe how ignorant I've been. The Senior House Officer shows me my B12 levels – bordering on that of Usain Bolt – and my iron. I'm fine. More than fine. I'm seriously healthy by the standards of western medicine. Physically, anyway. I do a lot of exercise, I eat a mainly vegan diet; I do my 10,000 steps a day without fail. But, I think back, when was the last time I had spent time in nature? Could it really have been longer than two months ago, three? For almost a year since I returned to office life, my life has not been defined by the nature that I had always prioritised in the past; full days from dawn till dusk at nature reserves, out on the crags, peering at wagtails through my binoculars and finding hidden patches of long grass to hunker down in and eat my sandwiches. I hadn't had my daily dose of lurking frogs and chirruping goldfinch flocks for so long now. I hadn't sat on a bank of moss and grounded my energy into the earth. Instead of wildflower meadows, my dreams were now often preoccupied with train timetables and unsaved Word documents. Where had all the wildlife gone from my life?

A 2011 study from the University of Houston confirms some of my feelings about the office. According to the research, our constant report writing, fidgeting with emails and the general multi-tasking required in the office environment can lead to feelings of fear and sadness, and can create emotions that have a negative consequence on the whole workplace:

> *Emotional contagion can spread in a group or workplace [in an open-plan office] through the influence of conscious or unconscious processes involving emotional states or physiological responses.*[1]

Bad bosses, towering workloads and the frazzle of the digital world all contribute to us feeling like nervous wrecks and, while we have all experienced some stress at work to a varying degree, how many people have you known who've had to get signed off work just so they can get their heads back together again? You might recognise the feeling – the seeping dread, the wide-eyed panic, the dawdling outside the front door at 8.58 a.m.; that's how it all starts. Another recent study shows that half of all sick days taken in the UK are related to workplace stress.[2]

But the real issue is that none of us, not a single person on this planet, was destined for office life. These kinds of work environments became popularised then normalised in the first half of the twentieth century, with the nine-to-five structure formalised by Henry Ford for his workers in 1926.[3] The culture of 'meetings' that we know today rose into being in the 1950s. As populations grew, so did the need for a more structured economic system; advertising and marketing grew to keep people buying the same things as the Joneses down the street, the two-by-five cubicle became the most efficient way to pack us in and keep us productive. Surely this life was paradise after decades of mills and smog? But as our means of earning money since the industrial revolution have expanded into job titles once unimaginable, so our access to bathroom breaks, conversation and natural light has diminished.

We have adopted florescent strip lighting as a mocking reminder of our circadian rhythms. We pad up and down concrete stairs to the coffee shop to fill ourselves up with artificial stress to keep our eyes on the prize all day long. These habits built on structure and reward have bled into my personal life so that when I take a run by the Medlock I'm counting seconds, footsteps and milestones, scattering young rabbits and blurring out the sound of blue tits with an enormous pair of Bluetooth headphones. I'm measuring meaningless successes, not connecting with anything around me.

A pre-Christian nomad, someone who once wandered freely where our houses, Tescos and Job Centres now sit, would be horrified by how most of us are living. If these people lived in our shoes for one day, with the fuzzing buzzes and vibration from the devices in our pockets and on our nightstands, they'd be able to see the labyrinth of trappings and expectations placed on us by a society that wants to boost global GDP at any cost. The age-old stones and trees around us experience the world through the slow turning of pebbles in the tide and the gradual wearing away of earth through centuries of storms. But humanity is racing ahead of the limitations set by our bodies and the boundaries that nature puts in place to help us all survive in harmony.

Put bluntly, I feel as if I can't go on living this way.

Having thrown myself back into a standard office setting once more, I have fallen away from myself. I crave a different way of life, but there are seemingly no plans for the world's cogs to start slowing any time soon.

Could I change the way I live though?

It's heaving torrential rain as I leave the hospital, my trainer socks squelching out North Manchester grit as I head to the tram stop. I'm not marching with my head bent against the wind; I'm almost skipping. By the time I get in the carriage back to the city centre, my tiredness is evaporating, the tingling sensation in the soles of my feet has drained out through my shoes and into every puddle I pass. It's like each breath I take is trying to heal me after the relief of the doctor's diagnosis. While I'm under no false impressions that a few sentences from a health professional were really all it took to knock me back into the world, I'm still delighted to be feeling something other than the sluggish strain of exhaustion coating my eyes. I'm hopeful for the first time in months, although frustrated that this realisation has taken this long; whole weeks, months, of my existence blotted out by anxiety and my lack of connection with the world.

But, if I'm not physically ill, then what is really going on? If I am honest with myself – I am aware there is an underlying issue here. I could be described as an 'up and down' kind of person; ever since I was a moody teenager wearing too much eyeliner, I have had periods of depression and anxiety. It's something I have often tried to get to the root of, without too much luck. However, as I reached adulthood these episodes became much more frequent and I was less able to get back to myself using the things I enjoyed. Such endorphin-making activities included going for a hike, reading a book and eating copious amounts of chocolate, but witchcraft has always been the one thing that has brought me back to myself with absolute certainty.

There have been so many times over the years when I've felt

entirely myself. These beautiful moments have been while out in nature, watching lapwings wheeling across the moors or walking through meadowsweet that smells like small crinkles of summer. But the other, perhaps more intimately happy, moments of my life have happened while sitting on my bedroom floor inside a circle of candles, feeling the powerful waves of magick play across my face like a warm breeze.

When I was fifteen years old and a practising witch, I performed an initiation ceremony while wearing a white dress. I lit the candles, conjured up the four elements and welcomed in the Goddess. In that small ritual on the floor of my childhood bedroom, I dedicated myself to witchcraft and promised that I would live my life in tune with the cycles of nature. But what had happened to that promise? I've been realising for some time that my spiritual connection to the world has been fading, power-washed away by city living. The practices that once filled me with such comfort have been replaced by my commute and having to zone out to prepare myself mentally for the working day ahead. I was getting further and further away from the person I knew and that skinny teenage girl who stood strong and tall with her face upturned to the light.

What am I going to do to stop my adult life being a cycle of trying and retreating, working and leaving, pushing myself and then falling ill? I know that *something* has to change. I have to break this cycle. I need to find a new rhythm. Now, as I take the long journey home from the hospital on a wintry November day, after an equally long period of musing, when the wind bites my fingers with ferocity and the brown-clouded sky threatens to splinter into a blizzard at any moment, I decide to begin again.

I know what I need to do next.

YULE

*

21 December

I'm crouching low on my heels between a high wall and a bare, black elm. It's three hours after sunset and I can't feel my feet or much else for that matter.

A quick check inside the cauldron tells me everything is burning away nicely despite the wind that whittles my knees, but I flick another match into the pot to make sure. The flame catches an edge of the paper and I see my handwriting coil and twist into smoke like a magician's disappearing act.

Behind me, on the other side of the park wall, I can hear two neighbours talking in animated voices at their front door. Who's sitting where at Christmas dinner and 'she spent *how* much on him?' I wince at my heavy chimney of smoke coursing their way, weaving into my hair and the lining of my coat, promising to remind me of this night for many weeks to come. I think of those neighbours leaving their warm doorway, moving towards the wall to find out where the smell is coming from, and I attempt to power-fan the smoke in the opposite direction. Luckily, their chatter doesn't falter; I think I've slipped by unnoticed.

A fresh splatter of rain falls on my forehead. I roll my eyes at the shifting cloud where the full moon should be shining down on me. Typical. The ground is a slippery, shifting bed of mud so my balance, and my patience, is being tested. But today is 21 December – Yule (*'yool'*), the first day of winter – if anything, this is an appropriate welcome into the darkest season.

'Great,' I say to nothing in particular, squatting down further to angle the lid of the pot and shield its sputtering contents.

15

THE WHEEL

Philips Park is my patch, one that I prowl and guard throughout all seasons; more than thirty acres of cropped grass and tree-lined pathways that sandwich a graveyard between another hundred acres of parkland called Clayton Vale. At this time of year, it's blissfully bleak. When I walk there just after sunrise, at around nine o'clock, there is no one else here: I hear my own footsteps wrinkling the frost, the peep of a robin following close by, hopping and turning in a form of primitive dance that I've become familiar with. Over the coming month, a flock of redwings will descend from the trees to pick the hedgerows clean. As spring appears, so will the kingfishers and dippers along the River Medlock, flashing out of the dark arches of pedestrian bridges. I'm looking forward to that time, but before then there's a mission I have to complete. It's one that has been a long time coming.

I'm burning something away. Something that has been clinging to my skin like branched lichen; like thick, breathing moss. Here in this dark, green space, I'm stripping myself bare with the fire of Yule and getting rid of the past few years.

It feels apt. Yule, the winter solstice, is an ancient fire festival, one that has been celebrated for thousands of years in the UK and across Europe. Fire is purifying; fire burns away the old and helps you to forget. Today, the Earth is at its furthest point away from the sun as the daylight hours dwindle and night takes over this northern part of the world. It is inevitably really, *really* cold. This peak point (when the exact winter solstice will fall) is viewed as a time of death, but not a sad one. Our Pagan ancestors knew that things must die in order to welcome new life, and this would be the time to slaughter livestock and dry it out or ferment it so that it could keep the village going as the earth hardened – a source of sustained life. Life-bringing. It's because of this central belief around death that Yule is seen as a time of rebirth, a festival of renewal and light – the longest and darkest day of the year before the sun begins to rule once more. It seems counterintuitive that we'd praise the coming heat of spring before winter has even started, but there's a hopefulness to this that I admire. I find that with all Pagan festivals, or Sabbats, each point of the year looks for the positive even as the world continues its tumultuous course. And, let's be honest, it feels good to chuck another log on the fire and forget about the cold nights, just like with the Christian holiday that follows Yule only four days later.

I started observing Yule as a teenager and I've always celebrated it with something quick (who has time in among Christmas festivities?) – a candle blessing on my windowsill followed by something delicious in the form of a Mr Kipling mince pie, before heading back into the realms of tinsel and TV reruns. The more food at Yule, the better. But this year, something else is needed. I want to use this day to mark a permanent change in my life.

I have just done the unspeakable. Earlier today, I quit my job at a large corporate company rather suddenly to focus on my writing. At least . . . that's what I'm telling everyone for now.

In Philips Park, I peer into my smouldering cauldron. The moon is the tiniest slither away from being full – and on Yule, too! The perfect time to let negativity die.

The sound of fire crackling through paper makes me focus. It's such a primal sound, the snap and pop of it making me watchful, alert – was that a footstep or the fire tripping? Even when I was first starting out on my witchcraft path, I always felt a connection with fire; it has the ability to comfort and strike fear, its purpose sometimes changing within seconds. I liked its unpredictability, but mainly I fell for its visceral hiss and bubble, the backdrop of many magickal nights. In the darkness of the park, a smile creeps onto my chapped lips – I feel like something much older. I am Cerridwen, the wise crone of Celtic legend (I'm one loose tooth away from being twenty-eight going on ninety), stirring her melting pot of prophecy and change at the rim of her cave.

What transformation will come from this burning ritual?

Inside my cauldron is a thick fistful of paper, old diary entries, work 'to do' lists, notes I wrote while I was in a bad place and feeling trapped in a life that was keeping my mind small and narrow; thoughts and feelings that were holding me back, keeping me tied to a time I want to let go of. These papers are flashes of lightning across a darkened room and I want them gone. As they curl and burn, twisting in black spirals like the farewell flourish of a travelling cloak, a sense of calm sweeps through my chest and shoulders. I feel it so strongly, like a blast of ice to my system, shivering out the old thoughts. I'm burning a path for something new to come in.

I stand upwind of my cauldron and take a deep inhale, rooting my feet down into the earth, feeling my energy in two striding pillars of vibration below me. I can feel the Earth's power; the wiry winter grass bending to the will of the Yule rain, the softening ground melding to my appalling choice of footwear – a pair of very porous trainers. The Earth is allowing me to be here with my pot of magic, absorbing my intent, inviting my energies to mingle with all the living things in this green space. The deep furled smoke is everywhere. My senses feel heightened and I can smell the damp soil – which reminds me of digging for worms in my childhood garden – and the scattered leaf litter gathering on the nearby icy pond.

There is a power building around me in the sights, smells and sounds of this space. The Earth is singing her winter song to me.

I close my eyes to let it all in through my skin. I imagine my body opening up to receive Her wisdom. That's when I feel it.

The crackling starts in my feet, where I am closest to the Earth. I feel it buzzing in the capillaries of my soles like static. It's a shifting pulse of air and light. The thing that's tingling there is neither positive nor negative, but it's an insistent, thrumming force that can be used to flush away the bad or fuse together to create the new. It's a beautiful thing that I can feel in my feet. It makes a giggle gather in my throat. As I breathe, I will the force to rise from the ground, up my legs, into my stomach and, with a sharp breath, I push it through to my arms and finally to my head, where it buzzes and seems to fill my eyes to bursting point. I grin with all my teeth showing.

This force is something I have felt many times before. It is called a great number of things in many ancient tongues and some not-so-old ones. I call it magick.

I feel it here now and I set it to work, decluttering my mind at the edge of this dark field. It is the wind and fire all at once, blasting through my thoughts and incinerating them from my mind. It is water and earth, cleansing me and keeping me rooted in my body. The magick sweeping through me feels like the power of everything on Earth rushing into me at once. If I'm not careful to ground myself afterwards, it will be easy to get swept away with it.

Perhaps this is a strange place for magick to occur.

Philips Park is one of the oldest municipal parks in England, one of the many Victorian spaces spreading out like a soothing green palm across the north. Packed out with bandstands, stone urns and fountains, these parks were built to be enjoyed by everyone; a reprieve from the grime-smudged buildings of working towns. My particular patch, not far from the old industrial hub of Ancoats, lies on a hundred years' worth of ash, rubble and poisonous chemical fumes. It might not be the perfect place to manifest a future, but where is the right place to practise magick? Earlier this evening, I completed the first half of my ritual indoors among candles and incense and a protective circle that I'd carefully laid on the floor of my spare bedroom. All went just fine but, as always, there was the issue of lighting a fire (setting off fire alarms is an occupational hazard for Pagans). Slag heaps and arsenic aside, Philips Park is as good a place as any for a spot of witchcraft.

As I stand here in the dark, my head feels scrubbed clear, like the inside of my skull has been polished to squeak. The crackling in my fingers and feet is still there but lessened now, so I crouch to look into my cauldron and check on the fire. The flames have died down. The acrid scent of burning Biro hovers in the air below the steady rain, another smell I'll be wafting from my jacket for weeks on end. I think we're done here.

The magick wants to leave – I've been carrying it in my veins and muscles for about fifteen minutes – so I place my hands on the grass to let it soak back into the earth. It floods down and out of me with the dull pulse of a headache. This grounding leaves me feeling numb after the thrill of power. The park is quiet through the hiss of rain and, although the moon is hidden, I can still feel the radiance of her, as though I'm bathing in her light on the shining backs of the clouds. As if it's just for me.

My cauldron is pretty weighty. I pick up two kilograms of smoking pewter and return to my block of flats. I go the back way so as not to pass the couple still nattering in a front yard. ('What have you got there?' 'Oh, just a cauldron of burning regrets.')

Once safely outside my front door, I realise there's no way this bad boy is going to stop spitting black ash any time soon. A few frantic trips upstairs for bottles, pans of water and a tea towel mean I can finally bring the cauldron back up to the flat.

I'm still buzzing with energy, although it's mainly fire anxiety at this point. I get back inside, holding the pot at arm's length.

Linnet hops down from the sofa as I put the cauldron in the bath, too terrified to take off the lid and welcome a black force field of smoke into my home. She jumps over the bath's ledge to eye the cauldron with suspicion before leaping out again and stalking down the hall. There is obviously no food to be had among charred paper.

When I first brought Linnet home, just over a year ago, I think I'd been hoping for a familiar. A cat who would help me to rediscover my witchy self, one who would sit nicely on my lap while I split herbs into bundles and wind around my ankles as I raised my arms to the moon. Linnet has turned out to be a cantankerous calico beast who enjoys clawing my favourite mustard-coloured armchair and likes being stroked as much as the average person likes being punched in the face. She definitely hasn't noticed my change in energy and, sure enough, I hear her snuffling in her toy box in the other room for something to bash against the skirting boards.

Despite her nonchalance, I feel calm, rejuvenated. I tip more water into the cauldron and hope for the best. Finally, the fire is completely out and the smoke seems to have settled. Some of the paper isn't completely charred so I swill it with cold water, mushing it until every pen stroke is illegible and gone for good. That's better.

Yule is a time of rest and rebirth and I am ready to leave my old life and accept the new one the Goddess will guide me to.

*

When I was younger, I used to get some puzzled looks when I said I was Pagan. I've only ever seen it used once as an option on a drop-down 'State your religion' menu. Even when I haven't been practising witchcraft for a while I would proudly describe myself as Pagan rather than anything else. More than a few times, the 'confused' look people gave me had progressed to 'startled face'. This was something I've speedily back-pedalled from and made me wish I'd just selected 'None'.

'Pagan' is a vague ID tag, a catch-all term for a multitude of beliefs, which means that, for some, it can be a bit of a minefield. Many have spent chunks of their academic career trying to define modern Paganism, but labelling those with alternative beliefs can be a tricky thing, as these people don't all come from the same walk of life and can have many shared or opposing practices. Your average Green Witch overlaps with the Druid, which overlaps with a shamanic practitioner, and Goddess help anyone who compares Wiccans to Traditional Witches. I could list all the paths here, explain their roots, their different beliefs . . . but there are plenty of 'Beginner's Guides to Paganism: The Dos and Don'ts' that already exist out there if you want to see what tickles your fancy. That's the thing with witchcraft and Paganism: this belief system is unique and fluid.

If we look at Paganism as a whole, it can be said that people who observe this path respect and revere the cycles of the Earth. They see nature as the divine and mark the passing of the seasons with rites and rituals in honour of the beauty of our green world.

Some Pagans use the seasons, the elements (Earth, Air, Fire and Water) and herbs that grow at certain times of year to create magick in their daily lives. This is something I identify with and use in my own rituals.

My path is a very personal one and has budded into a crown of interweaving beliefs taken from many different Pagan traditions. I'm not an expert on every element of Paganism but my own blend of magickal workings is one that draws on different forms of witchcraft and Neo-paganism. I often get asked about my beliefs by puzzled work colleagues once they've added me on social media and I always try to be as open as possible, but let's get a few things straight from the start: Pagans don't believe in the masculine god set out by Judeo-Christian religions and they certainly don't believe in the Devil. If you've picked up this book hoping to sell your soul to Satan, sorry, can't help you there. Pagans believe in something far more ancient and primal, something that speaks to our intuition and makes our bodies tingle when we walk on certain ground.

Pagans – now and long ago – are people who worship Mother Earth and the natural patterns of the world we live in. The word itself has its root in the Latin for 'of the countryside', something that rings true for me when I find myself deep in British woodland with my toes wriggling into a heavy bank of moss. In years long gone, lives were lived by the patterns of rain, steady sunshine and harvest. Festivals were dictated by the length of the day and the strength of the sun, not a strange book from distant lands; in fact, there are no key texts to follow within Paganism, only knowledge of herbs, weather and spoken words handed down and shared throughout the community.

In Paganism, cycles are everything.

Many Pagans subscribe to the Wheel of the Year, a circular calendar divided into eight sections depicting the celebrations observed throughout the year – usually enjoyed with a lot of food and dancing about. The name itself is a modern, Neo-Pagan term but the concept is an ancient one. The Wheel shows the eight Pagan festivals that are now widely celebrated, as well as the four seasons containing two solstices and two equinoxes.

There is so much to celebrate within nature, which is why we have so many festivals! There is always something new appearing out of the earth that makes me want to pick up the phone and tell everyone I know. These special festival days are sometimes called Sabbats and run around the Wheel as follows:

- The Witches' Year begins with Samhain, or Halloween, on 31 October. Halloween is the time of year we commune with hidden planes, as the veil between the worlds is at its thinnest. It is typically a time when we honour the dead and give thanks to our ancestors as we forge ahead into a new year.

- Yule (20–25 December). Yule is like Christmas but slightly earlier and a good excuse to have even more food. This Festival of Rebirth is also the winter solstice celebration, which marks the shortest day of the year and the hope of more light to come. At this time of the year when our light is at a premium, Yule is a good chance to remind ourselves of what makes us happy – whether that's family, friends, fairy lights or copious amounts of sprouts; I'll let you decide.

- Imbolc (1–2 February). Traditionally, this was when new lambs arrived and when the Earth was pregnant with life – the first glimmers of spring. While not many of us have access to a farmer's field anymore to see these changes happening in real time, there are other ways to get on board. Imbolc is a fire festival and can be celebrated through the means of a bonfire or flame, whether out in public or at home with a quiet candle. It is also a time to plant the seeds of what you want to achieve for the year and start to work towards it.

- Ostara (20–23 March). Spring is here! The spring equinox

brings with it the first wildflowers and the dawn chorus. This time is fresh, verdant and rich with symbolism, so you'll find many depictions of eggs and hares (the original Easter bunny) on a Pagan altar at Ostara.

- Beltane (30 April – 1 May). May Day is my absolute favourite Pagan festival. Everyone is well into the spirit of spring at this point so joy is in the air! Beltane is another fire festival but this time we celebrate the passion and sexuality of fertile spring – another excuse for a good old dance (clothing optional).

- Litha (20–22 June). Midsummer, or the summer solstice, falls when the world is pregnant with the world's harvest. It's a time to raise a glass to the steadily growing green things in the farmers' fields and beyond. Litha is another energy-filled festival to celebrate the sun's light, but we are also reminded that the long days will soon start to shorten – this is a good opportunity for us to honour ourselves, to reflect on the things we have and the practices we do which really make us shine our brightest.

- Lammas (1 August). Lammas, or 'loaf mass', is the first harvest of the year and is a day of abundance with lots of bread eating. Eating a load of stodge at the hottest point of the year might seem a bit counterintuitive but we are reminded of what our ancestors would have practised and to give thanks for the amazing bounty in the world.

- Mabon (20–23 September). The autumn equinox is when the days are perfectly balanced. Mabon is the second harvest of the year and a time to take stock of what we have as we move into the darker months of the year. It is also a time to examine the balances in our own lives and even make big decisions while weighing up all possibilities in equal measure.

Then the Wheel takes us back round to Samhain where we start all over again.

While not all Pagan folk subscribe to the Wheel of the Year, many of the larger festivals, such as Samhain, Beltane, Midsummer's Day and Yule, are celebrated by people in many different cultures, so ingrained are they in our ways of life. You'll find that many Sabbats reflect farming practices – the newborn lambs of Imbolc (or *Oimelc*, meaning 'ewe's milk') and the ritual loaf-making of Lammas in the harvest season – linking us to our ancestors that once ploughed the fields and could predict rain through the shape of a cloud or the sound of a cockerel's cry. With the prevalence of agriculture from around 6,000 years ago, our lives became dictated by the farming structure of the year we have been familiar with until very recent times. However, as nearly 80 per cent of people in our society now live in urban areas,[4] we are now perhaps not so familiar with the subtle natural signals our ancestors would have understood. Do we know the first signs of spring to spot before the flowers emerge? Can we sense a storm in the air? As we look to reintegrate ourselves into nature, the Wheel can be seen as a reflection of the turning seasons – the silver mists of winter rolling into the silky softness of spring wildflowers carpets – and what we can do to feel at one with it again.

We can all use the Wheel of the Year to tap into the Earth's cycles – to feel her swell and grow into summer then let the cloak of winter fall over her body once more. But the Wheel represents more than the shifting seasons – it is our ever-changing lives where we feel joy, excitement and sometimes a deep wintry sadness; it is our map to finding our place within the world.

The Wheel turns and so do we. This world is never-ending.

The Wheel is just one aspect of Paganism – a beautiful one – and there are many other ways that people choose to incorporate Paganism into their lives.

When I was performing rituals every month and living in tune with nature's rhythms, I would certainly have called myself a witch, first beginning to practise spells, divination and herbcraft when I was twelve years old. Not all Pagans are witches, but I would have classed myself as both Pagan and a witch. I worked with the seasons, made tinctures from herbs, and had been known to dance around in a circle by candlelight. I also liked to incorporate a few New Age twists along the way; I am a trained Reiki and crystal healer, I practised yoga and meditated to harp sounds in my spare room. I followed the lunar cycles, the seasons and the birth and death of wildflowers. I rose with the sun, ready to catch the first birdsong, and I spoke to the Goddess when I took a walk in the park. I observed the eight Pagan festivals of the year. I practised visualisation and divination within my rituals. I tried to limit the amount of negative energy I gave out because the world has a way of bringing it back to bite us on the arse, threefold. I practised the art of magick, invoked the elements and tended to chat to the trees. I've received quite a few funny looks in my time.

The Pagan calendar is all about balance, harmony and living seasonally, and my body is yearning for that way of living once again.

*

Have you ever felt like your mind was racing for no reason? You keep standing up from your desk and forget what you are about to do, or you're lying in bed and your brain is speaking two conversations over one another. You feel like you've competed in a high-intensity rounders match against your will. You're tossing and turning, you're in turn forgetful and creative; on the verge of tears and then ecstatic. Maybe you're just exhausted. Your boss won't mind if you left a couple of hours early today . . . right?

If this is the case, chances are it's a full moon tonight or the day before one. Go on, check.

It's easy to dismiss, I know. But we're all aware of the term 'lunatic', the howling wolf packs, the maxed-out A&E rooms at the time of the full moon, which we tell ourselves are just coincidence. We let out a nervous giggle to ourselves because the cold face of the full moon is a throwback to childhood ghost stories, to ghouls and flashes of vampires in the graveyard; their steps illuminated in the moon's quivering glow.

However, in my world, the moon isn't something you laugh at. In fact, I've only ever laughed conspiratorially with the moon: she's my comrade and mother all in one; she's my idol and my closest confidante. As a practitioner of witchcraft, the moon is something to be celebrated. Of course, the moon is revered by many other groups across the world – the Jewish and the Chinese calendars run to the cycles of the moon and she has been revered throughout history as a symbol of many different gods and goddesses, and sometimes as the deity herself. For millennia, we have celebrated her; we have mythologised her, sung to her and left her offerings – complete reverence.

Let's face it: I'm totally in love with her, and I'm not the only one.

Even though we have dimmed her significance with street lamps and neon strips in more recent years, the force of her power still shows. She controls the tides, our emotions (60 per cent of the human body is water – the moon's going to make you tear up once in a while), and her energy can influence the course of our lives. It can sometimes be difficult to see the true glory of her glow stretching out through suburban streets and grass verges, catching the sharp glint of animal eyes, but looking up at that spectral, changing face it is not hard to rekindle some of the hope and fear felt through past ages.

Traditionally, the moon is seen as providing a dark feminine energy to the world (the yin to the sun's masculine, fiery yang). This belief has never quite gone away and across the centuries, the moon has been reflected back at us time and time again in folklore, poetry and art, lighting up the shadows and the more hidden parts of ourselves through stories. For many cultures, the sun is a masculine force – commanding the plants to rise from the Earth to bask in its glory. The moon is viewed as the feminine; the soft, passive orb that is nice to look at on a clear night but doesn't really do much. Of course, this is a simplistic way to look at things – both have their creative and destructive properties; both planetary bodies have their direct place in shaping our landscape. We need the sun to nourish us, to grow the food we rely on for healthy, strong bodies, and to feel the pleasure of heat on our skin. But with too much of this heat, we are burnt to cinders, our food incinerated and our bodies too parched to move. The moon, cold and alone though she may seem, is intricately tied to us as she controls the undulating tides that ravage our coastlines and force new rock to form under the water's immense pressure. Shelley called her a 'dying lady, lean and pale', but our moon is very much alive and fighting fit, a guiding and empowering light. Artemis, Luna, Selene – these time-old goddesses are still the embodiment of the moon's feminine energies and there are people out there, an entire community, who work with her energies every month. The full moon for Pagans is a time for worship and letting go of past grievances, while the new moon can be a chance to work with the darker energies of the world or simply start anew as the lunar cycle begins all over again.

For many covens across the world, the night of 21 December is an esbat, an observance of the full moon's power and a time to celebrate another month gone by. There are twelve or thirteen esbats to celebrate every year (more food to be eaten – Pagans are big on cake). While the term 'esbat' has only been around since the 1920s, many people who have practised magick and nature worship throughout time have met to make merry on a full moon. A coven, or a group of witches, would do a ritual under the light of the moon and make plans for the coming month. As it is, I work alone, but the full moon's significance is by no means dulled by my lack of a coven. The full moon symbolises a time of letting go; letting go of a time in your life or a project that has done everything it can to serve you, or you may want to put a full stop at the end of a darker period that you wish to come out of. On these nights, the moon's power is at its fullest, it is ready to burst, it is ready to blurt out its energy in one enormous blast that can sometimes knock you sideways (and don't get me started on super moons). Only then, after that momentous night, will the moon recede, ebb into a waning crescent and fade into nothing, to begin once more. With so much energy moving around the skies, is it any wonder your mind is all over the place when the moon is at its brightest?

The moon is the top celebrity in a Pagan's world and we run by her rhythms, but stop and think for a minute: in our busy lives, when was the last time you looked at the moon? Actually looked out of the window or went outside just to stand and look at her glowing face rather than spotting it and being slightly surprised at its existence? When did you last look forward to seeing the moon?

As a witch, I have probably looked at the moon more often than most and, during my noted absence from witchcraft, I have missed her a lot.

The full moon is not only traditionally sacred to the witch, but to women everywhere. She offers safety for women after dark. Her glowing face, lighting up the sky, allows us to see where we are going without the need for a torch or anything that would draw attention to us, giving us safe passage through the night. Her cycles help us to keep track of our menstrual rhythms; her twenty-eight-day calendar running in time with our bleeding and bodily changes. In this way, she has been a companion and friend for many. For the witch, before the world was lit up by battery packs, her full form would have offered witches a light home after partaking in a ritual, visiting someone who needed our magickal assistance or doing something deemed illicit under patriarchal rule. Certain herbs when picked under the light of the full moon or at the new moon are said to have more potency. The moon really is the witch's guide. But throughout history, the moon could also have been the witch's lifesaver.

The term 'witch' has many problematic connotations and an even patchier history. If you'd have asked someone 'what is a witch?' at the turn of the twentieth century, you might have received some sniffy looks and mutters of séances and black mirrors. Rewind to the Middle Ages and you might have been tied to a stake just for uttering the word.

What is the first thing you think of when someone says the word 'witch'? With shops selling candles, incense and gemstones in every town, witchcraft – in one form or another – is experiencing a renaissance. Bags from popular high-street stores read 'We are the Granddaughters of the Witches They Couldn't Burn' and TikTok (or WitchTok, if you will) shows up a thousand videos on how to cast a spell. But ask anyone on the street what witchcraft is and you'll either hear 'bloody hippies' or 'that's all that Hogwarts stuff, innit?' The darker connotations have lost their meaning in a modern world where magick has been debunked or explained away.

Those who practise witchcraft fall into the bracket of Paganism, although not every witch is a Pagan as there are myriad forms of Paganism, as I mentioned earlier. Similarly, not everyone who practices witchcraft will label themselves a witch; they just like to tinker about with crystals every once in a while, or maybe they have another label for themselves. This loose definition allows practitioners to take from areas of different forms – a pinch of spellwork here, a little herbalism there – and this freedom is something that drew me to witchcraft in the first place. Witchcraft can be hard to define but some people have a great way of pinning it down.

In *Time* magazine in 2019, esteemed witch Pam Grossman, author of *Waking the Witch*, wrote of witches:

> *In fact, I find that the more I work with the witch, the more complex she becomes. Hers is a slippery spirit: try to pin her down, and she'll only recede further into the deep, dark wood . . . Witches have power on their own terms. They have agency. They create. They praise. They commune with the spiritual realm, freely and free of any mediator.*[5]

I absolutely adore this quote. For me, I have my own definition of the craft and how it fits into the overarching umbrella of Paganism; a witch is someone who is deeply in touch with people, plants and animals, and knows how to work with their innate power to bring about change in the world, usually through magickal forces.

It's no secret that witchcraft has long been dominated by women and those seen as 'other' to the straight-white-forty-something-cis-man who has sought to oppress us as a way of exerting control over our sexuality and our different, less linear ways of thinking about the power structures around us. However, since the 1960s, and more-so than ever in the past five years, we've seen a long-awaited retaliation from women and witches. With the rise of the #MeToo movement, we've seen women actively speaking out and using magick to hex men who embody the patriarchy, and we're very open about it. Writer Andi Zeisler, on the eve of the 2017 US Women's March, said: 'This is the time for getting scary. We need to go full witch.'⁶ This, of course, could mean whacking out the crystal ball and drawing some sigils, or it could mean women of all kinds – cis, trans or otherwise – asserting their full feminine power in a show of resistance against the dominant culture. Witches have always been linked to the feminist movement and feminist acts, with witchcraft itself being a way that a woman could earn a living throughout history without having to rely on a man. But is it any wonder that the confident, self-assured woman has always been feared by men and seen as a witch? She is capable of overturning the world as we know it.

Some Pagans and witches like to use gods and goddesses in their ritual work – invoking the powers of ancient figures to enhance their work, although they are not prescribed and are not part of everyone's path. Another way of looking at gods and goddesses is that they are the way a certain culture chose to represent the forces of Mother Nature around them – many peoples worshipped the goddess of the fertile land, be it Gaia, Demeter or Pachamama, to help bring in a good harvest and most cultures throughout time have revered a sun god – just think of Ra and Apollo to name two of the most known across the western world. For me in my practice, this way of practising Paganism has always appealed to me and I use deities from the Celtic pantheon in my work; as someone whose AncestryDNA test said that she was alarmingly British (97 per cent), Celtic seemed like the way to go. I worship the Triple Goddess – the Maiden, Mother and Crone – the three faces of the Goddess, which represent the cycles of life.

In some parts of the Pagan world and particularly for those following the Celtic pantheon, the full moon is represented by Cerridwen – the wise, elderly crone of the gods, the goddess of death and leader of the underworld. In other paths, she is Hecate, the 'dark goddess'; the moon is almost always a female deity and one with sinister connotations. Cerridwen is the last phase of the Triple Goddess's reign (the other two phases being Brigid, the maiden goddess of spring and queen of the crescent moon; and Rhiannon, the mother goddess of summer, the harvest and waxing pregnant moon). Typically, Cerridwen is seen hunched over her bubbling cauldron, her gnarled nose almost skimming the surface of its brew. The stereotypical hag-witch. Some Pagans see her full cauldron as a hearty broth to feed her followers, or containing a potion that gives the drinker knowledge and metamorphosis; either way. Judith Shaw of Feminism and Religion writes:

> When Cerridwen calls your name, know that the need for change is upon you; transformation is at hand. It is time to examine what circumstances in your life no longer serve you. Something must die so that something new and better can be born. Forging these fires of transformation will bring true inspiration into your life.[7]

Transformation, inspiration. Now you see why my ritual had to be done at the time of the full moon.

*

My Yuletide ritual has inspired me. I feel so vibrant, if slightly overfilled with sprouts. I'm glowing with the light of the moon and the power of the Earth that coursed through me during the ritual. This, this right here, is what makes me feel whole. Having tasted this sweet dose of witchiness again, I want to turn my attention away from the modern way of living I have become accustomed to, and reconnect with the two most important things in my soul – nature and witchcraft. For me, witchcraft has always opened me up to wonder, to search for what is hidden. It is both an empowering and lonely space of introspection, but one that has made me look upon the natural landscapes of Britain as my home and places of ancient knowledge.

Right now, I need to take action and reclaim the witch within me, for my own health and sanity.

Surely, we don't have to live in a world where we get sick to the point of despair, where we are too fragmented to remember how to be whole; where spirituality does not factor into our relationship with the natural world. There has to be something better than the way we are living now and I want to make it my mission to return to my witchy past, but also to the way our ancestors saw and experienced Mother Earth.

However, there are so many parts of me that still feel scattered and easily jangled, despairing and overwhelmed; I am desperate for the healing to begin and to reconnect to those calming natural rhythms of the world. A small voice in me wonders whether the answer to problems which are about the modern world and how to survive in it really lies back where I began my interest in witchcraft as a teenager. The darker emotions that I have experienced for many years were kept tempered by my Pagan practice; reassuring and mindful, magickal and enlightening. Is it truly possible to re-remember our links with the elements and the Earth when modern adult life does everything it can do to cut us adrift and keep us productive? I resolve to keep my mind open over a full cycle of the Wheel, and make sure I speak to people who I think could offer insight into my questions. Perhaps with these answers in my possession, I can really begin to heal.

Perhaps we all can.

*

It is way too early for this.

On Boxing Day, my parents and I head over to Lunts Meadow, a sprawling wetland in Sefton, Merseyside, only a twenty-five-minute drive from my childhood home. It's not somewhere that I could ever get to on my own and I give myself the 'you're nearly thirty, get a car' talk for the fifth time that week. My genuine appreciation of public transport is a bit outside the norm and something that makes me late for every social occasion and often stranded. I wonder if getting a car would allow me the chance to go out and enjoy nature more. There's something oddly comforting, reassuring even, about hopping onto public transport but there are only so many birds you can see when there's a nine o'clock train you need to catch.

I've been birdwatching for nine years so I've often been up at first light to travel to some far-off reserve in search of pied flycatchers. But over recent years, I've gradually been setting my alarm later and later and later. Today's 6:45 a.m. wake-up call feels like nails on a chalkboard, but Mum and Dad insist.

Will, my partner, is in Germany with his dad over Christmas. This is the first time we've spent it apart in four years so we can wake up with our respective families on Christmas Day. The flat felt cavernous without him and I have found myself speaking in whispers over the past few days so my echo doesn't bounce back at me. Now, fully into the festive period, I'm back in my family home, which is much cosier and has more snacks. Linnet has come back to Liverpool with me, an experience both my parents and I are dreading with similar ferocity.

I received some witchy presents for Yule, including a beautiful *vesica piscis* necklace from my friend Em, a silver circle with two overlapping circles inside it, like a sexy Venn diagram. Every time I wear it I feel imbued with power, protection and the friendship of my fellow witchy gal and it has already become a staple of my wardrobe; in fact, I'm wearing it today. The interlocking circles are reassuring to me and remind me that time always moves forward like clockwork.

It's a difficult Christmas; there's no other way to put it. My lovely, tiny grandad with the schoolboy laugh and the vibrant garden I'd grown up with passed away just ten days ago so we're all hedging our sentences and are full of half-smiles. It had been a long battle with Alzheimer's, one that we all wish had ended much sooner for his sake. Mum, Dad, Grandma, my sister Caroline, her boyfriend Adam and I piled around the dining table for Christmas dinner. It's nice, full of easy chat, a mountain of Aunt Bessie's Yorkshire puddings and several layers of Dairy Milk Tray, but something big is missing.

The village I grew up in, about half an hour from Liverpool, looks the same as ever except with more traffic streaming through it every year. There's the small high street with its post office, chemist, greengrocer and the little florist's shop tucked away in the corner. There are hobbled, cheerful, flat-capped old men who like to call 'Alreet!' across the street at each other. On Saturday mornings when I was still in primary school, small, vegetarian me stood outside the butcher's window keeping my eyes trained firmly ahead at the traffic lights so that I didn't have to see Grandma shopping for lamb chops. There is the library – where I'd spent a good chunk of my childhood – on the same road as the large, sturdy houses tucked in behind a fringe of beech and horse chestnut trees. I remember cracking the beechnut casings as I walked on tiptoes up to my grandparents' house after school, hand in hand with Grandad.

I always find it a relief to be back here, reassured that the relics of my village childhood still exist and I didn't imagine them all. I revisit the same tree every October, at the point where the village hits farmland, to add more conkers to my dried-out collection. It's a good place to spot buzzards hunting on long summer evenings.

At Lunts Meadow, much further out in the countryside, I walk on, trying not to think about who I really want to think about.

This reserve is a birdwatcher's treasure trove, a wetland hewn out of a curve of the River Alt and surrounded by several green miles of arable land. Sometimes when you look at it, the green seems blinding, like there's just far too much of it to digest in one sitting. This is somewhere I only seem to get to in the winter, a time when the mud splashes up to our knees and we have to abandon pathways every few minutes or so to avoid being swallowed up in pits.

The things we do for birds.

We're all feeling sluggish with too many roast potatoes, but there's a bright coolness to the day that makes my mind alert. A flock of fieldfare gets up as we round the first corner then there are shoveler, teal and the shuffling of moorhens on the scrape. The sun is blinding but welcome after not leaving the house all day yesterday. It comes through the bare trees at shattering angles, cutting across our vision and glaring up from the rivulets of the Alt. Dad is out in front as always, yelling back, 'Watch out!' when a patch of mud threatens to swallow him whole; Mum and I have our arms linked as we rise steadily onto a man-made ridge that gives views all the way across to Liverpool. The sunlight on the overgrown fields manages to blur out the city's edges so that it's only a smudge on our natural paradise. A man walks his pointer on the other side of the river and calls hello, while the dog creeps ever closer to a coot down in the weed.

Dad and I have been birdwatching together for almost ten years; it just felt like the right thing to do, a natural progression from Saturday hikes and National Trust outings. What started as 'just something nice to do at the weekend' while we blasted *(What's the Story) Morning Glory?* through the car speakers soon turned into a passion that devoured all our spare time and conversations.

'It was a juvenile!'

'How can you say that? It clearly had the yellow shoulders.'

'I can't even speak to you when you're being like this.'

In the early days, when I was still at uni, I turned down nights out with mysteriously vague replies like:

'Can't tonight. Big family thing tomorrow.'

'Deadlines – you know . . .'

However, it soon got out that I was getting up at 5.30 a.m. to see ospreys and bitterns with my dad, and people weren't quite sure what to do with that information. Birdwatching isn't something traditionally aligned with the cool kids and, I suppose, neither is witchcraft. But it's OK, I resigned myself to not being cool at quite a young age.

My burly Scouse dad and I have travelled all across the north of England, Wales and Scotland, from Anglesey and Mull to the Flamborough Coast, to get views of eagles and puffins over the past ten years. Mum sometimes came with us, although she was mainly glad to have a peaceful Saturday to herself without us rattling on about birds all day.

These days, Dad leaves the house at three o'clock in the morning to photograph gannets and seals before I've even hit REM sleep, so I mostly have to make do with the birds I see in my patch. Maybe that's something I need to think about, too.

We walk further on, traipsing across the tall ridge that overlooks the reserve. The river reflects the bright, cool blue of the sky and I find myself smiling because I can't remember the last time I heard silence and not the Velcro-pull of car tyres on tarmac in my city apartment. Despite the threat of lost shoes, I press my feet firmly into the ground with each step, mud squelching into the fibre of my laces. 'Anything?' Dad calls. We're all supposed to be vigilant, but I'm listening to the slow flow of the river and the shriek of an oystercatcher somewhere far away. I'm not on the lookout for what we've actually come here to see.

About ten minutes later, we're down from the ridge. This time, my eyes are wide and binoculars poised. Nothing. The reserve seems more deserted of wildlife than usual. Maybe it's time to pack up and head back to the car.

Dad freezes. Gaze trained on the field ahead. He presses the binoculars into his glasses as if to keep himself upright. Dad beckons us with his arm, keeping his eyes focused on the bird. 'There!'

We slow-jog awkwardly towards him. I nudge my binoculars through a gap in the high fence, focus and spot it.

A short-eared owl.

The shortie is perched on a low branch of a dead tree. Surrounded by reeds and at this angle, it's almost completely hidden, unexposed, or it would be but for the pirouetting motion of its head. Its focus spends barely more than ten seconds on a single spot, the owl's large eyes training on the ground below it then ricocheting away to the next patch. If I didn't know it was hunting, I would say it was possessed.

*

Owls have long been regarded as mystical symbols across the world and, most frequently, foreshadowers of death. During Diwali, throughout India and Pakistan, thousands of owls, such as the mottled wood owl and the rock eagle owl, are killed violently every year to bring good luck to the village and keep it free from sickness. In some traditions, owls are buried alive under a building to give prosperity to the inhabitants for the year ahead. Other folklore beliefs say that owl feathers are so terrifying they can be used to ward off bad spirits which come a-knocking at your door.

Short-eared owls are one of the five native species of owl in Britain: barn, long-eared, little, tawny and shorties. Less frequently, we are visited by the snowy owl – a handful of these owls find themselves swept over to Scotland from Greenland every year, causing quite a stir and making way for Harry Potter headlines across the country with very little consideration to how disorientated the birds must feel. However, our native owls can be seen all year round and it's much less difficult to spot them than you might think. The short-eared owl is equally as beautiful as the ethereal snowy owl and you can find them hunting mice and voles across wetlands and farmlands in the winter during the crisp sunlit hours before they head to their upland habitats as the weather heats up. Their raspy yap of a call is a shock of sound across the reeds, a short warning blast that sounds a lot like a grouse or an angry Jack Russell. With their dappled grey-brown backs and faces, they can look startling as the light hits them to illuminate their large amber eyes. As with all owls, shorties have incredible hearing. Their disc-like faces are designed to gather sound, with their asymmetrical ears (one higher than the other) meaning they can easily pinpoint the shuffling sounds of shrew families in the thick grass.

Powerful, silent, mysterious and deadly, is it any wonder that owls and witchcraft have always been linked? However, our short-eared owls are actually diurnal, so that busts part of the spooky myth. There are many legends about owls from across the world – an owl was the constant companion of Athena, the Greek goddess of wisdom and knowledge, and in some cultures the owl is seen as the Guardian of the Night, hooting to warn of death, bad luck or – traitorously – an approaching witch. In the Celtic Pagan tradition, the owl is the symbol of Cerridwen, the darker side of life, and is even sometimes called *Cailleach* in Scots Gallic, meaning 'old woman' or 'hag'. This isn't the kindly term you would use for your grandma – a *Cailleach* here is something intrinsically linked with the spirit world, ready to talon-grab you by the shoulders and whisk you off down a dark tunnel. It is something waiting and screeching just out of sight.

The Celtic Welsh myth about owls is perhaps one of the most interesting of all. The story of Blodeuwedd is written in *The Mabinogion*, the oldest book of prose in the British Isles, filled with eleven stories of magic and heroes with superhuman strength. In one of these tales, the Welsh hero Llew is cursed by his angry mother to never have a human wife, so Llew has one created for him by the magician Gwydion. The woman he makes is named Blodeuwedd (or 'flowery face') and, as the name would suggest, she is made of flowers. Blodeuwedd is sweet and innocent but is also in love with another guy. She tricks Llew into divulging the secret to his mortality, for he cannot be easily killed due to his magical powers. Blodeuwedd's lover almost succeeds in killing him but Llew is much too powerful and shapeshifts himself into an eagle to escape. Blodeuwedd is captured by Llew's uncle, who transforms her into a tawny owl, telling her that every other bird will fear her and she will be alone for the rest of her days.

It's no wonder owls have a pretty bad rep.

*

Here on the meadow, the short-eared owl is hit by golden light so that it looks almost white in the glow. Right now, it's not hard to see why owls are the ultimate witches' bird. The shockingly large eyes, the powerful hooked beak; everything about the short-eared owl screams predator. But they are also so incredibly gorgeous. I've seen shorties in flight here before, hovering cloud-like over the reeds and bulrushes; their silent flight is spectral, fantastical and mesmerising. But seeing an owl simply perched like this isn't something you can tear your eyes away from either.

The three of us watch as the bird continues to swivel and swerve its head, which must be filled with the sound of tiny claws scrabbling on dirt and the clicking of camera shutters that are being fired off around us. Dad is already aiming his in the right direction.

It soon becomes crowded as people catch on to what we're staring at. I decide to walk for a while on my own while Dad stays to get the perfect shot, and I head down the mown-grass track. Over on a smaller pool, I can hear teal whistling and the intermittent trill of a redshank. It's the first moment I've had to myself for a few days and I feel like my body has been vibrating non-stop. The pleasures of being an introvert during the holiday season. Right now, I'm shivering with my shoulders up to my ears. Voices drift by on the wind – a few Scousers, followed by a group of Americans. I find this hidden gem of wetland an odd place for them to be spending the Christmas break, especially as they're ignoring the lapwings wheeling around them and, as they walk further on, they wander straight past where the short-eared owl is perched, pivoting its hinged head. Surely, nature is the only thing worth stopping for.

Squinting against the sun, I take a few deep breaths of light, letting it sink into my skin and fizzle through my lungs. It is a soft, weak light, a hopeful winter sun, trying so hard.

In less than a week, it'll be the New Year. For the first time in a long, long time, I feel a sense of calm roll over me. Things will be different now because I'm making them different. I'm out in nature now, aren't I? While I haven't had too much time for magick over the past few days, I have a cool, multi-coloured calm in my chest. It's a new feeling; it tells me 'I'm out of that job, I'm free. I can do whatever I want!'

But I need to go one step at a time. There's a lot of repairing to do.

I take a deep breath and walk back to where my parents are still watching. The funeral is tomorrow and I don't know if even short-eared owls can distract us entirely.

*

My childhood bedroom has had many incarnations – baby-neutral yellow, neon-bright turquoise, goth-cave purple and now a crisp mint green that gives me a sense of serenity along with a clear message that the room is no longer my own. The books and white furniture have remained constant, however. I pluck out copies of teenage vampire novels and second-hand paperbacks, give them a sniff and put them back.

Linnet, by now, has scoped out the house and is making sure she leaves plenty of fur behind for my dad to sneeze at months later. Her favourite spots are behind the curtains where she can jump out on unsuspecting family members carrying full cups of tea, and the cupboard under the stairs where she emerges proudly covered in cobwebs. Mum has made her a little house from a cardboard box that has birds on the outside and her name over the front door so, of course, Linnet is defiantly not using it.

Currently, she is snuffling around under my duvet cover.

'You weirdo,' I coo.

Linnet is a keen observer of witchcraft. In fact, she likes to get incredibly close, something that's meant singed whiskers on more than one occasion. Once when I was three-quarters of the way through a new moon ritual after three hours of cleansing with tea, herbal baths, sage burning and charging crystals, Linnet came wailing to the closed door, claws paddling on the wood.

I crashed through my circle of protection charms and invocations, yanked open the door, only to have her stumble in like a drunk and run head-first into my incense burner. Will sheepishly admitted he had not performed his 'one job' of keeping her out of the way while I was going 'Full Witch'. Mouth set in a grim line, I started all over again.

It's bizarre to see her here, clawing the soft, innocent things of my childhood, digging those paws deep into the carpet and using it as a springboard to scamper down the stairs and back again in a calico flash. It's weird being back here in this small L-shaped room, because this is the room where I first started to learn about magick, something so closely bound up in my teenage years.

*

After discovering Wicca at a young age, I must have spent thousands of hours curled up in my room copying rites and runes into my Book of Shadows (a place where a witch records their workings in a diary format or writes out spells and rituals; at that point in my teenager years, my Book of Shadows was a purple spiral-bound notebook from WHSmith). When I was reading a book about witchcraft – whether it was on creating poppet charms, blessing candles or something bigger such as a Sabbat rite – I was engrossed. No amount of sunshine or sandwiches could tempt me away.

I was about twelve when I realised you could change your religion. A bit late to the game, perhaps, but I was a very 'good girl' who didn't like to challenge the status quo. We had RE lessons in my village C of E school where we made colourful posters with felt-tip pens and the loud kids got chosen for role plays at the front of the class where they could stand with their hands on their hips and their legs planted wide like they were head teacher for two minutes. There was a lot of talk of golden gods with lots of arms, special hats people had to wear and, of course, war. None of these things had really grabbed my attention. For me, religion was hymns in assembly about being 'cold and naked', long, dusty talks from local clerics who interrupted our classes at random intervals, prayers before bed to wish for the latest Barbie, and Sunday School, which I attended irregularly until the age of ten, mainly for the sweets and the painting.

All of this didn't fit in with the dark imagination that was running wild inside me. I'd been one of those children obsessed with *Charmed*, *Buffy the Vampire Slayer* and *Sabrina the Teenage Witch*. Witches made up the entirety of my media absorption. I read magical books, devoured the 'spells' in the back pages of *Mizz* magazine and dressed up as Mildred Hubble at the weekend. I liked Halloween. A lot. Witches were a bit of escapism that my grandparents tutted at.

Harmless stuff; definitely not like all those people burnt at the stake. All fun.

Looking back, it's interesting to remember the sheer amount of magical resources and paraphernalia that were targeted at tweenage and teenage girls – girls who alternated between tears, boredom, secret sharing and obsession – particularly back in the late nineties and early noughties. There are countless marketing reasons behind this, but it spawned a fresh generation of witches who would see the world in a different spectrum of light. The media pointed me with neon-lit light bulb arrows towards witchcraft. It told me it was fun to have a secret that you couldn't tell anyone about. Teenagedom is a time of exploration and pushing boundaries, and what could worry Christian parents more than tinkering with spirits in your bedroom? But by giving twelve-year-olds their own agency, and the ability to create something that is just theirs and done in secret, witchcraft gives many young girls a way to express themselves, perhaps for the first time in their lives.

That's certainly one of the things that drew me to it. But I'm also one for books with a flashy dust jacket. I can't resist.

When I was in Year Eight and stumbling about the Philosophy and Psychology area of my high-school library on a rainy break time, I came across a book labelled Demonology. There it was, just smack-bang in the middle of books about French verbs and how to do macramé. The book's cover was a stained white and it was decades old, but it was the illustration of a ram's head emerging from flames and women hung up by their necks that was pretty attention-grabbing for me. I checked it out before looking inside, my heart thumping hard as I approached the librarian's desk, like I was about to unleash a big secret that the high-school library had been keeping for many years. This book was something I opened in secret in my bedroom and couldn't keep my eyes off. It was the first time I had seen a book outside my teen fiction series and magazines that talked about magic and the possibility of things other than cars and fossil fuels and the inevitability of maths lessons. Other people believed in this stuff too and they had done so for hundreds of years.

Being raised Christian, I had attended church, gone to confirmation classes on a Wednesday night after school so I could take Holy Communion with the grown-ups, and never questioned any of it at all.

A simple 'Is witchcraft real?' search engine question gave me more information on what had been blooming in the back of my head ever since I could remember. There were hundreds of witches out there! Witches from across the globe, all practising different forms of the craft, swapping spells and advice on everything from how to prepare a witch's jar (don't Google it, it's gross) to hiding your magickal tools from your parents. 'Coming out of the broom closet' was a phrase I read countless times. As I pored through more sites, some with panpipe soundtracks and twirling pentagram GIFs, an emotion flared just below my sternum and I realised quickly that it was envy. Envy that they could be in touch with something that sounded so wonderful and free, something which celebrated women as much as it celebrated men and taught us that our bodies and emotions were not things to be frightened of. The protective chants, the surges of emotion, the circles and intricate patterns; all this allowed witches to tap into the world. This pang of energy inside me was angry that I would have no way of getting any of the magickal tools that these online witches said were intrinsic to spell casting and potion making, and I was angry that I had been praying non-stop for years to a deity that didn't speak the language I wanted to speak.

My demonology book safely stashed in my school bag and my mind sparking with ideas, I resolved to find out as much as I could about Wicca and witchcraft.

So it was by the miracle of dial-up internet that I became a twelve-year-old witch.

IMBOLC

Winter isn't so much a season, but a deep feeling that penetrates every lining of our tissue and each uneasy hip joint. While I know it's a necessary time of recuperation and rest after the scurrying and gathering of the autumn months, I'm just not built for it – the slowness, the waiting. Winter means chapped lips, low-level gloom and constantly slipping over on the way to the bus stop.

However, some don't share my superior viewpoint. The world is invariably divided into two sets of people. There are those who are normal and are only happy with the sun on their bare shoulders, wildflowers tickling their ankles and the buzz of young birds hovering just above their heads. Then there's the other type – the woolly jumper crew who wait impatiently for October to strike. These strange people like thick hardbacks by the fire, three pairs of socks and have a smile loitering on their lips whenever they hear rain outside their window. We all know the sort – you might be one of them yourself – but enjoying winter feels as unnatural to me as wearing a bikini on a ski slope.

You'll be pleased to know I'm one of the normal types of people. Caroline, my sister, is abnormal (as her closest blood relation,

I can say this with gusto) and is in her element as soon as the temperature plummets; striding out in five layers topped off with Thinsulate gloves.

I'm dancing from one foot to the other in the January chill when she pulls up beside me. She sighs with her entire body. 'Oh my *god*,' she says as I climb in the car. 'It's been a nightmare.'

She's half an hour late for picking me up from Bury station (I am still delightfully carless) after getting lost in the one-way system and looks completely exasperated. I'm eating a Greggs vegan sausage roll so am content, but chilly, but my sister is white-faced and looks like she might need a brown paper bag.

'Don't worry about it,' I say. 'Want some?' I proffer my sausage roll but am not dignified with a response.

We're just into the New Year, that strange in-between time where people still haven't taken down their Christmas decorations and have forgotten all their passwords to important work accounts. Most people have just done their first full week back, but I've been pretty smugly writing at home with the heating cranked up and Linnet glaring at me from a patterned cushion next to my desk. I'm back at the freelancing but mainly giving myself time to work on more creative pursuits and tinker about with the occult. I've never had the luxury of this time before and will most likely never have it again, so I'm making the most of this golden period for as long as I can. I feel myself being lapped by waves of creativity while I'm writing a new children's novel. My mood is better than it's been in months. I know that this experiment into witchcraft and Paganism is exactly what I needed. My mind and body are recovering slowly but there's a slither in me that wonders how long it'll be before I'm browsing TotalJobs again.

Caroline asks how things are going.

'I'm becoming more of a cat lady by the minute. I love it.'

'Are you sure about that?' She raises her eyebrows.

'Hey, just because I didn't get a lap cat, doesn't mean she's not a good girl, OK?'

'Yeah, but you could still swap her.'

No one ever thinks Caroline and I are sisters. People often do a triple take when we say we're related, and it's not hard to see why. Although we are the same towering height down to the millimetre, have the same hair colour and green eyes, we might as well be from different countries altogether. Caroline's mass of curly hair and propensity for burning in the sun versus my olive-toned skin and bumpy nose call our sisterhood into question on a regular basis. She's full of sardonic comments while I'm up in the clouds. It shouldn't work, but I'm glad it does.

I glance over to my right and am struck that I don't see her as often as I should. It's only thirty miles between Manchester and Accrington, but sometimes we can go months without anything other than a string of Instagram memes. I make a mental note to put more effort in; a delayed New Year's resolution.

Today, we're on a pilgrimage. We've got a pack of goodies for our walk and about seventeen layers between us.

*

When I was little, nine or ten, I'd ask Mum and Dad if we could go and see the witches. After a lot of eye-rolling and plenty of Chinese burns from Caroline, we'd be in the car with a pack of jam sandwiches, heading down B roads at speeds that still make me flinch today.

These were the parents who queued up outside Waterstones at midnight for the latest Harry Potter release, who took me to stand in stone circles in my teenage years and didn't ask too many questions when I sat outside in the freezing cold of the garden, wound up in scarves and blankets so I could watch the stars. They practically nurtured my becoming a witch, although I'm pretty sure they don't think of it that way; they might as well have handed me a broomstick on my sixteenth birthday.

When we, my dutiful family and I, arrived in Newchurch, Lancashire – a small village of blind corners and dark-windowed cottages – that's when I'd start craning my neck. I'm not sure what I was looking for, but perhaps nine-year-old me was hoping for a flurry of sparks from a bedroom window or a row of shrunken heads in a porch, like something from a witchcraft theme park.

We were in witch country.

The whole area of Pendle, Lancashire, is defined by the legend of the Pendle Witches. The area lurks just below the ancient Forest of Bowland, sitting almost squarely in the centre of England. When I think back over the time I've spent there hiking and witch-ogling, my visits have been made up of gnarled crops of moss, fence posts slick with rot and rain, black trees bent horizontal in the wind and the haunting whimper of curlew across the fields. If the fierce weather and sullen-fronted cottages aren't enough, the area of Barley, Newchurch, Roughlee and Blacko is dominated by the leering bulk of Pendle Hill – more than 550 metres of rock that seems to blot out the sun and conduct rain at all times of the year. This Lancashire moor seems even wilder than those of Yorkshire not so many miles away.

Newchurch lies close to the foot of Pendle Hill, with the old *kirk* that overlooks the graves of many infamous 'witches' carved with the Evil Eye to ward off their devilish suitor. My dad and I would get out of the car and I'd wander through the headstones and knee-high grass looking for secrets, a scrap of information everyone else had missed that would tell me the truth about the witches. I'd make this discovery and some local witch would take me under her wing and teach me all there was to know.

Caroline missed out on my magick obsession, probably because she could see my levels of intensity notching up over the years and got car sick on long journeys to the middle of nowhere. She would have much rather been cloistered in her room drawing pictures and making up cartoon strips. Even now she prefers sketching and *Grand Designs* binges; however, she did move to a small village with Pendle Hill visible from her bedroom window. Maybe she did get the witchy influence after all.

*

We drive to Barley and it seems like half of the North West has chosen today to come and stretch their legs here. I'm annoyed, OK, I admit it – this is witch turf. This lot aren't here for the witches, they're here to pick up dog poo and have a mulled cider at the Pendle Inn. Some of us are here to breathe in the witchiness of it all, to put our hands in the frozen mud and feel the tingling of the earth under our fingers. My frequent visits have made me oddly protective of the place.

'Look at them all. Look! That dog has shoes on. God, I hate them all.' I'm in the passenger seat, shaking my head into my Thermos.

'Wow, Jenn. Wow.'

'But they don't get it!'

'They're just walking their dogs, OK? So what if that beagle is wearing a puffer jacket?' She's right but I carry on.

'Remember when we were kids though? You never used to get anyone here. We were left alone to enjoy the witchiness in peace.'

'*Some* of us enjoyed it . . .'

I heave a dramatic sigh. 'We'll have to pretend they're not here.'

We find somewhere to park, which involves a fifteen-minute walk along a line of cars back into the village of Barley, and get going in the direction of Pendle Hill. But as we're walking, I notice something is missing.

'Where is it though?'

'There!' Caroline says.

'Where?'

'Well, it's supposed to be there.'

The January mist has completely engulfed Pendle Hill and there is nothing to be seen but an opaque wall of fog. On the drive from Bury station, we'd debated actually climbing up it – Caroline is training for the Yorkshire Three Peak Challenge so any chance to scramble up a slope and post a Strava update, and she's usually there. But today, it's impossible. People around us are chattering away, oblivious to the looming hulk of stone just out of sight. I've been up the hill a few times in recent years and always manage to get lost on the summit. At the top, I've got my head pointed skyward to follow the graceful arc of skylarks and end up falling over a clump of sod onto my arse. I have genuinely broken bones while birdwatching, but I try not to hold it against them – birds can't help being so enticing.

In the summer, once you get to the peak of the hill, the world below drops away to another plane and there seems to be only miles and miles of moor crackling underfoot. The surrounding view is a staggered pavement of fields and reservoirs and wind wraps around the hill in a continuous vortex, making standing still by the edge for more than five seconds completely impossible. Pendle Hill is not somewhere to go if you want a quick climb and a chippie tea – there is another world on top of it, completely invisible from the cluster of villages below, that needs to be explored. The peaty surface, furred over with sphagnum moss, gorse and heather, is the perfect habitat for partridge, meadow pipits and, in the autumn, migrating dotterel. Pathways thin out into narrow V shapes that leave you stranded, up to your ankles in bog. It's easy to spend hours on the maze-like plateau without finding your way down. Gorse and golden studs of tormentil work their way into the grooves of your boots until you feel rooted to that landscape – you are just a swathe of moor and open sky.

I remember once just narrowly catching the last bus out of Newchurch for the evening, struck with panic that I'd somehow be stranded in this strange, mythologised land as the sun was lowering its gaze away from me. Even now, there's still a flutter of fear attached to the landscape of Pendle Moor; Pendle Hill has overshadowed the many lives lived in this valley and it has touched a part of me too; I am the travelling witch come from afar (well, Manchester) to hear the dark stories of the witches who lived under its eye.

Knowing the mires that can still linger at the top of the hill on even a blindingly sunny day, I'm glad Caroline and I have decided to stay on level ground today. I snap on my gloves and take a deep breath. Inside Pendle's enclosure of hills, fog and high stone walls, I feel wrapped in the story of this area.

*

It's not so much a legend but well-known history, particularly across Lancashire. Ask anyone around there about the Pendle Witches and they'll automatically assume ghost-story mode. The rivalry, the hatred, the curses and the fears are great for scaring small kids. The borough of Pendle was thought to be 'contaminated with witches'[8] and ten men and women were sentenced to death at Lancaster Crown Court for having bewitched sixteen people to death 'by devilish practices and hellish means'.

As a child, I wasn't scared by the whisperings; I was obsessed. I latched onto the story like it was a fairy tale. In 1612, almost a decade into the reign of *Daemonologie*-author and magic-denouncer James I, witch hysteria had been unleashed across the country, the pyre fire and superstition having swept over from Central Europe. In among the hubble and bubble of accusations and Devil-fearing that sprang up in cut-off rural areas, a case of witch-fearing broke out in Pendle, Lancashire. It's here that an intense feud between two families had been simmering for years – a 'he said, she said' argument that would never be settled by an act of kindness. At the head of each family stood two women of 'ill-repute'; Elizabeth Southern (also known as Demdike) and Anne Whittle (known as Chattox) were demonised by the village as trouble-makers, layabouts, prostitutes and witches.

The two families were incredibly poor and lived in flea-infested conditions, often sending their children out begging along the winding roads around the moors of Barley and Blacko. It was on one misty morning that a pedlar was heading across the moors, carrying his wares through bog and marshland, when he met a young woman – Alizon Device, Demdike's granddaughter – who wanted to buy his pins. When he refused to sell to her, she cursed him. On reaching the next village, the man had a stroke, telling people that the wild girl up on the hills had caused it with her curse.

Boom. Witch fever.

The whole area was on high alert, watching out for the next person to choke at the dinner table or fall down face-first in the street. More 'supernatural' events kept occurring that year. A blighted harvest, stillborn children, mysterious illnesses; more rantings and ravings which only sought to exacerbate the fear. The Southern-Device family was at the heart of the whispers and accusations, and it didn't take long for the villagers to ensure their arrests, alongside several members of the Whittle family.

'They're witches, the lot of them!'

'Hang them all.'

The families blamed each other, hurling insults in the street, only adding more heat to the fire. The people of the area were up in arms against them, convinced they consorted with Satan out on the moors. Many people came forward to say they had seen the 'witches' talking to their animal familiars, which were actually the Devil in disguise. Evidence was called up from the strangest of places, including from the mouth of a nine-year-old girl, Jennet Device – another granddaughter of Demdike – who testified against her own family at Lancaster Castle in 1665. There is much indication that she was schooled by the local magistrate, Roger Nowell, on what to say so eloquently in front of the magistrate's court as the words recorded verbatim in the court registers were certainly not the words of a snotty-nosed little girl.

In total, ten people were hung for the crime of witchcraft and 'sorcerie' in Lancaster. Now, much like Salem, Massachusetts, the area of Pendle has become synonymous with toads, warts and witches. The tourist industry has gone to town with the idea and there are statues, placards of poetry, 'witch trails' scattered across the area – you name it, and Lancashire has it. We're so proud of our ghoulish history. There are even little white witches on brooms across our brown tourist signs and a few years ago I took the 'Pendle Witches' tour of Lancaster Castle where you could see the courtroom they were tried in and the chains they strained against. Even without the legend and history, there's something about the area that – akin to the wily, windy Yorkshire moors – makes the skin prickle and your shoulders rise, like someone's about to emerge from the fog to give you an unbidden, icy tap on the shoulder.

Of course, the reality of the story is a sinister one and everyone concerned must have been incredibly scared – and rightly so. Even if the women and men tried for witchcraft weren't actually casting spells on the community by the jagged light of their hearth fire, theirs would have been a short, brutish life (as Thomas Hobbes might have put it). The threat of hunger, plague and the Lord would have been ever-present and may have haunted the dreams of these villagers as they settled down on their dirt floor and hay for the evening. Sometimes it's easy to forget the privileged world we live in where we sleep under our duvets with a full belly of cocoa and the promise that our incantations and incense stocks won't cost us our lives.

This wasn't always the case, but it doesn't stop me from falling for the romantic view of the Pendle Witches when the clouds scud across the sky in a certain way and the setting sun casts shadows across the winding streets of Newchurch.

I'm not sure where I had first heard the story; my parents weren't into scaremongering but maybe they'd seen the word 'witch' on a pamphlet and thought they'd pass it my way. I might have read about the Pendle Witches in a service station leaflet and became obsessed.

Still am.

*

'Are you sure it's this way?' I ask Caroline, eyeing the path ahead of us. We are walking towards Aitken Wood where she says there's a nice walk. However, it turns out we'll be completing the walk alongside everybody else in the county.

'You want to go back?' she raises an eyebrow into the density of her bobble hat.

It's not that. I just don't want to share.

We climb the steep ridge towards a heap of black trees perched precariously on top of the hill. As we walk, my eyes wander off the path to the rivets of moss that twist around the ankles of trees to form large hollow banks around their roots. Moss banks are one of my favourite things in the world – you step on them and could just tread on a sweet-smelling, springy bed of green, or you could fall right through and break your ankle. They're deliciously dangerous.

At the top, we find ourselves plunged into darkness. Even without leaves, the trees are tightly packed and conspire together to weave a canopy so thick that all daylight is blocked out. Children's shrieks can be heard somewhere deep in the wood but everyone else's voices seem to have dampened, absorbed by the tendrils of winter mist and the thick carpet of pine needles softly decaying below us. No redwings rustle in the tangle of last season's brambles. The same fog that has swallowed up Pendle Hill is roiling around our ankles like in a high-school horror movie, breaking only occasionally to reveal a slick of dark green moss below. Underfoot the mud is frozen into ridges, hollowed out by rangers' Land Rovers, moulded into peaks and troughs making us walk lopsidedly through the tracks. Despite the hiking boots and wellies, this place has a stillness to it; its own special breed of magic. It is a capsule of icy winter, reminding us of our place on the Wheel of the Year.

Imbolc isn't far away; the first Pagan holiday of the typical western calendar year. Imbolc ('*IM-bulk*'), celebrated by Pagans on the first or second of February, is all about preparing for the coming spring, welcoming the first lambs and anticipating the early glow of blackthorn blossom. But here in this undercover labyrinth of trees, I find it impossible to imagine the reverberating bleat of lambs and the retreating snow when everything looks like *this*. Talk about bleak midwinter.

*

Statistics show that only a small percentage of the population suffers from seasonal affective disorder, a condition where the darker days and lack of access to sunlight to bookend our nine-to-five hours mean that we get depressed. This condition affects just 3 per cent of the population, with people reporting low mood, insomnia or sleeping too much, not being able to concentrate and other common symptoms of depression; but if you counted the heavy sighs of people as they flicked from their emails to their first spreadsheet of the day, I think many more people would be on the SAD spectrum than they let on. My own experiences with SAD have caused many lost weeks; periods of time where my memory is hazy with low thoughts, and where not a lot seems to make sense. I have longed for someone to pop out of the ether with a magic wand and whisk these feelings away so I could go out with my friends or take a yoga class, something that would uplift me again to my normal happier self. I know that it's going to take more than a magick spell to zap my depression and anxiety, but I'm still trying to unlock the reasons why I feel this way so badly throughout the winter months.

Everything is so much harder in the winter, especially in January and February. However, Imbolc is a time of hope in the darkness, a beacon of light in the limbo period between Christmas and Valentine's Day – two holidays where we are told to eat as much Cadbury's as our pancreas can handle. The word comes from the old Gaelic – *Oimelc* – meaning 'ewe's milk' and is the first of the Julian year to be associated with the Celtic goddess Brigid, the maiden of spring. Despite my feelings towards winter, Imbolc is definitely a time to be celebrated. As we move through the Wheel of the Year, Cerridwen, the dark goddess, is put to rest and the lithe goddess of promise and youth emerges like a seedling from the earth. Her influence touches the hawthorn buds and causes seed casings to burst open with a sound inaudible to human ears.

This festival, the next on the Wheel after Samhain and Yule, brings to mind a time of farmsteads long gone where sheep heavy with matted coats were cloistered away together over the darkened winter months, their babies tangled and stirring in their bellies. This was the real beginning of spring for our forgotten farming ancestors; the time when planning could begin for the year ahead, even though the first green shoots and the dawn chorus are not even a flicker in our consciousness yet. As with many Pagan festivals, Imbolc was adopted by the Christian church as Candlemas or the festival of St Brigid – to ease those unlawful Pagan stragglers into the new ways – turning the old celebrations away from the wind-tight barns filled with straw and into the draughty church hall.

*

Imbolc doesn't fall until February so January holds a vast expanse of foot stamping and icy cobbles ahead of it, which I'm not looking forward to, even though I have Caroline by my side. However, Aitken Wood holds several treasures. The trail we're walking along has been created to cause nervous giggles and make kids squeal. There are faces carved in the trees, a hag-witch emerging from behind a rock and, oddly, a unicorn with muddy flanks. It could feel cheesy but I like this nod to the spirit world. No actual witches are lurking behind the trees, the purposely laid-out boulders or the hanging bats, but I feel glad for this space and the stories it inspires in those who visit.

Caroline and I do a loop of the trail, posing for pictures with spooky creatures and talking non-stop about whatever it is we natter on about, waving our hands around. We pause close to the unicorn.

'Do you want a picture?' Caz asks.

'Um, yeah!' And I practically sprint over to get my photo taken. 'Do you?'

'Don't be ridiculous.'

I take her picture anyway, evidence of our day-retreat into the mist, and we both post them on Instagram. I know my sister.

Without looking at my face she asks, 'How are you doing?'

'All good,' I say. 'I'm becoming a cat lady, remember?'

'But are you doing all right being at home all the time and everything?' Her eyes are low like she's preparing for the answer to be a blow. She knows it's been a tough few months leading up to this point.

'No, you know what, I think it's actually fine. Genuinely.' I'm waving my hands around. 'I go to yoga nearly every day, I see my friends, the freelance writing is going well.'

She nods. 'OK, that's brilliant. Are you looking for a job?'

'Not yet. I can last another couple of months before my savings run out. I just . . . yeah, I just need some time out.'

We pick our way through the mud patches in silence, arms out for balance. It's hard to explain why I need to take this time away from standard nine-to-five work. I need some space to reconnect, and even more time to understand what it is I'm reconnecting with in the first place. I want to thank my sister for asking though. I link her arm on our descent back to the valley.

On the way back to Bury, we have Smooth FM on and they say it will snow soon. I don't doubt it.

*

When you're in hibernation mode at this time of year, you've got to get your kicks in other ways. Aside from exploring the natural world, writing has always offered me solace. Both have gone hand in hand for me for many years. By trade, I am an environmental writer and have written articles on birdwatching and nature conservation for national magazines. But before I took the plunge to become a freelancer I had worked for the Royal Society for the Protection of Birds (RSPB), getting excited about birds on a daily basis, so much so that once I raised money for hen harrier conservation by hurling myself off a crane in a sponsored bungee jump. Passionate? Yes. Crazy? Maybe also yes.

I've always had that love of nature inside me and have felt the urge to sneak out of the house early in the morning, even before the first blackbirds rustle their heads from their wings, to see it at its most incredible. It's been the same with writing.

Writing, for me, has felt as easy as magick. It tickles the same deep-rooted feeling in me like it's coming up from the core of my being. There are times when I am writing where time doesn't seem to exist like I'm in a trance state or in the depths of a ritual.

But another positive aspect of the passions of witchcraft and writing is the community they create. While I have been out of the witchcraft loop for some time, I have been following like-minded individuals on Instagram and Twitter, allowing me to keep a tentative toe in the witchy waters. This has led to many longing-filled hours of scrolling, just wishing I had the energy to be as active and dedicated as these people with their flowing dresses and candle magick tutorials. Just step onto social media for two minutes and you can really feel the love and the passion people put into their craft – whether writing or witchery. Type in the magickal hashtag of your choice and get ready to fall down a rabbit hole of knowledge; all at once you're wrapped up in the cosmic folds of astrology or plunged down to the spongy roots of herbalism. As someone who has attempted to draw my star chart on numerous occasions only to realise I can barely count or draw angles, reading the nuanced online posts about sun, moon and rising signs has been so helpful to my development in astrology. While there are many staunch defenders of gleaning your knowledge from a long-awaited book, having access to free content has been revolutionary in my development as a witch and to those I know.

'What can I use as a substitute for amazonite?'

'How do I dress a candle?'

'What are the properties of holy basil?'

Ask any question and within seconds Google's magic mirror will whisper the answer. I've ordered many a book or picked something up in a second-hand bookshop only to find the writing dry, condescending or just plain ill-informed. Online, if you know where to look, you can find the platform that really steps up your development.

There are many of those in the online witchcraft community who are welcoming and willing to take a young witch under their wing (but please always be careful who you approach as your teacher) and I have always tried to do the same and give out helpful information about my own craft in the past and point people towards resources that have helped me on my own journey.

Perhaps, one small step I can take to return to the witchcraft community is to reach out to people on Instagram. I need to remind myself that witchcraft is something that can fit around, and be incorporated into, my daily life. It doesn't have to be shooting sparks from your fingertips and extravagant fire rituals under a blazing full moon; it could just be a chat with your favourite witchy people. Stir your morning coffee with intent saying 'I will be resilient today'; if you find yourself anxious in a crowded cinema, close your eyes and imagine your energy stretching right down to the earthen ground deep below the building's foundations – Mother Earth is there to catch you in the most unlikely of places. Look just about anywhere and you will find her.

Surrounding myself, even digitally, with people who I know are on the same wavelength as me feels like a step in the right direction.

It was on a chilly day in January that I decided to reach out to Ambrosia Hawthorn. Ambrosia is the editor of *Witchology* magazine, a celebrated author among the Wiccan community, and is on the editorial board of witchy resource Witch With Me. I've written for *Witchology* a few times in the past and I love how the magazine normalises witchcraft and allows us to connect with other magickal folk via their websites and social media pages, alleviating that sense of being 'the only witch in the village'.

Ambrosia is a like-minded person who didn't have access to a lot of resources when she was stepping onto her path many years ago, so the online world has been a great source of joy and knowledge-sharing for her too.

With my own path in mind, I ask her how she stays on track with her own witchcraft calling, even when modern life gets in the way.

'For me, there are lots of little instances that invite wonder and magic into my life. My relationship with the natural world is everything. I respect and work alongside nature and the cycles of life. I do feel that a nature connection is important to any path and most of the tools we witches use come from nature. Is a nature connection necessary? I don't think anything in witchcraft is truly necessary. Magick is a choice to create change that's entwined with intention. Symbolism also plays a large part in witchcraft and can be often substituted for items from nature. Don't have a candle to light? Draw a symbol for fire instead.'

This thrifty and resourceful view of the craft can be a blessing for anyone caught without a pocket of herbs and is great for anyone just starting out with the craft – you don't need a set of magickal tools, you only need yourself, your breath and the moon shining in through your open window. Ambrosia identifies as a Wiccan and a witch and has a focus on herbalism, divination, energy work and astrology as part of her daily witchcraft practice. She works with the four elements of Earth, Air, Fire and Water, which bind witchcraft to the intricate patterns of nature. Working with the elements doesn't really need special tools; it just requires time and the ability to step into a deep connection with the natural world: 'For my Wiccan practice, I mainly focus on following the Wheel of the Year, observing the moon and performing Goddess rituals. Much of my recent work over the last few years has also been in Water magick, but I have slowly started gravitating towards earth or green witchery as of late. My natal chart in astrology is heavily based on the Earth elements and I am missing Water almost completely. I like to think that my lack of connection to Water magick is either from an earlier life's mastery or a vital need in this life.'

Despite being happy working witchcraft alone, as I have done for most of my life, Ambrosia does believe meeting like-minded people is important for not only honing your craft but for feeling a sense of connection, particularly in your teenage years when you might feel like you're the only one who really sees the stars at night.

'I realised I was a witchy person when I was around thirteen. I grew up hearing stories about my ancestors on both sides of the family. On the one side, it was the Yup'ik ancestors (the indigenous people of Alaska) who read dreams and practise healing magic; on the other, it was the Puerto Rican folk healers who also liked to divine futures. These stories intertwined with my own life when I started picking up dream interpretation books as a teenager. From there I discovered Wicca, then witchcraft. My search for knowledge of the occult has never stopped since.

'*Witchology Magazine* was a special online project I started in 2018 to reach out to other witches and those who were interested in witchcraft. The magazine helps give a voice to witches by witches; there are many Pagans, Wiccans, witches, heathens, Druids and healers with knowledge to share. The core of the project focuses on no right way or path, but highlights many ways people can connect to the magick around them. When I was a teenager I didn't have access to many books, nor did I have a witchy community as I do now. My practice was heavily influenced by my internet connections and the magazine was born from those connections.'

This witchcraft community has always been a great help in more ways than one, both for myself and for Ambrosia, and I'm glad I reached out today. It's warming to know that even though I might have abandoned witchcraft and Paganism for so long, the inclusive online community is thriving and still giving people a place to nurture their beliefs. While I'm lucky enough not to have faced too much opposition to my beliefs among my family and peers – although I'm not sure my Year 10 RE class in 2005 was ready for the revelation – there are many who have been forced to keep their beliefs a secret from parents and colleagues for fear of discrimination. So, in a world of polarised views, how does a full-time witch deal with the haters?

'That's definitely a tough hurdle to overcome for many,' Ambrosia muses. 'Personally, I have always been a private person, which has extended to my craft. However, I also have first-hand experience with family members not understanding me or my beliefs. A sad but true example of hate that I worked through was with a family member who would turn my photographs face down because I was thought to be evil. They made many attempts to purify my soul in their own way. My only advice is to hold firm in your beliefs, try not to be too confrontational and find support from the witchy community around you. I have spent many days online looking for connections to a path I knew in my heart was valid and that was enough. Today, I have a truly supportive sister and husband that I can share everything with, free from hate.'

Ambrosia's story sounds familiar and I'm sure rings true for many others who discovered their path as a teenager. Of course, there are hundreds of thousands of people across the world without access to the internet and with many people around them who do not let them practise witchcraft freely, so we are in an incredibly privileged position.

Knowing that these resources are still available to me, and that there are supportive people out there looking to lift up other witches, is a real help. I might be in my pyjamas and scowling at the weather outside through my window but I feel reassured that there are small ways I can reconnect with my path and get back on track, without having to put on a pointed hat and cackle at the moon. At least not just yet.

*

1–2 February
Imbolc comes while driving through a snowdrift on the most treacherous road in the Peak District.

I feel pumped up; Joss and I are singing along at the top of our voices to the songs we've just been moshing around to for the past three hours – a Welsh rock band that screams about feminism, empowerment and heartbreak; only the best subjects, of course. It's past midnight now and we've been checking the news for road closures all evening. Tonight is the first night in a week when the Snake Pass has remained open although there are still reports of black ice. We're two lucky ladies to be getting back from Sheffield to Manchester tonight.

I hope we make it in one piece.

Joss and I have been friends since uni. I do some quick mental maths and realise that's eight years and we're seriously old now. After almost a decade of friendship, I know that Joss is one of the most practical and capable people on this planet. If I smashed a wine glass on her kitchen worktop (I haven't done this), she would already have ordered a whole new set through John Lewis '1-click' because it's likely the rest would soon follow suit. At uni I went to her for dating advice and what to wear on nights out; now, I ask her about how to tile my kitchen and cope with mental breakdowns. She's incredibly versatile with her advice.

As we're practically ancient now, I'd wondered if our gig-going would tail off somehow, but we still seem to average one a fortnight and our eyeliner and Dr Martens will not be put to rest. A few years ago, Joss spent an entire concert shielding me and my broken arm against the front barrier so we could see one of our favourite childhood emo bands – not even shattered bones will stop us.

The bends up here are getting pretty tight and I'm gripping the door handle. Joss's face is unflappable as always. The waning crescent moon is not exactly a guiding light when the roads are armed with dull ice slicks and potential rock slides, and I feel totally powerless. The weight of craggy heath several hundred metres above on the mountainside presses down against us as we ricochet through the gorge. Joss's phone, our Satnav, rattles ominously, propped behind the gearstick. Luckily, our music is so loud it drowns out the fearful sound.

We turn a corner and the headlights scream against a thick wall of snow clinging to the mountain wall. On the next stretch of road, we find an abandoned car and a single, lone hubcap. Another turn and our lights illuminate a barn owl on a fence post. As we tear back into shadow, the owl turns and flies away, its body arched like a white double fish hook. I tighten my grasp on the door handle.

We can't see the owl anymore, just another stretch of dark road, but it's then I remember. I check the dashboard clock. 'Oh! It's a Pagan festival today.'

'Oh, right!' Joss says. 'What do you do for it?'

'It's a fire festival called Imbolc. So, traditionally people lit bonfires to welcome the coming spring. It's the start of lambing season, but now people just tend to stick to the fire thing.'

'How many festivals are there? I know you do the Halloween one.'

'Samhain. Yeah, there are eight of them. It starts with Samhain, then it's Yule – Christmas – then Imbolc is this one today.'

'It sounds cool.' After a few beats she asks, 'Do you think they'll tour again this year?'

'Who?'

'The band.'

To be fair, witchcraft isn't something that comes up for us in everyday conversation and she does already listen to me talk a lot about birds.

Joss drops me off outside my block of flats and we're both grinning with relief that the mountainsides didn't crush us, maim us or send us hurtling into a ditch. Linnet is intrigued to find out why my back smells of other people's beer.

I'm feeling on top of the world, still pumped up with adrenaline. I'm in no way in the right mindset for an Imbolc ritual and am too unprepared to do one later in the day. Instead, I opt for something simple. I scavenge a tea light from the bathroom cabinet and light it on the kitchen worktop. It's just your average tea light in its pre-packaged silver cup, no wider than an espresso cup, standing on the corner of the worktop by the draining rack. When you light a candle, sometimes there's no way of knowing how large the flame will be. It could be a small bubble of light, no bigger than your little fingernail, or the size of an entire mound of earth pushed up by a thick and greasy slick of light. This one pops out of the wick as a round, fizzing ball, bouncing around like a balloon on its frazzled black string. I glance around at the usual sights of our kitchen; the cat bowls, the recycling box, back issues of *BBC Wildlife* on the dining table and Linnet two inches from my feet hoping for a second supper – all the usual messes and sights. And then there's my little flame.

It's waving with a Mary Poppins sort of cheeriness. I nod back at it only to find it bopping back and forth again in acknowledgement.

In the modern form of Paganism that I have followed over the years, I have worked with the Triple Goddess taken from Celtic myth. Brigid, Rhiannon and Cerridwen are viewed as three aspects of one goddess – they represent three phases of the year, three phases within the moon cycle, the three phases within our own life. They are the Maiden, Mother and Crone and show us womanhood through the ages. Imbolc is the time of Brigid – we have emerged bleary-eyed from the darkest days of winter and are looking to the pale and wintry sun to guide us into the light. Brigid, this Maiden form of the Triple Goddess, is often represented by a waxing crescent moon or as a tall, defiant girl just coming into her womanly body; her chin held high and a burning torch in her right hand. She is the spark that starts our year. She is the ignition of daylight and the bringer of vitality.

I look down at the worktop. This little flame holds the renewed hope of spring. It's barely anything at all, a minute firefly reflecting off the cutlery and plates, but when in darkness, we always look to the light. She is my small spark of Imbolc fire.

*

Witches can be tricksy so-and-sos, they're difficult to find. It's not that they're hiding in caves in the Outer Hebrides, but you won't find them under every stone at the bottom of the garden. As it goes, I know very few witches in the flesh. You can't just pop in for a cup of tea at the witch's round the corner, as she might be thirty miles away. Pagans don't have a physical church to visit on Sunday mornings – they do their form of worship outside in nature or the comfort of their own homes. The internet is brimming with fabulous people willing to share their craft or post an arty shot of their latest herbal concoction. But you're unlikely to see your local suburban witch advertising tarot readings in the village hall down the road. That's what makes it all the more special when you find another practitioner who lives close by.

Saying that, there are all kinds of Pagans and witches living in the UK today; in fact, the 2011 census said there are over 53,000. When you come across a witch in real life, the chemistry can be electric – like love at first sight, but more like, 'Oh my goddess, you're a witch, tell me everything.' You can find them in the most unlikely of places; you may find fellow Pagans in your yoga classes or city-centre workplaces; you just need to know what to look for. Some may be more private about their practice than others but, in my experience, witches can sense other witches.

This is quite a common experience as a 'hedge' witch or solitary practitioner. Those who practise magick solo sometimes label themselves as hedge witches, coming from a witch's love of nature and all things green, but it has come to mean someone who practises witchcraft alone (but maybe in a hedge if they fancied it). The term itself was popularised by Rae Beth in her book *Hedge Witch: A Guide to Solitary Witchcraft* in 1990 – a series of letters written from Rae to two new witches who were each studying alone – although the term has much older roots. The book details the seasons, festivals and how to get in touch with nature if you are just opening yourself to the craft, and it was one of my guiding lights when I was returning to the craft in more recent years. The hedge lifestyle has always suited me and it can have its perks; finding a quiet spot among the trees to sit and connect with nature is something that brings me great joy.

As I write, of my current circle of friends, flung all across England, four of them practise some form of hedge witchcraft. Covens, on the other hand, are a tightly knit group of people who want to practise ritual work together and dozens of them exist all across the country, but they are often elusive and very exclusive. But how do you get in the know about where to find a coven when there is so much secrecy and stigma still surrounding the Pagan path in the first place? I don't think it will come as a surprise to hear that hedge-witchery can get a little lonely.

It was at this time of year (cold, wet and miserable) that I first found Treadwell's. There isn't an equivalent of Treadwell's up north, or anywhere else I've found, for that matter; the world is severely lacking in Pagan bookshops. I'd moved down to London for a new magazine job three years before, and I'd felt completely cut adrift from my life. Having just left Lancaster where I'd been living since university, one of the greenest cities in the country, and been dropped into Acton, west London, I'd lie awake wondering what I had just done with my rural, countryside life. Every day I was woken up by ring-necked parakeets skittering blue tits off the garden fence, nothing like the oystercatchers that had echoed up the Lune.

I quickly found the WWT Wetland Centre not too far away in Barnes, where I watched bitterns and siskins at the weekend. It was a haven in this clunky, drawn-out city, but it was a speck of calm, not a sanctuary. I was having a great time making amazing friends in my fancy new office and drinking wine on a weeknight, but I didn't have somewhere I could feel grounded. London left me reeling twenty-four seven.

After a bit of research, I found what I was looking for.

Treadwell's is down a long, dark side street in Soho. If you weren't looking for it, you would have no idea it was there, a bit like Diagon Alley. I like to think that witches and esoterically minded folk just end up drifting there, pulled to it like to a vortex of all the supernatural happenings in south-east England.

It is the middle of January, and I am bundled in a long grey wool coat I found in a charity shop in Chiswick; I thought it completed my 'London look'. I keep my head low as I enter the shop, sure that everyone in there will turn their heads. 'She's not a witch!' they'd say, and fling me from the door with the power of their minds. As it goes, no one notices me apart from the friendly shop assistant who nods and checks me in. He asks if I've come far tonight and points me in the direction of candle anointing oil.

Everyone is chatting merrily against the downpour outside. There are around twenty of us, all different ages and nationalities, London residents and passing visitors, each of us ready for the Open Circle ritual we've signed up for online. An Open Circle allows you to take part in a ritual with others, without being part of a regular coven.

As the clock on the wall clicks over to seven o'clock in the evening, we're all told to file behind a woman in a floaty dress, descending a concealed set of stairs into the basement.

At that moment, it is difficult not to think *I'm going to die here.*

The basement room is lit by candlelight; long tapers and thick, sturdy pillars. Our hostess and High Priestess for the evening tells us what the evening will centre on – the coming Wolf Moon. Every full moon has a name depending on the time of year and 'Wolf Moon' seems pretty apt for the wildest of months. After letting us know what our evening would be like, the visualisation we will be doing and arranging us into a wide circle, she leads the ritual, which goes something like this.

We chant:

> Enter the circle,
> Enter the circle,
> Bring what you have to give,
> Take what you need.

We call the quarters and the Goddess in the usual way, then each of us reads a line from a poem:

> Out in the dark over the snow,
> the fallow fawns invisible go
> with the fallow doe;
> and the winds blow
> fast as the stars are slow.
> Stealthily, the dark haunts around
> and, when the lamp comes out without a sound
> at a swifter bound

than the swiftest hound,
it arrives, and all else is drowned.
And star and I and wind and deer
are in the dark together – near,
yet far – and fear drums on my ear
in that sage company drear.
How weak and little is the light,
with all the universe in sight;
love and delight,
before the might
of the vast and wary night.[9]

After this, we sit and listen to a candlelit story told by our High Priestess; wily wolves, shadow-filled forests and rumbling snow. It's so clear in my mind's eye I could reach out to grasp a fistful of thick wolf skin and furred sinew, to feel the power of that wild animal in my hand. Furrowed in candlelight, we begin a guided walking meditation with our eyes focused low on the ground, moving in a circle around our leader to the low beat of a stretched-skin drum.

It is exhilarating. In my meditative state, lulled by the incense and the patterns of our shared breath, the wolves from the story find me in a crisp forest clearing. A part of me, the part that is hardly in this world right now, sensed them coming; they sweep me up and now we are all running together. The vision of their lean muscle and raised hackles is something that fills me with strength. I urge myself on, knowing the group and I are all experiencing this together. I am comforted by the wolf's might.

I've no idea how long we do this for. It feels like years and seconds all at once. So is the power of magick. The energy of our breaths and quickened pace spirals upwards and it's possible to feel the weight of the hundreds of rituals that have been performed in this space over many years.

It's then that the drum slows and we are asked to bring the energy we've created down to the floor, to ground it. As we stop, I feel immense power rushing through my feet and hands into the basement floor. When it has all flowed out of me, I'm left with the sense of oneness, not only with myself but with these flushed and smiling people in the room who I don't even know by name. We all look up to find ourselves grinning, wolfishly, at each other across the High Priestess and her drum. Community, trust and support.

After the ritual's ceremonial closing is done – thanking the elements for supporting us and the Goddess for giving us power – a few of us exchange numbers, and I even end up heading to a woman's house a few weeks later for our own Imbolc ritual. I think back to those tightly wound communities that would have visited their village cunning woman for potions and tinctures – who would have relied so heavily on each other to get through the harshest peak of winter around the time of Imbolc.

As we have shifted into a society that values individual productivity over almost anything else, the sense of community felt in the generations even so close as our grandparents is something which has gradually faded away in westernised parts of the world. In times of need, plenty of which we have experienced in our all-too-recent history, having people who know us and genuinely care about us in close proximity has literally saved lives. The glowing buzz of a WhatsApp message from a friend who lives on the other side of the country just isn't the same as a quick hug and a cup of tea. But standing here among the smiling, flushed faces in Treadwell's basement makes me long for these vital meeting points to exist far and wide. These communities are a miracle for the lonely, the lost, and those who want to find a new way of living.

*

Coming back to my little life in Manchester, I know that the past year has been a train wreck for my mental health. In February, I feel like I'm still processing the strange, unnerving and familiar world of work as well as my intense emotional and physical reactions – the crying that seemed like it would never stop, the strange rashes and the clumps of hair that came out in the shower, the panic attacks on the tram before I had to snap on my smile and be a cheery workmate for the day. Over the next few months of my journey, I want to make it part of my mission to search for the small magickal communities and find my people.

OSTARA

'I'm all floppy, but just drag me along, yeah?'

Readjusting to an old way of life is knackering.

It's been a bumpy month. My eyes are a little dry and creased from too much time bunched up on pillowcases. I feel like I've slept non-stop for weeks. The low winter sun glares into view at eye-level and makes the world seem impossibly bright, like I'm seeing everything under fluorescent light; I'm an insect under an interrogative microscope trying to come to terms with my new surroundings. I thought I'd feel rejuvenated, filled with beans and sassy quips, but my body is taking longer to get with the programme than I thought. Part of me is filled with the jittering anxiety that millennials are so used to – I always feel the need to be on the go, ripping between side-hustles, back-to-back brunches and the usual nine to five. It's like I've been on the go for so long that I'm still sprinting in my mind when what I'm really longing for is a good old potter about a garden centre. There's another part of me that just aches and aches, like the sinew between my fingers is wedging the bones apart, making every flex agony. Why this strange affliction has decided to narrow itself down to my fingers and joints,

I don't know, but taking myself from A to B without a sit down in between is hard.

Who'd have thought it would be so hard to *slow down on the inside*? However, I do feel prepared. At home, I've cleared out the second bedroom to use as a ritual space. Candles and chunks of crystal stand on the upturned wooden crate I use as an altar; my sacred space that holds my ritual tools and is the hub of all my witchy work. It is something I can store neatly under a chair when the parents pop over or bring out to dance around under the moon. It centres me and reminds me that magick exists everywhere, even in my second-floor city-centre flat. I'm forging forward with my mystical goal for the year, just incredibly slowly.

Today, I'm getting out of the city. The idea seems fantastical like I'm about to head out on the trip of a lifetime (Disneyland, Australia or Mordor) after so many sluggish rainy days in bed. It's been ages since I had a good hike but I wish I'd brought my walking poles to prop myself up like the elderly lady I've become. Luckily, I can use Laurie as a leaning post and I hope he doesn't mind too much.

Despite my distinct lack of witchy pals, I'm very lucky to have a group of friends who are absolute diamonds. Laurie is one of these glimmers. The pair of us have been friends since we met at four o'clock in the morning in the pitch darkness of a nature reserve. It was during a 'Dawn Chorus' walk and, if I remember correctly, it was pouring it down, our tightly pulled drawstring hoods revealing about three inches of face. I thought he looked impossibly cheerful for a pre-sunrise amble. I think I was wearing a head torch, but that's by the by.

I wouldn't say we are unlikely friends in the slightest – there's a level of understanding between us that comes alongside our mutual interest in birds, weird folklore and crazy levels of exercise. Crazy full stop, really. Although we don't look alike per se, our shared characteristic feature is gangliness and a perpetual stoop from carrying too much birdwatching gear or having to bend low to talk to incredibly small, normal-sized people. I love Laurie for many reasons, but what I like the most is that while many people might try to make you act 'normally', sometimes you cry over the first swift of the season, and that's OK; we both get it. In our five years of friendship, we've been birdwatching across Europe, lived together as housemates for six months back in Lancaster, swam in a few cold rivers and lost wellies in many a field. There are few people I value more in my life than my best nature pal and few, come to think of it, who I can babble along with incessantly for six hours straight.

We're scarfed and hatted at Leighton Moss, the same nature reserve we met on, and we're on a slightly reminiscent track.

'How close should we get to it?'

'Right up there. Like last time!'

We shuffle along the length of a wooden barn; we're being covert, devious sneaks. The barn's walls are etched with moss and patchy with age, and the structure borders a scrap of ancient woodland. Half a tractor spills out from the open entrance but the inside is neatly stacked with carefully tessellated hay bales. The old farm buildings on the Leighton Estate look as rounded and ramshackle as the rolling hills around them, morphed over the centuries into something more approved of by the landscape.

In the murky light by the barn door, Laurie and I look up to the highest rafter where a box the size of a rolling suitcase is skulking in the gloom.

We crane our necks. 'Anything?' I whisper.

'Nothing.'

Four springs ago, we had assumed the same positions, slightly crouched with binoculars poised. I was a resident volunteer here at RSPB Leighton Moss in Silverdale, Lancashire. I'd saved up all my money to take up an enviable six-month internship and was fully immersed in the wild with no phone signal, miles away from the nearest place to get a Twix. When I look back on that time, I feel an immense sense of peace send its glow over my chest; it was a surreal segment of time, fuelled by a fierce passion for nature and shed-loads of homemade cake. I felt like I had been given the greatest gift of all. Of course, the daily practicalities of it weren't always rosy and I had more than my fair share of anxiety being so cut off from everything I knew, but it didn't take long to get into the slow, ambling pace of life that mimicked the meandering patterns of the seasonal shifts.

The internship was something I'd wanted to do for years and was born from the yearning for the wilderness that I felt so keenly, so intensely, and not just in a normal, socially acceptable way. I wanted it inside every pore of my skin and woven into the fascia of my being. I felt like I just couldn't exist without being totally consumed by nature.

In my eyes, few more perfect wildlife spots exist in Britain and I certainly wasn't disappointed during my stay. Twilight badger treks, lake-skimming ospreys, and tiny otter pups twisting over themselves like eels. I learned what felt like a lifetime's wealth of information in just half a year while I marched over the limestone crags in search of butterflies.

In a country that saw just eleven breeding male bitterns in 1997, the extensive reed beds of Leighton Moss played a pivotal role in bringing this bug-eyed, eerie bird back from the brink. I've always thought they looked like a heron's creepy cousin with a hangover. The reserve is now home to several pairs of mating bitterns after measures were taken to repair its ravaged reed bed a couple of years ago. Although I have been coming up to Leighton Moss for ten years, I have only ever seen four bitterns; they remain tricksy, secretive birds. But that's not what I hope to see in this barn.

The perpetual green of Silverdale and Arnside, an area of Morecambe Bay stretching up the North Lancashire coast to the border of Cumbria, is an Area of Outstanding Natural Beauty. It is home to some of England's most sought-after birds, several almost-extinct species of orchid including the lady's slipper orchid (Britain's rarest flowering plant), butterflies such as the high brown fritillary and the Duke of Burgundy, and more than 500 species of moth. The array of wildlife is intense and being in this landscape of hills, reed, wetland and beach always feels like coming home to me, like I have been craving my fix of this concentration of nature until I set foot here again. When many people think of Morecambe Bay they think of quad bikes on the Prom and seagulls nicking their ice cream, but Morecambe Bay isn't all about the delights of Morecambe itself. If you get to the highest point above Leighton you can see north around the curve of coastline to Ulverston, Grange-over-Sands, Kents Bank and Humphrey Head; this delicate fishing line of villages and towns all marked by the Victoriana of their bygone seaside holiday days. At night, they twinkle in a meandering constellation hovering slightly over the mudflats.

But there's a tinge of darkness to the area which has been the source of many works of fiction and many very true horror stories. The flats of the Bay are dangerous, life-snapping things where no sane person ever goes. The hidden tidal channels of the Kent River and the shifting sands are constantly on the move, with the one sure path you took yesterday lunchtime completely gone by the next. The sands are meshed together in an iridescent kaleidoscope of patterns like a deadly snowflake – they can never be replicated. Very few people can navigate them, giving them the sinister air reserved for old sailors' stories and tales of Atlantis. However, there are some who can predict their snakey ways – Cross Bay Walks are led by an appointed Queen's Guide of the Sands (there has been one in place for every generation since 1538) that until April 2019 was local man Cedric Robinson MBE. During his fifty-six-year position, he led hundreds of walks across the perilous sands, often barefoot. Despite warnings, there are still those who must work on the Bay or try to cross it alone; every once in a while, cocklers, tourists and locals are killed by the swirls of quicksand, their bodies never to be found.

The fishwives' tales hang like bait over the Bay.

For a decade, I've spent every spare moment I had in this area, lurking in fields long after dark to listen for woodcock or to catch sight of a snuffling badger, transfixed by the magic of nature.

A mission statement leaflet from OBOD, the Order of Bards, Ovates and Druids, reads:

> *Through the work of the Druids, we are able to unite our*
> *natural, earthy selves with our spiritual selves while working,*
> *in however small a way, for the safeguarding of our planet.*

While this is specifically about Druidism, this statement applies more broadly to most Pagan beliefs. The Earth is a friend, not something to plunder, and it is rare to find a Pagan who is not involved with some kind of environmental activism, whether that's winching themselves up a threatened tree or spreading wildflower seeds to help pollinators.

When I worked in nature conservation at Leighton Moss I didn't come across any Pagan folk (that I knew of) but the way the team talked about the landscape like it was alive and breathing struck a deep chord within me. People spoke about the Leighton Moss reed bed with stately reverence.

For me, this place – where you can spend a day getting lost in the greenness of it all – is somewhere that retains ancient knowledge. It speaks to me and I think other avid wildlife enthusiasts, like Laurie, get that.

*

It had been a warm evening during my internship, nearing summer so the sky was lilac and orange on the horizon with drawn-out flecks of gold. I'd heard a rumour of a barn owl living on a nearby farm and had rarely seen them in the wild so couldn't wait to see if my sources were correct.

On the easterly edge of Leighton Moss there is a long causeway, a rift in the reed bed which offers up a vast expanse of sky above it. When you descend the slope of the path, the reeds either side of you rise above head height so the only way to look is skyward: male marsh harriers practising food passes to their harem of females; broad-bodied chaser dragonflies muscling across the path; bearded tits pinging from one side to another, bobbing and dancing until they are engulfed by the thick microphone heads of bull rushes. It is a magickal place. In late March to early April, depending on the phase of the moon and the way the wind blows, you'll find wardens and avid birdwatchers stationed at regular intervals down the causeway listening out for 'gull call' – that uncanny and almost unpredictable few moments when overwintering bitterns emerge from the cloistered spaces between the reeds and scream like black-headed gulls as they rise up and fly away to their summer homes.

It's around seven o'clock on that summer evening when Laurie and I begin heading down to the causeway. The weather is warm and the pool at Public Hide seems impossibly blue after a never-ending stream of grey, cloud-patterned days. Shovelers, teals, cormorants, lesser black back gulls and a circling buzzard do rounds of the mere, marvelling at their own reflections in the clear water.

We approach the barn at Leighton Farm and wait.

As if manifested from our breath, a barn owl glides silently over the field below us. One downward motion of her wings – nothing more – and she is halfway across the green, pulled along on an invisible string. We stand as if the blood has solidified in our veins, in awe of her. She swoops around us into the barn and lands close to a box in the rafters that neither of us had even noticed. The bird dips her elegant head inside the box and is met by the squall of four haggard creatures. A host of chicks!

Just a few weeks later, I would have the joy of holding one of these chicks while it was waiting to be ringed by the Leighton Moss rangers. It sat like a splayed out kitten in my hand, staring comically up at me with its round eyes. But it smelled like a rat's rotting arse and I gagged until somebody, thankfully, removed it from my presence.

*

So, we are here at the barn once again except it is very early March and we can't feel our fingers. Laurie and I stand shivering. We aren't going to be so lucky today. Either the birds are hunkered down low in their nest box or they have found a better spot this year.

'Ah well,' we smile, bitterly disappointed.

I'm feeling slightly better by now and the sun is shining. There is even some blue sky. But I'm still knackered, with Leighton's best bird-friendly coffee yet to permeate my icy veins. We decide to find somewhere to sit and eat.

There is a log up ahead surrounded by a light covering of trees and I plop myself down so heavily it almost splinters the wood under my bum. The underside of the log is speckled with the knotty black balls of King Alfred's cakes and long, thin strips of lichen that are smooth to the touch; the log's wet mossy surface shifts under my weight, but its body is grounded in a way that calms me – a good spot for a weary traveller or a knackered witch. There is a quick-flying stream to my right, running into the west so it glints in the low sun. I lift my binoculars occasionally to watch great tits and robins in the trees around us. It's too early in the year for the undulations of birdsong; the world remains still. I'm glad to have got out of the house and to have felt the cool hands of winter sun on my cheeks but we've seen hardly any wildlife and I'm not the most adept of conversationalists right now. Poor Laurie!

Just then, he jolts and his eyes look over my left shoulder.

I burble, 'Wha——?'

I swivel around to see a stampede of seven red deer stags hurtling across the fields directly behind me. They're running at full pelt, led by the alpha, holding his heavy head high. The stags are of varying ages, one with only the banana stubs of antlers to prove his sex. There is a synchronised thud as their delicate hooves hit the hillocky grass, but surely no noise could ever come from the body of something so otherworldly?

They're coming straight at us. A beat of silence and they leap over a fence in almost perfect unison then hit the ground again. Their hooves thunder past us, across the path and into the tree cover where they slow to a trot and then a long-legged saunter. The mass of antlers immediately merges with the saplings until there is no traceable evidence of their appearance. The whole thing could have been a vision.

The field is cold again now. There is no aftershock, no stirring of the air to recollect their presence. Laurie and I sit in wide-eyed silence, watching the trees where the deer are no longer in sight until we aren't sure if the whole thing happened at all.

*

These incredible creatures can be seen at all times of the year, but red deer like these ones are found in very few parts of England, with higher concentrations of them in Cumbria, Norfolk and Cornwall. The natural habitat of red deer is in the deep woodland realm but, in the modern world, this kingdom has been taken from them so they have to get creative. At Leighton Moss, red deer carve deep paths in the reed bed, their myriad tracks visible only to the birdlife flying overhead. These paths can change the course of water, redirecting mere channels until the reed bed itself changes shape, causing havoc for nesting birds. Such is the trouble with forcing wild beasts into small boxes. At this time of year, the does are carefully cloistered away, harbouring curled up fawns in their stomachs. Stags, never the most paternal creatures of the animal kingdom, are left to roam in their own herds.

Ask anyone in the street what the most beautiful native British creature is and they're most likely to say a deer, so intrinsically linked are they to their elegant bodies, their knowing stares and their secretive nature, making it seem that they materialise like ghosts from thin air.

Typically, we might spot a small herd of red deer on the sheer highland mountainsides, raising their shaggy heads before cantering off into the distance. Roe deer can be found all across Britain, interspersed with the smaller population of Bambi-spotted fallow deer. They are always a joy to see and, due to their generally quite small numbers, it's still always a bit of a shock!

Deer, particularly stags, are bound up with magick and feature in so many Pagan myths and legends it's hard to keep up. From the Ancient Greeks and the Romans to Mayans and Ancient Britons, deer are one of our largest yet delicately featured land mammals and have entered our consciousness perhaps like no other animal.

In Celtic myth, some followers of the pantheon worshipped the horned god Cernunnos. The lord and protector of the forest, Cernunnos is depicted in many ways but most commonly as a hulking man with leaves twisted into his long and shaggy beard and many-pronged deer antlers protruding from his scalp. There is certainly a connection with the half-goat, half-human satyrs of Ancient Greek myth and this god of the wild lands and mountains; the archetypal figure of half-man, half-beast has been seen in many lands and passed through the minds of many. In other places around the western world, Cernunnos is linked with the Green Man, the guardian of the ancient forests and the very land itself.

As with many Pagan gods and goddesses, the Christian church took Cernunnos and adopted him as its own. But unlike Brigid (St Brigid) and other virgin goddesses that were channelled into the peaceful portraits of the Virgin Mary, Cernunnos did not get such a good rep. The Bible doesn't really like things with horns – in fact, they get pretty mad about them – so Cernunnos, ruler of the woods, became synonymous with the Devil and all that goes with that nice, shady character.

Among some more modern Pagan traditions, Cernunnos is the virile companion of the Great Goddess – her equal and counterpart.

I have worked with this god on a few, limited occasions. Last summer, for the festival of Lammas, I meditated with him and felt the warm land giving up its bounties in the form of fruit and well-fed animals. But Cernunnos – antlers twisting from his skull in what looked like a painful way, the bone towering over his sullen expression – only hovered in my peripheral vision. He was small and shaded, very unlike my clear-browed, open-chested Goddess who comes to help me out and only need rest her hand on the ground for something beautiful to bloom there. I work with the Goddess on a daily basis but the god's power didn't sit well with me, like an ill-fitting shoe or a mispronounced word. Perhaps I haven't found the right god for me just yet, but femininity and feminine power drew me to Wicca and Paganism and – you know what? – maybe I'd like to keep it that way.

While Cernunnos is the embodiment of all that is traditionally masculine, in Ancient Greek and Roman myth, deer have a much deeper connection with the feminine. The Greek goddess Artemis (Diana in Roman mythology) is often depicted as carrying a bow and arrow and was the goddess of many things, including the hunt, the moon and purity. As a protector of chastity, she is often most associated with the springtime and the young virgin goddess who is just budding into her power. Her most famous story tells us of the hunter Actaeon who patrolled the mountains that Artemis frequented. One day, the hunter stumbled across Artemis and her nymphs bathing in a pool and stopped to stare at Artemis' beauty. Artemis was outraged and cursed Actaeon so that he would never speak again and reveal her beauty to others. If he tried she would use her magical powers on him. But the man heard his hunting party roaring in the distance and tried to call out to them about what he had just witnessed. As soon as he spoke, he was transformed into a stag. As he ran, his own hounds spotted him and immediately began the chase. He was ripped to shreds by his own dogs and companions thanks to Artemis' curse.

Deer are one of my favourite creatures – I love the way that fawns gambol awkwardly on stilt-like legs and the way the sun glints off their backs. I also get a thrill over the fear they can strike in our chests. Several years ago, on another Leighton ramble with Laurie, we stumbled over the fields before dusk and into Cringlebarrow Wood (which needs a mention just because of its incredible name). We lapped around this Tolkien-esque place, slightly giddy with its beauty. If there was one place on Earth where I wish I could spend a quiet day lying in the shade with a good book, it would be among the gnarled boughs of Cringlebarrow Wood in the soft drifts of vibrant moss that cover the roots of trees that had seen many lifetimes. The moss slopes downwards on either side of the path and is thick enough to lose a hand in.

In this wood, darkness fell very suddenly and we realised we were nowhere near a gateway. We quickened our pace and, in the thick folds of the forest, we could only hear our breath on the still air.

Then suddenly, we heard a haunting bellow somewhere to our left. We froze, shoulders hiding our necks. Owl? Serial killer? Werewolf?

The raspy warning from the heart of the wildwood came from a male deer, out of sight in the gloom, and very angry at our presence.

We made our exit at a run.

This wasn't the first time I'd been shouted out of a wood by deer and I wonder what fairy tales and ghost stories this sound has laid the foundations for over the millennia.

These beautiful and sometimes fearsome creatures are lost to many of us now and our love of them makes us shocked when they are culled from nature reserves across the country. Without their natural predators, which we hunted to extinction over the past millennia, their numbers sometimes exceed what is possible for our current landscapes to uphold but it's our job to create habitat corridors to make sure these incredible beings can always find their way home to the wildwood from whence they came.

*

Ostara (*'o-STAHR-uh'*), 21 March, lands roundly on the full moon this year. We have scattered daffodils around the house and the place feels like spring's biggest fan. Winter has stuttered into the new season with faltering British awkwardness. Surprise heatwaves during the week give way to frost and slippery pavements by the time the weekend comes around like the world is going back on its word.

But today, the sun comes through our bedroom window and sprinkles my face with the yellow light of a summer's day and it seems like an invitation.

I can't help but feel like my health has been renewed by the heat that has been gathering over the past three weeks. Chiffchaffs and willow warblers have sensed it too and have landed back in the UK to give their distinctive springtime calls. My mind has finally caught up with my body after three months of trudging through the fog. It's like I've recovered from a major illness and all that's left now is the feeling of intense relief, like everything is shimmering green ahead of me. I might not be 100 per cent there but there is a glow to my face that wasn't there last month. There are fresh blades of grass growing on the underside of my skin, tickling my veins and encouraging my blood to whirr faster, pushing out my lungs to full capacity until I'm breathing into every corner of my ribs. That evening, I shove all my crystals on the windowsill to charge in the moonshine and skip around the house zhuzhing up plants and singing at the top of my voice.

'How are you doing, love?'

The weekend comes and that 'green feeling' is still here. As Will and I lie next to each other, I do a quick body scan. 'I'm good,' I say. 'I'm good!'

'Then let's go!'

It's Saturday morning and we leave the house with a bag full of houmous-y sandwiches and our jumpers tied around our waists. By the time we reach the end of the street, I'm almost skipping and I giggle as Will swings my arm up high into the air. It's one of the things about Will; his ability to keep me buoyed up when things aren't so rosy in my mind is unparalleled. I swear to the Goddess he was put on this Earth to just be a happy soul, breezing around with a mouthful of sardonic humour and to make people roll their eyes at his awful puns. My blond-haired, German-born lad with an adopted northern accent doesn't half make me smile. It feels like the perfect nerdy romance between a birdwatching witch and a train-spotting lawyer.

We board a train from Manchester Piccadilly to Huddersfield and then a small commuter chunter train on the Penistone line to Denby Dale. Will is obviously in his element and I can see his mind whirring to calculate distances, whizzing down rail routes that haven't existed since 1962. Trying to get any sense out of Will while we're on a train is pretty much impossible. If we were driving while sitting side by side with only rolls of motorway ahead of us, surely he'd have to talk to me? I smile as he practically bounces around on his re-stuffed Northern Rail seat.

The day is crisp and the night's frost crystals have only just dissipated. As we step out of the carriage onto the shady platform, high up on a man-made ridge, the cool air nips my hands but the sun is warm on my cheeks. This area of Yorkshire was once an industrial hub, a key cog in the revolution that swept across the smoggy north, but is now mainly famous for baking gigantic pies. Only the towering arches of the nineteenth-century viaduct remind villagers of their coal-soaked history. We scoot under one of the twenty-one arches and take a small footpath that hops a stream and leads through a new-build estate. Once we're through, we're out in the open farm fields with their twittering hedgerows and sliding, mud-slick paths which almost send us flying at every gate.

I've only ever been to this tiny one-street village to visit the RSPB's Yorkshire HQ, just training courses and hot-desking while I worked for the organisation a few years ago, so I never actually got to explore the lush Yorkshire hills around it. We're following a rough route from Will's phone which consists of the muddiest path I've ever seen but the fields are shooting green up from their cores so that everywhere we walk is patterned with small arms of fresh spring life. Lesser celandine sprouts in yellow lion's mane tufts from the shady verges and sparrows clutter around in the undergrowth.

It's a beautiful place to be for the spring equinox, otherwise known as the Pagan festival of Ostara.

Ostara is named after the Germanic goddess Eostre, the ruler of spring and fertility. We can see her counterpart across many cultures where spring is represented by Persephone, Freya, and my personal favourite Brigid. Eostre, however, comes from the same root as where we get the word oestrogen and is also where 'Easter' comes from, so it's clear to see why Ostara is heavily lined with egg symbology. Eggs, the sign of new life just about to burst through, are an ancient symbol of fertility (not a lot to do with the rock rolled away from Jesus' tombstone although I remember that being the explanation for Easter eggs from my local Sunday School). The round and potent egg also makes us think of a full breast ready to give us the drink of life. But the other main symbol of Ostara is perhaps not so obvious.

For many thousands of years across the world, people have revered the hare, the sacred animal of many a spring goddess. The symbol of the moon-gazing hare, its face upturned towards the sky and its ears flopped in wonder against its back, is a classic fertility image seen in many different cultures. Hares aren't such a celebrated symbol of spring these days as back in the 1600s they took on a more sinister role. Witches' familiars, while more commonly thought of as black cats and toads, could take many forms and, when snitching on witch activity to the local council, people often reported seeing the accused men and women walking across the fields with a shadowy hare at their feet. Sometimes a dog, sometimes a goat, but hares cropped up in superstition many times over.

On this day of the year, Brigid is in her element – the crone well and truly put to bed. Just like at the autumn equinox, night and day are perfectly balanced and we celebrate all that is equal. However, with the promise of so much brightness to come, it's hard to focus on the dark. Now is a good time for getting up early with the birds, doing a sun salutation and spending time among the flowers – don't let the winter creep back in, please!

We round a hedged corner into the next field and I make an incoherent noise. Will looks at where I'm pointing.

I manage to splutter out, 'Yellowhammer!'

My usual routes don't follow farmland; I've always been more of a coastal and reedbed kinda gal. Yellowhammers aren't too fond of the beach so this is something pretty rare in my eyes.

Gaudy and noisy, yellowhammers really are a striking bird to find at the dark end of winter. Their heads and breasts are bright yellow, making them quite the eye-catching fixture on their brambly perches. These birds begin their nests in early April so I've caught this one just before its major job of the year. Their eggs are something beautiful to behold – gorgeously marbled with calligraphy squiggles. These intricately decorated eggs have led to their pet name of the 'scribble lark', which I just love.

The bird bobs up and down once and then burrows itself into the hedge. I'm standing in a toothy open-mouthed grin. I look over and Will's doing the same. We do a mini 'yay' dance and carry on across the field but now I'm hypervigilant. When we're almost out of sight of the hedgerow, I hear the bird's distinctive 'a-little-bit-of-bread-and-no-cheese' call that makes me giddy all over again.

We've been walking for a good couple of hours now but we haven't seen another soul other than a few incredibly woolly sheep begging to be shorn. We don't even see many other birds apart from Yorkshireman Ted Hughes's crows and a smattering of circling buzzards, and the Pagan hares elude us too. I start to wonder whether we've shifted planes and this walk will actually go on forever. We are in fairy territory after all.

*

Yorkshire's Cottingley Fairies captured my imagination at a young age. The whimsical childhood film *Fairy Tale* came out when I was about eight years old so the idea of two young girls finding fairies at the bottom of their garden was basically too much for my imagination to handle. I became obsessed with leaving out little cups of milk for fairies in my back garden and was on the prowl for all kinds of legendary birds and beasts whenever I left the house. The film, of course, was based on a real event where Frances Griffiths and Elsie Wright, two cousins in

West Yorkshire, 'discovered' fairies in Cottingley Beck, which ran by their house, and took pictures of them. In 1917, the photos became an international media sensation and it was only towards the end of their lives that the women admitted the photos had been faked. However, both maintained that they really had seen fairies at the bottom of the garden.

I've since been to an exhibition of the photos and have tried to appreciate that special effects weren't a thing in 1917, but ... those fairies are pretty 2D.

Over the years, reports of fairies (or faeries) have been pretty common, maybe you've even seen them down your way. The 'Fae' have been a large part of British mythology for thousands of years and are something we can see in Celtic history. The Celtic mythology of Ancient Ireland tells of a race of people called the Tuatha de Danann (the Children of the goddess Danu) who were rulers of Ireland and who are sometimes referred to as fairy folk. This secretive race, with their love of magic and war, were tall, graceful and terrifying, spreading their music and art across the land before retreating to under the Irish hills to their home Tir na n-Og (the Land of Youth). More recently, in the seventeenth century, Reverend Robert Kirk from Aberfoyle in Scotland had long studied fairy folk and collated a book called *The Secret Commonwealth of Elves, Fauns and Fairies* in 1691. However, this book became his undoing. On the night of 14 May 1692 it is said that fairies carried him off for revealing their secrets, to be their captive forevermore.

Stories similar to Reverend Kirk's have appeared across Europe for hundreds of years, most of them not ending well for us human folk. Pixies, brownies, changelings, elves and nymphs – tricksters and kidnappers, the lot of them!

Perhaps the fairies symbolise the repercussions of man's intrusion into a mysterious green and spiritual world; as we know, nature does have a habit of reclaiming what is rightfully hers once humans let down their guard. At least, I'd have liked this metaphor if I hadn't had my own dealings with the Fae.

Recently, I was heading to a place called Boggart Hole Clough after a challenging week at work and hoped this green space would clear my head. Even though I'd lived in north Manchester for four years, I'd still not managed to get to this piece of ancient woodland and a bit of stress relief was the perfect excuse. I liked the idea of the place's history: a boggart (yes, the same as in Harry Potter; the ones that transformed into your worst nightmare, those ones) was supposed to live there. A clough, to we hardy northerners, is basically a ravine, a steep-sided rock face eked out over millennia by a freshwater stream; the knots and fissures in the rock of Boggart Hole Clough left plenty of places for nasty little goblins to hide out.

From what I knew of boggarts, they were once renowned in Lancashire and were tricky little blighters who loved to get up to no good. However, some more sinister disappearances in the Blackley district of Manchester in the past few centuries have been attributed to the boggarts of the clough. So, of course, why wouldn't I want to go and relax there?

I walked the long hour and a half to get to this enchanted wood and felt all the better for it. Boggart Hole Clough was mainly a dog walkers' paradise now and the pathways were slick with newly blossomed mud. Fungi sprouted from fallen branches, coating them like bubble wrap. But, stand still for long enough and you could feel the creaking of the roots under your feet; under the thin smear of tarmac, you were wholly supported by this network of interlaced trees. They were speaking to one another, passing on messages in an elaborate game of Chinese whispers, letting each other know who had entered their midst – friend or foe.

I don't know what the trees thought of me but I had not been walking under their canopy for long when I started to feel ill.

It started with a wave of dizziness, a prickling sensation in my upper back like I knew someone was watching me. I decided to find a quiet spot off the path where I could put my head between my knees and take a deep breath, except I would have if there wasn't something falling from the tree branches. *Pat, thunk.* Something about the size of a bat with its wings outstretched. It was July, definitely not the time for falling leaves. I tried to zone in on what was happening around me, tried to spot what was falling from the trees, but I still felt dizzy.

Then came the weirdest thing.

A kitten was meowing from the calf-deep ferns and tangles of thorns. I couldn't see it but it was meowing every twenty seconds or so. Lost and all alone. My latent maternal instinct kicked in and I tried to move closer towards it, but the nearer I got the quieter the noise became. If there was a kitten here, I was going to have to scoop it up and take it home and give it to Linnet as something to bat into submission. But I'd never heard of a kitten in the woods before and there was something about this place that was making the hair on the back of my neck rise. The rustling in the trees was getting louder and things were spring-boarding from the branches, landing with the 'dun dun' of two feet hitting the floor. Suddenly the trees around me felt very close like I had been transported to Birnam Forest with their roots crawling towards me and wrinkling the surface of the soil. Something wasn't right in this place.

When I got home, shaken and feeling like the lining of my intestines was knocking at my throat, I switched on my computer and googled boggart: *A malevolent, demonic creature of English folklore tied to a single location – a household, a bridge, a woodland – known for turning milk sour, making dogs lame and abducting children. Other names include bugbear and the bogeyman.*

Note to future self: always do your research before going to creepy parks.

*

Back in Denby Dale, I'm stunned by sunshine for the first time in months. Will and I stumble up to a piece of ancient woodland, hopefully goblin-free. You know that it's ancient woodland for several reasons – the sprouting dog violets pushing their delicate purple heads defiantly through the leaf litter, dog's mercury unfurling a string of poisonous white flowers from its spear-like leaves, the oaks so gnarled and bent over one another that their trunks look ready to explode with age. You could be under the watchful gaze of green woodpeckers and goshawks, dappled in the foliage light. But it's not just the flora and fauna that give it away. Amidst the ancient woodland, there's a shift in the air. It's like a reverse vacuum chamber; there is *so* much air and it is dense, as dense as the tree canopy which weaves over itself again and again to infinity. I almost feel my heart slow down. It's as if our bodies have a primal reaction to it. When I'm in that space, everything feels connected.

The periphery of the land is scattered with broken machinery; tractor hulls on their side, an abandoned plough. Cast aside like this, they look defeated by the wood, swallowed up into the ground by the labyrinth of roots and spat out again a little chewed around the edges. We slip through a gap in the stone wall surrounding the wood and suddenly find each other's faces marked by the shining edges of leaves and our hands seem green, the etching of every living thing above us traced onto our skin.

While mighty and beautiful, ancient woodland is massively under threat in the UK. As HS2 plans progress, the protest shouts of environmentalists are getting louder and Twitter is abuzz with fearful cries. This particular development (although there are many other man-made constructions causing a similar effect), if realised, will see the destruction of 693 local wildlife sites, 108 ancient woodlands and 33 legally protected SSSIs (sites of special scientific interest), which is something that makes the green-beating thing in my chest ache.

As I've said before, you can't be Pagan and not care for the pulsing life force of the Earth. How people can be so intent on destroying something so necessary for all life, I can't quite grasp.

One of the commonalities across all Pagan beliefs is the idea that nature is sacred and we should treasure and conserve it at all costs, taking only what we need from nature and giving back just as much, if not more, is fundamental to this way of life. Speaking on behalf of many Pagans, from the conversations I've had with friends and witnessing the stunned panic in the face of yet another road through precious habitat or another bird of prey's nest destroyed, I will say that people who share this belief in nature often have to cope with despair. It is very difficult to live in a society that seems hell-bent on furthering humanity's iron grasp on the planet and not listening to the pleas of the natural world.

When Highways England announced plans to create a tunnel under Stonehenge, there was much uproar among the spiritual community. It felt like a personal affront: a place where people go to celebrate their connection with the cycles of nature, haunted by the rumble of man-made vehicles just below the surface. Stonehenge, perhaps one of the most revered nature temples in the entire world, would have part of its identity taken away because, in the short term, machinery can do just as much damage as the forces of nature. At the time of writing this, there is still a good chance that the construction might go ahead,[10] endangering Stonehenge's status as a UNESCO World Heritage Site.[11] I'm still hoping that a resourceful group of witches might be able to change the government's mind.

I often look for those good news stories on the Guardian Environment page or when I'm doom-scrolling through Instagram – I want to feel that feel-good buzz of a new tree-planting initiative. One hundred new jobs in the green sector – great! Swift box installation on new housing developments made mandatory – fantastic! Biodiversity net gain measures to become a legal requirement in the new Environment Bill – bloody brilliant work! But for every positive story I see around the environment sector, there are six stomach-dropping tales of woe to be heard. Wildfires, flooding, pesticides and hunting. I'm not so hot on my Bible studies anymore but it does sometimes feel like the end of days out there.

Humanity is a very recent addition to this world, with our first human-like ancestors emerging on the African continent around six million years ago. Long before us, somewhere in the 4.5 billion-year lifespan of the Earth to date, plants, sun, water and air nurtured the planet's soils and grew forests to spin oxygen into the ether. This beautiful symbiotic system is something we've been gifted with – we're just 4.4 billion years late to the party.

Thankfully, this existing system helps us to thrive – giving us food, water and shelter but so much more. Spending time in the woods is proven to lower cortisol levels. This stress hormone courses through our bodies as that big deadline looms or we worry about our upcoming rent payment. Visiting forests can improve mental health issues such as depression and PTSD and even lengthens our attention span. The IGNITION project in Greater Manchester collated a database of all the benefits trees and green space (known in the planning and construction industry as 'nature-based solutions') give to us and found that for every 1 per cent of green space and tree coverage a person can see out their window there is a 4 per cent decrease in anxiety and mood disorders. This, coupled with the fact that a single tree stores up to 5.5kg of carbon from the air every year,[12] makes me wonder why we're not more head-over-heels in love with trees as a society. A recent study by Forestry England showed that spending time among trees exposes us to phytoncides, a chemical released by the trees to protect themselves from infections and insects. By breathing this in, trees can actually boost our immune systems, making us more resistant to infection. Trees can help us on a physical, mental and, I'm going to say it, spiritual level, weaving together the health and happiness of humans and wildlife across the planet. I mean, is there anything they can't do?

But how can we as modern-day citizens help our ancient woodlands and trees thrive? It is said that 2.7 million green jobs could be created between now and the early 2030s,[13] although the prime minister has been keen to remind us that these jobs won't be all 'bunny hugging' and frolicking about in the fields bottle-feeding baby fox cubs. Many of the jobs that Boris Johnson talked about will be in the green energy sector and not necessarily helping nature conservation on the ground, but they could help to maintain energy sources that do not involve cutting down trees. I'm all for making new jobs that help us live more sustainably and create a circular economy, and I know that many conservationists have high hopes for the Environment Bill. But to be honest, those bunny-hugging jobs sound great; where do I sign up?

Social prescribing is now being used by doctors to help patients improve their health through interaction with nature. These prescriptions are nature-based activities such as walking and cycling, tree planting, community gardening and food-growing projects all designed to help people overcome mental health conditions, become more physically active or combat issues like chronic loneliness. In 2021, Greater Manchester received £500,000 of government funding to improve their social prescription service across the city region and the stats show just how much this is needed.[14] As part of the funding bid, 4,000 of Greater Manchester's citizens were surveyed and this revealed that on a scale of one to ten, people rated their happiness as 5.2, life satisfaction as 5.1 and anxiety as 5.6. When asked what would make their local area a place better for their wellbeing, one-third of people said that the most useful thing for their mental wellbeing is open green space. Even with these stats, the government is not providing new parks or better-maintained green space; in fact, funding for councils' park maintenance has been cut drastically. Councils are therefore looking to other means to fund the upkeep of their local green spaces such as establishing Parks Foundation Trusts. Within this model, funding is generated by on-site cafés and activities. People paying for yoga classes in the park, guided wildlife walks and the use of BMX tracks goes towards clean toilets, wildflower planting and lawn upkeep. But should well-maintained local green space be classed as a luxury or a necessity?

I'm enjoying my phytoncide exposure in this ancient Yorkshire woodland so much that when Will says 'I think we've been here before' I don't even register. I look up dreamily and say, 'Hm?'

It's then I realise we're well and truly lost. We get the area up on Google Maps but the GPS on both our phones has conveniently dropped out – sabotaged by nature once again. I can't see the edges of the wood anymore.

'This way!' I say with my chest out and my head held high. Ten seconds later, I lose my foot in a bog. It hasn't rained for over a week but this ancient place has decided to store up all the weaponry it can against poachers, doggers and innocent witchy nature lovers.

Will dutifully yanks me out then says of the mud, 'Guess it's that way, hm?' He points over his shoulder and I trudge behind him with my hands in my pockets. I'm trying desperately not to tread on the shy faces of violets with my muddy boots but they keep popping up in front of me. I am an intruder to their springtime sun-basking; a blundering Alice in the face-filled gardens of Wonderland. We loop around the space a few times, lost in the spiral of trees, always trying to keep a higher-up ridge of trees in our eye line. The space can't be more than a quarter of a mile across but it's like the forest wants us to get lost.

We take an easy step over a tinkling brook that whispers across the bottom of this tree-lined valley. It is shady here and the trees look comfortable in this space with their mixture of saplings and old, bent and twisty ash trees; the old welcoming the new into the natural mix of things.

Then I see them. Wood anemones!

'Will, look!'

Wood anemones are one of the first flowering plants of spring. In my eyes, they are like quartz crystals burst open. White stars about the size of a fifty-pence piece – and there are hundreds of them studding the forest floor here, alternating from dove-grey to snow-coloured as the dappled light makes them shine. I've never seen so many all in one place and my eyes are darting further and further away from me to see how far the reach of the wood anemones extends. They coat the base of this small valley, popping up close to the stream and in the places covered by the densest trees like they are wary, delicate, blind things emerging from the dark after many years. I look over at Will and see he is not as ecstatic over these tiny flower faces as I am – I'd hoped some of my nature excitement would have rubbed off on him over the years but he is stoic as ever, planning out the next stages of our route in his head like carefully laid train tracks.

I gaze at them as if they have appeared from another planet. In this hidden place of ancient lichens and mosses clustering at my feet and climbing the arms of long-forgotten trees, I can believe there is a world that opens up only to those who want to find it. Call it the Realm of the Fae or whatever you will, but there is a place that the soul goes to when we are in the dappled light of trees that is not quite of this Earth.

We walk for another couple of hours, holding hands and taking slow, lazy steps down farmers' lanes, the air now warm and pleasant on our wrists and cheeks. On the train home I'm exhausted; not like the extreme tiredness of the past month, but with the clear-headed yawns of someone who has tramped through mud and thigh-high grass and has used every square inch of their lungs that day. I feel connected with the world, the crystalline flash of wood anemones under my eyelids.

*

HSP. That's Highly Sensitive Person to you, thanks.

I only found out about the notion of Highly Sensitive People quite recently. I'd always pegged myself as an introvert, preferring my own company and being unfazed by a week on my own here and there. If there was a good paperback, a cup of tea and maybe a nice cat around, I'd be just fine.

Getting rattled by violent films, having stories constantly sizzling around my head and being extra sensitive to noise came with the territory, right? I'm told that, actually, no. Not all introverts have the same visceral reaction to external stimuli as I and many other people do.

The more HSPs I meet, the more witches I invite into my life. Witches seem to be highly perceptive people and hypersensitive to the feelings, flickerings and actions of those around them. It's something I see time and time again. Witches can read the 'aura' of those around them, understanding on a subconscious level why the person next to them is a bundle of nerves or wanting to get up and run from the room.

While some witches have been known to practise 'black magick' and the darker side of the craft, I've found this to be rare as many witches live by the Wiccan tenet: 'And it harm none, do as ye will.' Your average witch on the street doesn't go around throwing curses and fanning purple smoke at people. The witchcraft community is generally a very peaceful one. Personally, I believe that witches have always gravitated towards helping people and healing them through plants and holistic means. Perhaps your massage therapist or aesthetician dabbles in witchcraft on the side. The social worker in your office, the physio you see for that twinge in your lower back. Hey, maybe your therapist is, too.

OK, maybe I'm tarring everyone with the same brush, or magic wand, but I've seen it with my own eyes. We witches are highly sensitive; you might know more than one of us on your street.

Being highly sensitive to our environment and the seasonal shifts feels like an archaic idea, something reserved for serfs and farmhands looking at the clouds and predicting rain, or maybe nineteenth-century Romantics who carried smelling salts in their pockets. But there are so many people in this world who experience reality very slightly differently, whether that's having to cover their ears because there's a fire engine going past two streets away or falling asleep to the sound of the rain because it feels like a lullaby. Human beings are not made to be around sharp sudden noises. I read recently that when we go into a coffee shop to relax and read a book, we are actually entering a world of random, disconnected sounds that put us into fight-or-flight mode. Coffee grinder. Nokia ringtone. Yapping poodle under the table. Those things combined with an espresso shot are enough to send us flying out the door leaving a trail of cortisol in our wake.

Nature, on the other hand, activates our parasympathetic nervous system, the part of us that tells our bodies to rest and digest. It nourishes the body and soul.

While I didn't grow up roaming across the Yorkshire moors or through the cornfields of Shropshire, my love of nature came from an early age. I didn't leave the UK until I was fourteen, on a school History trip to the Somme, having spent a week every summer in the country lanes of Pembrokeshire, Devon or Cornwall with my nature-loving parents. Back home, I had access to the birds in the garden and a rusty pair of Grandad's binoculars. I remember being amazed at school when I saw a goldcrest on a spindly tree growing in the courtyard, unnoticed and unnamed by those around it.

Becoming a nature writer was something that bloomed out of my magazine articles at the BBC and I found myself with a platform that allowed me to introduce others to nature for perhaps the first time in their lives. I loved researching the innards of owl pellets and the secret autumn rituals of hedgehogs – I enjoyed speaking to young people and inviting them to look further than their kitchen windows. But, as time went on and the more I delved into the environment sector, the more urgent my writing became. The more I grew to understand the impacts of organisational actions as well as our own, and I began to appreciate nature on a level where I was reduced to tears when I saw the devastation of overfishing, coral bleaching and fracking on the news. I'm sure our ancestors would have felt the same.

Our senses have become dulled. We have lost our hypersensitivity to the world.

> *You ask me to plough the ground? Shall I take a knife and tear my mother's bosom? Then when I die she will not take me to her bosom to rest. You ask me to dig for stone? Shall I dig under her skin for her bones? Then when I die I cannot enter her body to be born again. You ask me to cut grass and make hay and sell it, and be rich like white men! But how dare I cut off my mother's hair?*[15]

It's hard to believe that this speech was uttered less than 150 years ago. These are the outraged comments of Smohalla, a member of the Umatilla tribe based in modern-day Oregon. The tribe had inhabited this region in the Pacific North West for over 13,000 years, following the great Columbia River to take only as much fish as they needed to survive.

Smohalla's words would have been part of commonplace belief in pre-agricultural Britain.

Again, it's difficult to believe that just over 6,000 years ago, the plains, forests, mountains and marshes of Britain would have been inhabited by no more than 9,000 people in total. Humans would have played a very small part in the ecosystem of the day, just one of the many animals with fast-beating hearts looking for a dry place to sleep for the night. Living a nomadic lifestyle in tribes of 20–200 people, moving with the herds of red deer that roamed the highlands, was the practised way of life. Scientific studies have shown that the pre-agricultural nomad of 6,000

BCE would have lived an active lifestyle on a primarily vegan diet. One 1.3-metre stag would have been enough to feed a tribe for a month with the rest of the daily meals consisting of plants, roots and berries.

When we think of hunter-gatherer people we often conjure up images of ferocious tribes – the woad-clad bandits of the wilderness – armed with spears, flint daggers and a mouldering set of teeth. This is certainly the image I had of our ancestors until recently. However, anthropologists have made many discoveries that suggest these people were incredibly peaceful, each person playing a vital role in bringing up the young of the tribe and helping to prepare communal meals. There is evidence to suggest that in the absence of crops to tend, much of the tribe's time would have been devoted to storytelling, play and appreciating the natural world around them.

We no longer live in such close relation to the Earth. We are not sensitive to its minute fluctuations. In *A Short Philosophy of Birds*, authors Philippe J. Dubois and Élise Rousseau capture our mundane, everyday relationship with the natural world perfectly:

> *Leading largely sedentary lives, indoors for hours on end, we cut ourselves off from the natural elements that are waiting there to surprise us every day, every hour, every minute. Staring at our screens until our eyes hurt, we hardly notice the little morning rain shower happening outside the window . . . 'What's the weather like there?' asks a far-off relative on the phone. We're almost ashamed to have barely noticed. 'Hang on, I'll look out the window . . . Yes, it's a bit cloudy . . .'*

It seems the world has been undergoing a gradual process of forgetting. Spring is no longer lying in the 'cowslip pips'.[16] Autumn has morphed from the 'season of mist and mellow fruitfulness' to pumpkin spiced lattes and plastic Frankenstein masks. According to environmental charity Hubbub, 2,000 tonnes of plastic waste are thrown away every Halloween in the UK alone[17] in the form of costumes, plastic jack-o'-lanterns and party decorations.

Witches' Samhain celebrations tend to be rooted deeply in the spiritual side of this holiday; there is no need for dressing up, in fact, you're very welcome to take all your clothes off if you want. The closer you get to nature the better. We enjoy the festival for the sheer delight of worshipping nature, eating nice food and laughing at all the spookiness with the people we love. There's a thrill and an excitement to Pagan festivals that doesn't need much embellishment, something I think our society could learn a lot from. You definitely don't have to be an HSP or a witch to pick up on the state of our world and our climate. However, it gives me so much hope that people around the world are embracing a low-carbon lifestyle, buying local produce, raising awareness of environmental causes and spending more time in nature for the benefit of their health. Who knows, we might even be able to reverse the effects of climate change by recharging our spiritual connection with the planet and rethinking our relationship with the Earth. Maybe then we'll be in a position to tap into what the Great Mother is trying to tell us.

She is telling us to go outside and breathe it all in.

*

21 March

A sprig of hawthorn blossom has fallen to the ground in Philips Park. I pick it up gingerly, narrowly avoiding its thorns between my fingers. This will look beautiful on my altar.

A witch's altar is a place where we carry out our ritual work. It is usually inside the home but it can be anywhere – at the base of a favourite tree, out in the garden or on a rock looking out at the sea. An altar can hold your ritual or spellcraft tools or maybe just some crystals or candles to represent the elements as you meditate. While not a necessity, an altar can be a grounding, centring place to come and worship the Goddess or hex your ex.

My altar is an upturned wooden crate covered in a velvet cloth. In the centre, I have a dark wooden plaque containing the symbol of the Triple Goddess – the Maiden, Mother and Crone – a round full moon flanked by a crescent moon on either side.

My sacred space changes from season to season. In spring, I'll add a small, framed image of the sun and a vase of cut daffodils, checking on them each morning to see if their crackly sepal casings have burst open to reveal a cloak of gold. I put out a pale, milky rose quartz. Rose quartz is very symbolic of friendships and love, but also has links with the spring festival of Ostara. I pop out some shimmering pale green aventurine for health and wealth, and add a small chunk of moonstone, my favourite. Moonstone, for me, is such a feminine stone and allows me to tap into a kind of inner peace – my engagement ring and future wedding ring both contain moonstone, because I want to feel close to its energy always. As autumn creeps in, I add a fallen, lichen-pocked branch I found on the floor after a week of high winds. Its silver-green mossiness looks like something you'd find over the lintel of a witch's cottage. I also bring out a pine cone I found a few years ago that fills the whole space in between my palms when I cup my hands together. I remove the small image of the sun and change the set of crystals, opting for darker colours – a hunk of red jasper for balance during blustery October, golden tiger's eye for focus and clarity, and black tourmaline for protection and to welcome in the darker months.

There are also some evergreen elements of my altar, including my tools. I have a wooden athame, or dagger, which is definitely ceremonial and not used for anything else. An athame is a very masculine, phallic symbol and can be used to mark the boundary of a circle before a ritual or to invoke masculine forces, balancing out the feminine power of Mother Earth. The Mother and Goddess is represented by a dark ceramic chalice filled with water. In many rituals within Wicca and other branches of witchcraft, the masculine athame can be dipped symbolically into the feminine chalice to bring about fertility, love or passion. I also have a long stick of selenite, a pentagram or five-pointed star, an incense burner, several candle holders and usually some conkers or a bundle of herbs, collected from nature or the dark and hidden witchy shops across the UK. Owning tools is a very modern privilege within witchcraft; 'cunning folk' of days gone by would have used their kitchen knives to chop herbs, crystals would not have been in regular usage for normal people and any candles standing in a sacred space would have been the ones used to light the home after sundown. In our modern homes, in the soft and hazy fug of incense, it can be all too easy to imagine ourselves as performing the rites of ancient peoples – but many of these tools would not have been accessible to our ancestors. We may be walking in their footsteps, but we are definitely performing modern iterations of the rituals of yore.

Nevertheless, I find my altar to be a soothing place and I often find myself just entering the room to look at it for a few seconds before trundling on about my daily business.

When I get home after my blossom-filled walk, I put the white hawthorn blossoms in the centre of my altar, right on top of the goddess symbol. It feels right, and perfect for the ritual I have planned for today.

Hawthorn has a mixed reputation in folklore and superstition. As the tree's frothy white flowers begin to appear in late April, it is often associated with fertility and the abundance of May Day festivals. It is also closely tied with the Fae, sometimes known in Ireland as 'the fairy tree', and said to have magickal properties. But despite hawthorn's links with reproduction and the new life of spring, the tree has long been associated with superstition and death – one of the reasons for this is due to a chemical emitted by the hawthorn tree to attract flies to help pollinate its flowers that smells like a decomposing body. It's because of this smell that people have historically feared the hawthorn tree, saying it's unlucky to bring any hawthorn flowers into the house.

I look at the branch on my altar, covered in white bursts of flowers like the foam of waves, and am only reminded of the beauty of spring, nothing more. Hawthorn will only ever be a symbol of joy and bright days for me.

I have already taken a ritual bath with Himalayan salt, patchouli oil and frankincense this morning, taking my time, to get in that slowed-down, dreamy state that's needed for a ritual, as well as being cleansing to both the mind and body. When I sit among the candles and the rising steam of my darkened bathroom, I imagine white light glowing all around me and I breathe it in deeply. With every exhale I gather up any negative or busy thoughts that are clustered around my temples and I breathe them out in a ball of blackness, watching it fall with a heaviness down through the floor and into the street below. I think of it absorbing into the Earth and neutralising, no longer the fug of hectic thought it was inside my head. I always emerge from these baths feeling regal, like my bones have been fortified with the glow of candles.

My altar is set up in the study. I position it in front of me so I'm facing out of the window. The sun, after heading to bed before the end of the workday for so long, is now setting after six o'clock in the evening. It feels like a miracle to have its rosy glare splintering the edges of the low-rises around us, and into my eyes through the window. On the altar cloth stands a thick white candle I use to represent the Goddess, my athame, a clay bowl of salt, a chunk of cleansed rose quartz and a green candle to promote healing, all bathed in the last rays of the day.

The study, if I put the swivel chair in the hall and re-angle the IKEA furniture, is just about big enough for a witch to sit in her circle like the room was made for witchery. A circle is a witch's cleansed sacred space, a place where her energies are magnified and where magick can be performed safely, without outside forces having an effect. A circle is a boundary for magick to be contained – you are keeping the world safe around you and keeping yourself safe from the world.

I slip into an outfit I reserve only for ritual work, a pink and gold wrap-around robe that feels soft and natural against my skin, and begin.

I sit in the space for several moments, taking some clearing breaths to make sure my head isn't filled with the nonsense of train timetables and the Latin names of birds. My mind is only on the intention behind my ritual – to feel renewed and refreshed; to feel better.

Today, I want to harness the rebirth of spring and Ostara. I want to be rid of these strange symptoms for good. I want to be a new version of myself. But first, I must create my circle.

To do this, I stand up – my robe finishing just above my clean, wiggling toes – and take my athame, holding it with the wooden blade pointed out in front of me. I begin at the north point of the compass:

'With this athame, I mark my circle.'

I spin in a slow clockwise circle three times, arms outstretched in front of my chest. In my mind, I envisage pale orange flames springing up around me where the athame hits. They are protective flames promising to keep my magick inside the circle while making sure any unwelcome spirits or forces stay firmly outside it like uninvited vampires. I am burning away any lingering energies from the room, keeping myself protected.

I then take the bowl of salt and sprinkle some around me in the same clockwise, or *deosil*, motion:

'With this salt, I purify my circle.'

The salt hits the floor, grains shooting off at angles, and coats the soles of my bare feet like fresh clean sand.

If I half-close my eyes, I can see the shimmering outline of pale flames around me, metallic and protective. My robe is soft against my skin, making me feel cut adrift from the sharp edges of the everyday. Everything is gentle here. I whisper, 'The circle is now cast.'

I turn myself back to the north and raise my arms skyward. It is now time to welcome in the elements.

'Hail to the guardians of the Watchtowers of the North. By the powers of Earth and stability, I welcome you into my circle. I invoke thee, I invoke thee, I invoke thee.'

With this, I root my feet down into the ground, imagining the element of Earth holding me up, strong and tall, hardening my body with strength.

I turn to the east.

'Hail to the guardians of the Watchtowers of the East. By the powers of Air and inspiration, I invoke thee, I welcome you into my circle. I invoke thee, I invoke thee.' The Air element is more of a butterfly feeling – I picture it blowing my hair, tickling my fingers as it flies into my circle.

The south is next.

'Hail to the guardians of the Watchtowers of the South. By the powers of Fire and passion, I welcome you into my circle. I invoke thee, I invoke thee, I invoke thee.' A sudden warmth hits my face in the orange sunset. Hello, Fire.

And lastly, I turn to the west.

'Hail to the guardians of the Watchtowers of the West. By the powers of Water and emotion, I welcome you into my circle. I invoke thee, I invoke thee, I invoke thee.' The cool cleansing wash of water laps at my feet, cooling me after the blast of Fire; Water has arrived.

With all the elements now hovering around me in the confines of my circle to support my magick with their power, I can then invite my last and favourite guest into the space. I sit down cross-legged and raise my arms up once more.

'Brigid, Goddess of spring, the banisher of winter. I welcome you into my circle on this day at the very start of the season. Come to bring light to this space and hope for the year to come. I invoke thee, I invoke thee, I invoke thee.'

As I finish my words and take a deep breath through my nose, it's like all the light from an early morning spring mist has filled my body, taking refuge in my chest before spreading out like ripples on a clear pond into my fingers and nailbeds. I feel a presence in the room.

This realisation is instant. My eyes are partly closed in the sun's glare and through the slanted rays of rose gold, there she is.

For a moment, I am speechless.

Brigid sits before me, cross-legged, folded arms resting on her knees. She does not sit like a goddess; she has the slouch of a child who has yet to be told what to do in an adult world. She is the May Day Queen, an excited, flattered girl, barely allowed out of her mother's sight. Her blond hair is loose and topped with a flower crown. She is freckled, bright-eyed and filled with childlike joy. But despite her gangly teenage appearance, I feel the power radiating from her in thick humid waves. I daren't open my eyes fully for fear of losing this apparition.

This isn't something that happens often. I can't usually just light a few candles and have mystical beings pop in for a brew. Many times when I'm performing a ritual, I might feel the faint buzz of magic around me. The sensation of water over my feet when I am working with that element. But, here she is, right in front of me. I wished I'd had a go around with the Hoover now.

You might ask me who she is, or *what* she is, and the reality of the matter is – I don't know. But what I do know is that the Goddess, Mother Nature, our Earth Mother – whatever you wish to call her – is more than just a symbol or a parable told to children around the kitchen table to help them make sense of the world. Today, I have tapped into other worlds and this vision of the maiden, in a form I can understand, feels like all the proof I'll ever need. This being fills me with absolute awe that expands my heart but also a deep sense that I have more to learn about the world than I could ever possibly understand.

Another thing I know is that my connection with the magickal realm has been getting stronger this year ever since my journey began again. It's like she is here today to nudge me in the right direction. I sit in her presence, tears in my eyes, for another minute or so, then I forge on with what I came here to do.

'Brigid,' I say, my voice cracking, 'I ask you to take away my illness and to bring in light. Take the suffering and leave only brightness.'

I repeat these words again and again. I take some deep breaths, feeling them in every cell of my body. Magick uses visualisation to bring about a change and right now the hum of magick in the room is making my chest vibrate, making my heart quicken as the power threads itself like gold through my veins and into the fine cells of my long loose hair.

With the virgin goddess in my room (in my actual spare room!), I know that she can help to bring about what I need.

Without thinking, I reach out and feel someone press their hand against mine ever so gently. I jump, shocked by the confirmation that I am not alone in this room. The incense smoke wafts over us and, under her gaze, I feel it taking my aches, my pains and the fatigue that still knocks me out for days on end. All those wasted hours, lying with the blinds drawn and maxed out on painkillers. *Brigid, take this pain away from me. Renew me.*

My eyelashes flicker as I wait for her response. I look down at her green dress under narrowed eyelids to make sure she is still there, that her attentions haven't been called elsewhere. With her hand grazing mine, I feel her transferring something to me. If I was to put it into words it would be a shining orb, but it is just glowing energy, coming from her ethereal body. It feels golden, or how the colour gold makes me feel; invincible and happy. I don't want her to stop because once she does I know she will have to leave.

The light flows through me, intensifying the vibrating feeling that is making my body sing.

'Thank you,' I whisper and she flashes a girlish giggle of a grin at me.

I sit in awe, filled with healing light and wonder.

The sunset light in the room has faded now, replaced with the violet shimmer of twilight, and I know it is time to close the circle. I release Brigid from the borders of my sacred space, feeling the absence of her in my chest once she has disappeared, and turn to each compass point in reverse order to thank the elements for their presence and assistance.

I realise now that I've been crying the whole way through, completely blessed by the beautiful presence of Her.

THE WHEEL

*

I first met the Goddess when I was a teenager, very young, maybe thirteen or so. She came to me in a vision; an astral projection method I had found on one of those panpipes websites of the early noughties that I frequented with obsession. I am still saddened that they don't exist anymore. This particular meditation allowed you to meet your spirit guides, the ethereal beings that give you guidance in your physical life and watch over you. I had a wild idea that they would be the eight-foot-tall angels I'd seen in the stained glass windows of my church, the one with the golden eagle lectern that was polished by a rota of pensioners every Saturday morning. I, of course, had zero experience in astral projection, just excitable tendencies, and, to be honest, I wasn't sure I even believed in spirit guides. The website talked about totem poles and tents filled with sweet smoke that didn't speak to my rigid Christian upbringing, but I was up for trying anything new and magickal. I lay on my bedroom floor with its short-cropped yellow carpet under the crazy-coloured walls I'd been allowed to choose when I was nine: turquoise, dark purple and 'sexy pink'. I wasn't allowed candles, although I flouted the rule several times and ended up with wax embedded deep in the weave of the carpet. Whenever I'd sit on the floor I would play with those scraps of wax between my fingers trying to pull them out like they were chewing gum but I never could. I lay on my back, meditating with the lights dimmed low, and imagined myself in a happy, beautiful and safe place. For me, having visited the Pembrokeshire coast with my parents a couple of years before, the place I chose was a beach where I had spent a day sunbathing, bodyboarding and exploring hidden rock pools before burying my sister in the sand. As I pictured it, I felt totally at ease there – at once childlike and serene beyond my years.

A staircase made of ethereal matter appeared to my left where I sat cross-legged on the beach inside my mind and I ascended into a glowing mist, making it difficult to see where I was heading. When the cloud thinned, I was in a never-ending sun-shot grassland. The grass had green wheaty heads as big as my hand and the sun was shining with a blinding intensity that left me dizzy and small in this strange world. Minute though I was within this landscape, I felt like I had the capability to zoom in and out, seeing just myself and then for many, many hundreds of miles. These were the days before Google Maps so maybe my head was onto something.

The brightness felt like the blaze of the midday sun but the light seemed to be coming from every angle, rising like evaporating dew from under the blades of grass around me. I looked to where the light was most dazzling and saw a dog padding towards me – no, a wolf. By its side, a tall and elegant woman was emerging from the light. Her long auburn hair seemed to glance off her body as she walked as if it wasn't allowed to touch her radiant skin. The grey wolf's mouth was open but its tongue wasn't lolling like a happy dog. Instead, it looked at me with such wise eyes that I couldn't help but kneel.

The meditation I was doing told me to ask whoever I met on this new plane a question, but what could I ask? I was in awe. Who were they? Where *was* I? Was it all in my head or had some part of my teenaged-self managed to transcend the confines of my body and visit some mystical realm?

In my eyes, she was a goddess of spring and summer, filled with kindness and light. She was so warm. She spoke to me – standing like a reed of light next to her canine companion – offering me reassurances when everything in my high-school life felt like a bad amateur drama and gangly boys with braces and blazers they'd grow into were being particularly unpleasant. She put me entirely at ease. I carried this experience with me for many years and still do; that radiance and calm is a place I return to when my adult life feels like the first few pages of a discarded play.

When I was seventeen, after a little pause on astral travel to dabble in make-up, My Chemical Romance and boys with long hair, I returned to my witchcraft studies. I was in sixth form college and pretty stressed out with learning Chaucer quotations by rote on little flashcards in my bedroom, so I decided to get a taste of stillness by returning to the beautiful field that went on forever. I was surprised at how easy it was to get back there but when I arrived there was no one waiting for me. No wise wolf or glowing goddess. Instead, I walked for a long time under the glow of a full moon until I came across a campfire. I approached with caution only to find a large bird using its ruffled feathers to cover itself from the night. A pelican. What a strange thing to find by a campfire in the deep recesses of eternity.

It looked a bit scruffy but in a wholesome ragamuffin way, and not like a dodgy backstreet Fagin. I asked it where my usual companions were and it looked at me with a beady eye ringed with yellow like a solar eclipse.

I'm here to help you now.

This strange character didn't appear to me again but sometimes I caught a flicker of that campfire in my mind and wondered if it was still out there in some realm watching me. I never saw the wolf or the ethereal woman again.

It was many years before I chose to work with the crone goddess Cerridwen or even dared to. Cerridwen, the goddess of the cold, dark and shadowy places and the gatekeeper of death itself. Why would I move away from the lovely motherly comfort of Rhiannon, the summer goddess, or the kind and friendly spirit of Brigid that so embodied spring? Cerridwen was akin to something straight from the pages of my demonology book, my frightening nightmare read from the school library. The crone was the fearful scrabbling in the film *The Cabin in the Woods*. She was the hook-nosed fiend of many a fairy tale, clothed from head to toe in a black robe that hit the angles of her ragged bones. Why would I trust her?

I wanted to stay in the warm glow of the assured and stately goddess from my astral vision.

But, of course, the Wheel of the Year teaches us to embrace both the light and the dark. Without the two, we can never live a whole life.

Cerridwen, Hecate, dark mother – I'll meet you again later in the year when Brigid is tired of springtime and Rhiannon needs to rest in the shade of autumn.

See you on the next full turn of the Wheel.

4

BELTANE

May! May is nearly here. Let's sing it from the hills!

October may be the witches' month, but there's nothing quite like the transformation of late April and May to slap joy into your heart.

The earth is spattered with the golden dust of silver birch catkins as I leave the house for my morning run. The days are now alarmingly bright before eight o'clock and the dawn chorus kicks my early-bird senses into action. It is the final days of April at 5.30 a.m. and I'm out in the park. The cold air hits the back of my throat making me gasp as I do my usual lap. All around me, nature is turning over its palm to show me hidden, just-sprouted beauty.

I feel as though I've been woken up. Moving my body like this, quickening my pulse, is welcoming spring in. Every day, something new appears in the park – a burst of forget-me-nots, a fragrant swathe of wild garlic. The hawthorn and cherry blossom cloud the sides of the path so that every walk in the park feels like I'm in some kind of rom-com and a man on a horse is about to come galloping into shot with a love letter. All those wintry walks stamping the blood back into your feet, and fighting through sleet to beat your Strava PB – they don't have the same effect as the reawakening of spring. Give me a mountainside walk with the sun on my face, heading west on the descent. I just want to wear shorts again, OK? Spring is the driving force of the year; it pushes the great Wheel forward, spinning it into a fresh cycle of seasons.

As I run, I round a corner where the old bowling green used to be and freeze.

On the hill before me is a deer. A beautiful female roe deer. She turns her head inquisitively, but not fearful to see me. I am barely breathing and my brain is telling my heart to stop the noisy movement of my blood. The deer is watching me, seeing if I am a threat – this small pillar of black Lycra and bed hair. With a short springing motion, she morphs herself into the trees and shrubs, no longer seen by any living creature in the dense greenery around her. Deer! In my local park! How could this be? The traffic from the A6 offshoot on the other side of the trees hasn't started up its smoker's cough yet. To have deer going about their daily business so close to the centre of a large city feels surreal like I've stepped back in time to the mists and marshes of what might have lain on this ground many hundreds of years before. A couple of years ago when it snowed here I remember seeing the light pointed prints of a deer crossing a path into the trees. I couldn't believe what I was seeing, convinced that it was a hoax or, failing that, the deer must have been lost, lonely and far away from home. Now, I know the deer was just where it meant to be and I feel so grateful to live so close to such a beautiful and unexpected creature. My chest swells with pride for the voracious way that nature can return when you give it space.

Throughout history, deer have often been seen as symbols of fertility. Stag antlers can be seen throughout the millennia as being a part of fertility rites. After all, deer definitely do make quite a noisy show of their mating rituals each autumn. Of all the Pagan Sabbats,

Beltane (*'BELL-tane'*), or May Day, is the one most closely linked with fertility, virility and passion. In some traditions, it is the time of year when the God and Goddess are wed and the classic Maypole that people dance around after a few wines is actually just a big old penis sticking out of the village green. It's no wonder May is celebrated for its fertility, of course; the dawn chorus is now at its peak with the mating trills of birds elongating across the fields and the titter of early chicks sounding from the tangles of the hedgerows.

Beltane is also a fire festival. The word 'Beltane' itself means 'the fires of Bel', who was a Celtic god of fire, the sun and farming. As Bel was the one who blessed people's livestock, cows were often passed through a bonfire or another type of blaze to honour him and ask for prosperity for the coming year – after all, Bel's name means 'bright one'. In a ritualistic sense, the fire can be seen as burning away any negative energy and supercharging the atmosphere for the months to come.

While some Pagan Sabbats shift their date on a yearly basis to coincide with the equinoxes and solstices, there are some with fixed dates and Beltane is one of them. Come 1 May, the witches are out in their flower-crowned droves. Aside from Samhain, I'd say that Beltane is one of the big ones.

OK, so you might have heard the rumours about us. We witchy folk do have quite the reputation for getting naked and dancing under the full moon. All those 'sky clad' rituals out in the woods have raised quite a few eyebrows over the years – it wasn't me, honest . . .

In years gone by, Beltane was the time when people could head off to a hidden spot outside with a partner they weren't married to without the promise of scandal waiting at their front door the next day. It was a chance to be at one with nature while doing the most natural thing in the world. All those May Queens crowned as the image of beauty and fertility; all those baskets overflowing with spring flowers; all those young lovers entwined in the woods. In the UK, we still get 'May Day' off work. If we were supposed to be frolicking around in our underwear every Early May Bank Holiday, I missed the memo.

With this in mind, I decide to try something I've rarely done before, outside of Yule last year, and take my Beltane ritual outside – but I quite like wearing clothes when I'm parading around the parks of central Manchester, sorry to disappoint.

The park is blooming. The blackthorn has given way to white bursts of hawthorn blossom, the sweetest smell of spring. The migrant chiffchaffs now have their 'chiffchaff chiffchaff' song in full swing after a few croaky starts as spring began. The dog walkers are out earlier and earlier each day and I begin to wonder where on earth I'm going to do my ritual. I could drive to our allotment a few miles down the road but there isn't really anywhere to sit in between the raised beds. Nowhere big enough to draw a circle, anyway. Could I go to the park before dawn?

The graveyard feels like a safe spot. I've been spending time there just after sunrise when the somewhat creepy space is filled with the piercing, clearing light of spring mornings – graveyards can be unsung paradises for nature. In among the old melodious Lancashire surnames, I am often surprised to see nuthatches, jackdaws and a buzzard as they use the stones as an elaborate game of the floor is lava. They hop from one stone to the next, tapping their toes fondly on each one as if in remembrance of the person lying deep below.

I'd like to say that this early morning wandering is down to the newly regrouped migratory birds chirping softly in my ear, dusting off their choir sheets after a long winter break. But really, Linnet has decided that the first hints of daylight mean breakfast time. I'm equal parts flattered and pissed off that she decides to sit on my head at five o'clock in the morning and not Will's.

*

Several years ago during my internship at Leighton Moss, I was an assistant guide on a dawn chorus walk through the reserve, stopping at each hide under the cover of nautical dawn. Even now, I'm surprised at how many people joined our group, some having kipped behind their steering wheels in the car park over the road to meet us at three o'clock in the morning. I had stumbled out of my cottage accommodation on four hours of sleep and no coffee – it was going to be a long time until breakfast. Luckily, this was the walk where I met Laurie so we spent most of the subsequent four hours sniggering at the back of the group.

Birds like a sense of order to the mornings; an unspoken ranking system. First, the robins start up, with their melodious swoop of notes. I have mistaken a robin's call for a blackbird many times, its cadences making my heart swell in a similar pattern. Next are the wrens and tits with their more scattergun approach to singing. The great tit's insistent 'teach-er, teach-er' call, for me, is like a tic at the back of your head, reminding you of something you've forgotten to put on your shopping list. Next are the blackbirds and the song thrushes – two of the UK's top-rated singers – platinum all the way in my eyes. I think there are few more hauntingly beautiful moments than listening to a lone blackbird chant and chime about its dreams from the highest branch of the tree.

This time of the morning may be useless to birds who want to search for food, but it is a great time to flex your vocal cords. If you've ever woken at the crack of dawn and gone outside, you'll know that this time of the morning has a different quality to it, and the birds know it too. As the air is often so still and quiet at this early hour without the rustle of human life to fill the air – machines are at rest and car doors won't begin slamming for another few hours – the air just after dawn can physically carry sound further, twenty times further in fact, making it the perfect time to make yourself heard.

On our official dawn chorus walk, we stopped every couple of minutes or so to hold our breaths and close our eyes to listen for small, stalk-like feet dancing over the spikes of the hedgerows. We were led by one of the reserve's most knowledgeable birdwatchers. At first, we were all silent as we moved our tired feet around, but then people began to get braver, pointing out birds they'd spotted raising their heads to the coming dawn and asking questions to our main guide. Of course, he knew all the answers; the size of each brood, the underwing feathers of a chiffchaff, how many small scuttling insects each new chick needed to eat to become strong enough for the flight over the Sahara Desert at the end of summer. His passion for nature really shone through. From the back of the group, I wondered if our guide had ever stood with his eyes closed against the soft heat of the spring sun, the twig-like lines of veins clouding his vision, and imagined himself rooted to the earth, moss growing over his walking boots until he was another tree for the birds to nest in. What he might have given to grow with them and watch the intricacies of their lives play out on the outstretched tips of his fingers – to be part of the natural world himself.

*

May Day

The day arrives.

It's Beltane – May Day – and I have so much to be thankful for.

I've been feeling stronger every day. The fatigue has lifted, evaporated like it hadn't ruled my life for the past ten months, and spring has buoyed me up. It really is my favourite time of year. I flip through my Book of Shadows to a page where *Beltane* is underlined in biro at the top. I haven't kept a Book of Shadows since I was about fourteen years old but many witches find it useful to have a notebook where they write down their rituals and spells. When I had just discovered Wicca in my early teens, I used to write down everything, every little charm, every astrological correspondence, pages and pages of Futhark runes and Theban characters. It was like taking an extra class in ancient philosophy, myth and meditation every night while my maths homework lay gathering dust.

Until the late 1800s, many of the people who would have practised the craft – working-class and lower-middle-class folk – had neither been to school nor would have been able to read or write. The 'ancient' *books of shadows* went no further back than 1920, penned by the likes of Gerald Gardner, the founder of Wicca, and other middle-class witches.

Other practitioners had their traditions passed down orally around the kitchen fire. While the idea of a Book of Shadows is rooted in Neo-Paganism, I would definitely recommend keeping a record of your magickal journey and workings, that way you can keep tabs on how far you've come.

Like many people in the community, I prefer to use the word magick with a 'k', to differentiate it from 'rabbit out of a hat', 'dove up my sleeve', 'rainbow hankies in my pants' kind of magic. However, if this doesn't suit you and is a little too Neo-Pagan for your tastes, feel free to substitute it with 'magic'.

But what is magick?

In his book *Pagan Paths: A Guide to Wicca, Druidry, Asatru, Shamanism and Other Pagan Practices*, Peter Jennings writes:

For me, magic works best when I take a natural process and encourage it to be stronger, or alter its rate. We then descend into the thorny subject of what magic is, but I would agree with the definition of projecting one's will to alter the course of events on both a physical and spiritual plane.

Magick can enhance, influence or change the way something happens. For example, you really want a promotion at work – you can wish and wish for it without success. However, by using mystical forces or a 'spell' a magick-worker can find themselves with a pay rise under their belt. There are many ways that a magickal practitioner can do this, whether through the combination of herbs and incantation, lighting a flame and imbuing it with intention, or invoking the great Goddess or 'Spirit' to carry out your wishes. Doing this involves a strong sense of self, knowing your own will and being aware of the magickal correspondences of the planets, herbs and times of the moon cycle to enhance your power. These are, of course, just a few ways that magick can be carried out. I'm not really one for everyday spells but it's something I use to bring about change every once in a while.

My ritual is written out clearly and I pop the book inside my rucksack alongside a lighter, candle and a piece of pink ribbon. It is a simple ritual, welcoming and honouring the festival of Beltane, my favourite Sabbat of all.

It's early, around six o'clock in the morning. I'm about to leave the house in hiking boots, a camouflage jacket, leggings and a long pink robe tucked up in a round bundle inside my jacket like I'm about to give birth, when I catch a glimpse out the window.

It's pissing it down.

Beltane – what are you doing to me?

I leave the house, hood up, and quickstep across the park, squelching as I go.

I've scoped out a good spot – an elm tree right at the back of the graveyard, shady and out of the way. I sling my rucksack up against the only side of the elm that isn't getting hammered by rain.

'This isn't what I had planned,' I laugh to the tree. I place my hand on its trunk to steady myself and take stock of whether I will be able to continue the ritual in the downpour. A slight movement catches my eye. I look at my hand and only an inch from it is a small bumblebee. She is a bundle of fuzz, almost invisible against the dark tree bark. Did she spend the night here? Or were her early morning rounds scuppered by the sudden rain? I'm honoured to be sharing this space with her. I take a closer look at the tree and find a spider who'd had similar ideas and some small flies are also resting their wings in a hollow just above my eye line. Who would have known that one tree could offer a resting place to so many creatures during a storm?

I place my candle at the base of the tree and take off my shoes and jacket. Everything is so soaked by now that there is no chance of anything being damaged by the flame. The tree's branches are wide and mark their own circle above me. I walk around this circle clockwise to cast my ritual space, but the rain doesn't seem to understand this magickal boundary and I'm drenched in seconds. However, the water and bubbling grass between my toes feels calming. When I have found stillness, I call to her.

'Brigid, I invoke thee, I invoke thee . . .'

From the centre of my circle, I feel a presence. It is not as strong as the one in my Ostara circle and I know that if I opened my eyes right now I wouldn't see her face looking back at me. It's like Brigid is in everything around me, her intense power diluted by the downpour and spreading into the soil and living things in this natural corner of the graveyard. I breathe her magick in — so verdant, letting this green luscious energy swallow me up as I perform my ritual. On the strip of pink ribbon I have brought, I write 'Bless this new world' and tie it to the branches of the elm, honouring this time of growth and new life.

I'm standing with my feet in the fresh mud, my hands outstretched by my thighs, when a niggling feeling tells me to open my eyes. I peer over my shoulder. Sure enough, there's movement close to the graveyard gate. I position the elm tree directly between me and the onlooker, feeling like I've just been caught pulling faces behind the head teacher's back.

Someone is coming towards me and I freeze. Why hadn't I done my ritual inside like a normal person? Stupid, stupid. But I squint and realise the person isn't a person at all.

A deer ... no, two deer! They're moving slowly through the gravestones, each careful placement of their hooves is calm and serene. I watch, stock still, my hair in tendrils and my face slick with rain. This is their place, their home, and I'm the lurker, peeking out from behind the elm tree like a burglar. Is this the same deer I saw a week earlier? Is it with another pal? Is this a mother and child, or two sisters, who have found their way into this strange, urban world? The pride in me almost bursts my chest once more and I feel a single hot tear on my cold cheeks.

When they are out of sight, I finish my ritual, thanking the Goddess, the tree, the rain and the two glorious deer that chose to honour me with their presence today. My feet barely register my boots as I jam them back inside, so numb with spring rainwater and the wet dense earth. But I don't care. As I get inside, my socks are sodden, but I feel like my day has been blessed. Blessed Beltane, blessed cleansing rain and blessed be the heartbeats of the wild creatures living so close beside me.

*

Lottie is one of my oldest and dearest friends. Every time I see her, her hair is green, or pink, or purple, or half-shaved off and she's thrusting some new gem or tarot card set into my hands. In her career she's been a massage therapist, a social worker and a burlesque dancer and is now studying for her PhD; she's also been doing rituals with me ever since we were fourteen years old in her parent's garage. She radiates the delicious feminine energy that I associate with the highs of spring and the dark coils of winter. Lottie is intense chaos energy so there's never a dull moment around her ... which is why I've decided to go along with her plan.

It's a rainy Saturday morning in Hunt's Cross in Merseyside. We pull up outside a modern-looking brown-bricked church close to the main road on the way to Speke. Not the typical place to dip my toe into Shamanism.

My knowledge of Shamanism and Shamans is limited and conjures up vague images of Amazonian tribes and psychedelic visions. It is not the sort of practice I would expect to find next to a Liverpudlian industrial estate. For me, Shamans are robed, mysterious men who chant and dance in dark tents filled with pungent smoke and I don't know how much this has to do with the Pagan path, if anything, but I've decided to go wherever this cycle of the Wheel takes me; I'm willing to try most things and the universe has certainly been nudging me in this direction. Over the past few months, Shamanism has been dropping into my lap more and more often; I'll open a second-hand book and find notes about shamanic practices scrawled in the margin or I'll see bunches of tribal 'smudging' feathers at a local fair, said to be used in shamanic ritual. I had an in-depth discussion about homemade *ayahuasca* (the potent psychoactive brew and purgative used by Shamans within some South American tribes to enhance spiritual work) with a Scottish witch only a few months before and it spoke to the part of me that is interested in astral journeys. It isn't something I've researched too much but Shamanism has been trying to enter my consciousness for some time.

Inside, the arch-ceilinged room is filled with the steam from two-dozen mugs of tea. The clunky church hall radiators are clicking and rattling into action because, although it's approaching June, it's been grey and raining since Beltane. Lottie and I take two seats among the twenty chairs positioned in a wide circle in the centre of the room. I feel at ease immediately in the scents of white sage and green tea. We've been asked to bring a blanket, cushion, yoga mat, scarf and a notebook, so the room is draped with our home-brought soft furnishings and I fight the urge to nestle down into a fuzzy ball on the floor.

The session is led by a woman called Chris – a tall, elegant-looking Scouse woman with a friendly face and a mane of Celtic, auburn hair. There's a lot of Irish blood in this room of lilting Liverpudlian accents, myself included. Chris is wringing her hands as she chats quietly with the men and women closest to her before our workshop starts – the room is pretty full. Fifteen years ago, I wonder if people would have shown such an interest in practices like this; how would they have heard about spaces like this? I'm heartened by the people in the room – I've been to many 'New Age' events in my life and sometimes the room can be thick with spiritual jargon; people with their chests puffed, talking about their training in the mountains of Nepal. This isn't unique to the spiritual community, of course, as we've all come across 'that sort' in our running clubs, our neighbourhood watch or down in the queue for the bank – however, this kind of experience within the yoga and esoteric world has often led me to seek my own spiritual practices, confining me to my room with a candle and a soothing book. Here, in this circle of steam and cushions, people talk about their journey through the Kingsway Tunnel, the relentlessness of the English summer rain and their favourite kinds of biscuits. It's so *normal*. My nervous system feels calmed just listening to the same patterns of speech I grew up with and, in my segment of the circle, I pretend quietly that I am normal too.

Chris calls everyone's attention. 'Hi everyone, I'm so glad you've braved the rain to be here today!'

Today's session, I've been told by Lottie, is a brief introduction to Shamanism: where it comes from, what it is used for, and we will have the chance to take part in a 'journey', which most intrigues me. The workshop starts with a history of Shamanism. I'm surprised by how much I've already picked up from books or friends, like this has been part of my consciousness for many years, but there are some key bits of knowledge that I'm missing. Shamanism is a practice that has been around for millennia, with archaeological findings showing that it has been used by almost every culture throughout history if we turn back the clock 10,000 years. Shamanism uses trance work and altered states of consciousness to commune with nature and beings from other astral worlds, allowing a Shaman to seek healing for themselves and people among the tribe through a practice called 'journeying'. Through Shamanism, we can speak to the essence of a plant, a rock or a tree – its true spirit – and find healing on a physical, spiritual and emotional level. Although it is a spiritual practice, Shamanism would have been part of the everyday existence for many peoples across time, vital to both how they experienced the world around them and how they would have respected the animals and plants they shared their lives with.

The word itself comes from a Mongolian/Siberian set of tribes and means 'one who sees in the dark'. I like to think that at the beginning of humanity we were more in tune with everything that lived in this world, like birds who can sense the turning of a storm or a shark smelling dinner half a kilometre away; but we would also have been more connected with the unseen places, the 'other worlds' and realms. Spirits, goddesses and gods, the things most people dismiss as myth and legends, would have played a large role in people's lives and their relationship with the land, influencing the everyday.

Back in these ancient cultures, Shamans were spiritual people within the community who trained for many years, sometimes isolating themselves from the main group until their services were called on – they were said to have a foot in both worlds; this reality and another. These people would have been deeply in touch with the other worlds, the ones unseen, just on the periphery of our consciousness, but so intricately connected with our own. Shamans are still important figures to remote communities in places such as Siberia, Tibet and the Amazon, and work with local people to alleviate physical, emotional or spiritual problems.

This is all new to me and I'm scribbling down every word Chris says with such intensity that the spine of my notebook cracks and a page flutters loose onto the church hall floor.

Chris explains, 'Within Shamanism, there are multiple different worlds. We, in our physical form, live in the Middle World.' I immediately think of myself as a hairy-footed hobbit. 'This world is filled with our everyday lives and mundanities, our relationships and traditions. But it is also full of fast-moving technology, war and people with bad intentions. The Middle World can be a confusing place for many of us who feel we have lost our connection with nature and are being forced to keep up with the fast pace of modern life. But this world is the one we have to deal with on a daily basis.'

I keep my face neutral but I'm filled with a sudden ache. The words about *connection with nature* have focused my attention. Once again, my mind tries to comprehend how many people must feel this way and I think of all the people in their apartment blocks with a view of power stations and car parks. How many people in their daily lives don't see a single tree that isn't held upright by concrete?

My intuition is telling me to stop fidgeting, breathe, and really pay attention to what Chris is telling me. It is telling me I'm here to learn something.

She goes on. 'However, it is not the only world that exists.

'A Shaman is someone who travels among the worlds; this Middle World reality and the Other Worlds. There is also a Lower World, a vast spiritual plane filled with nature. Here it is wild, healing and safe to wander without the problems of the Middle World we live in. The Lower World is the realm of animals, plants, rocks and trees, untouched by the hand of humanity. Shamans often go to this realm to seek deep healing for those in the Middle World who are physically or mentally sick. They help to bring back the connection between Mother Earth and those existing in an unbalanced, unhappy world.'

My eyes flick up from my notebook. This Lower World sounds familiar. An untouched green land filled with animals and plants. Could I have been there before? I think back to those astral journeys I took as a teenager – the worlds I saw that were grassland that went on for infinity. The red flowers and the dazzling sunshine. Could I have been practising a form of Shamanism without knowing it while I was hovering between the worlds? I look over at Lottie with my mouth open but she is busy writing – maybe she has also been to the place that Chris is describing.

Chris also talks about another realm; the Upper World. One populated with goddesses, angels, gods and other higher beings. It is a celestial realm, made up of ethereal white palaces. Just as I think to myself, 'It sounds a bit like heaven', Chris chimes in to say, 'At one point we were connected with this world and used its imagery in our own architecture, trying to build a piece of heaven on Earth. You'll see these beautiful churches and halls – take Liverpool Cathedral – all being made in the image of the Upper World.'

When I got up this morning, I definitely thought I was coming here to meditate and have a bit of a sing-song. I couldn't have been more wrong and I'm thrilled.

What amazes me most is that, from the things Chris is saying, these places are all accessible. People practising Shamanism can reach these other realms by getting themselves into an altered state of consciousness. A few people dart their eyes at each other but Chris assures us with a grin and a shrug that there are 'no drugs here'. As humans, we can reach this state of consciousness through many other ways – fasting, ritual dancing, breathwork, meditation and a repeated rhythmic drum beat. Today, we will be using a drum.

Chris explains that the aim of this introduction day is to meet our Power Animal – our animal guides that will lead us safely through the Lower and Upper Worlds. These Power Animals are what is called the 'over soul' of a creature – they are not a particular creature that has a name or an age – they are not your long-lost Jack Russell – but rather a representative of a whole species. Again, a shiver of recognition goes down my spine. I remember the soft and rustling bird I once met by the campfire while travelling to another world in an altered state of consciousness.

Chris mentions that, when we go on our shamanic journeys today, we can ask our Power Animal a question that we want to know the answer to and they will be able to nudge us in the right direction. We can ask them for help, or simply ask if they have anything to show us. The animal might give us medicine or show us something that could bring meaning to a situation we are facing in the Middle World. It sounds quite similar to searching for an answer in a spell or Pagan ritual, except just travelling through space and time. A bit different, then . . .

I suddenly feel self-conscious, wishing I had honoured this practice with more than yoga pants and a high ponytail. The group is smiling, ready, and a low hum of contentment seems to glide over us. We are filled with wonder and recognition.

Chris smiles back at us, sensing our thirst to move on. 'We'll now be doing a shamanic journey to the Lower World. In this world, remember, there is only pure nature. Trees with deep roots and wide rivers that have not been modified by man.' A warning note sounds in her voice now. 'You will not see the influence of humans here. If you come across a fence, cotton clothing or something metallic, you've not gone deep enough.'

I nod fervently, overeager to get started. I want to return to the serenity of the Lower World, skimming over the thought that springs to mind, *What happens if I don't go deep enough?*

Chris says, 'First of all, we will go to our axis mundi – our world's axis – a natural place on this plane where we feel safe, a place we can conjure up in our minds easily. This could be a tree we feel a connection with, or something like a mountain we've visited and where we felt really calm.'

My beach. The location is immediately in my head. I've travelled there before many times in my mind while astral journeying. My axis mundi is a place drawn carefully on the inside of my head – my quiet, empty cove of beach that I visited fifteen years ago, although I've never called it my axis mundi. It has been an ever-present place in my mind; a place that straddles my last memories of childhood and the unknown of adolescence; it is a place that has become tied to the very first steps I took on my witchcraft journey all those years ago. I know how easily I can find it again.

I remember it as a sunny day where the sand was scorching underfoot. I moved along the beach slightly away from my parents and sister to the west where I found a rocky cove – an almost perfect circle of sand surrounded by barnacled rocks, some slippery with kelp from the morning's tide, some rough as sandpaper from the blasting sun. Just beyond the cove was a sheer cliff, disjointed from the land. Between this cliff and the rise of the mainland, the sea was framed and shaped like a photograph of another world. I don't know how long I sat there that day but I lulled myself into a calm daze as I watched the waves crashing against the cliff far out of reach. This is the place I have returned to again and again when I want to feel that surrender to the beauty of the world – when the neon glare and clacking keyboards get too much. When I first used it in that long-ago guided meditation as a teen, I had wanted to experiment with the new world that my interest in Wicca had opened up. Looking back on this now, a young teenage girl astral projecting herself out of her bedroom with no guidance or protection of what other worlds could bring was probably a mistake, but it did let me flex this portion of my brain. I was just a gangly child adding her presence into other worlds. Ever since, I have been able to slip easily into this meditative state of consciousness and float myself into permanence on another plane.

As the years have passed, I've wondered how much was actually an astral meditation and how much was my teenage imagination.

Of course, we've all heard of kids who have recounted past lives or toddlers who have spoken to 'the man in the corner of the room' when there's nobody there. Studies have shown a link between HSPs, or those more sensitive to their physical environments, and experiences with the supernatural. But there's always been part of me that has wondered whether my experience was the product of reading too much teenage fiction. I guess I was about to find out.

This journey with Chris and the group will just be ten minutes long – a test run. We all move to find a quiet space in the room and roll out our yoga mats. The lights go out and I'm so cosy in my little corner with a blanket wrapped around me and a scarf over my eyes to block out all the light. I listen for instruction and am met with the sound of expectant breath around me. Chris begins to play the drum. Slow and rhythmic at first. Another shiver goes down my spine – my body is aligning itself with this primal sound; the reverberating thuds of the beater on stretched animal hide stirs something in the room. My heartbeat picks up as the drum quickens. I'm expecting very little but I seem to be already slipping into another state.

This is it.

Under my eyelids, in the back of my mind, I'm at my axis mundi on my beach, sitting cross-legged with the sea reaching my ears in steady streamers of sound. I know this place well. Behind me, a vertical rock cracks open inaudibly and I feel the space widening in my consciousness. It's a dark crack lined with long strands of sea moss. It has the same pull I felt as a child when I saw a cave along the beach, that intense desire to explore and peer into the shadows, maybe to hide there. I walk over; to touch it feels like stroking a wild animal's dense fur underwater.

I turn sideways to slide myself into the opening of this narrow cave.

My hair and skin catch on the rough surface of the rock. I'm heading into the dark unknown as I inch myself inside, then suddenly the space opens out into a womb-like dome and I'm relieved to be able to flex my arms like it has taken me a very long time to get to this cave.

Before me, there is another opening. It is bright and green. It is filled with sounds I'd only ever heard in a David Attenborough documentary.

The slice of jungle before me is enticing and I step forward into its lushness. It is all around me, emitting the sounds of colourful birds and the scratchings of hidden claws and feet. These are trees I've never seen before, each growing from vivid-green moss that covers my ankles. I crane my neck and see the trees hold pendulous white fruit. They are bulbous with white nobbles and when I reach up to touch one – soft as a peach – I press my thumb into it and am met with a deep red liquid with a wine-like scent. Juice runs down my hand and I watch it, amazed, like I'm in a slow-motion romance scene.

Chris had told us that we would find metaphors and symbolism in the Lower World and I ponder what these sexy fruits could mean.

I walk through the trees, drawn in by their sounds. This place feels safe as I was told it would do; the patterns of sunlight through the canopy make me feel like the path before me is being lit up like the Yellow Brick Road. As I walk, I get the sense that a lake is up ahead and I should go towards it. It will be cool there after the jungle's humidity and I might sit and put my feet in the water. These simple thoughts drift to me like I'm slightly intoxicated, dreamy and not fully in my body, or like I'm catching the tail-end of somebody else's whispers.

The tree branches become lower and thin out as I approach a clear pool of water.

And there he is. His long bill gives him a mournful look as he turns to face me.

My Power Animal.

A pelican with white-grey feathers and a yellowish bill is bobbing on the lake before me. I shake my head, incredulous. It has been many years since I've seen this creature. The pelican I once saw by a small campfire is now paddling towards me, holding me fixed in his yellow-ringed stare.

I chuckle slowly to myself in this dreamlike way I seem to have in the Lower World. A pelican, really? I'd been a birdwatcher for many years but I'd never come close to seeing a pelican. A few years ago, I was invited on a birdwatching trip to the south of Spain where I saw vultures, flamingos and Spanish imperial eagles, but never a pelican. So, this was my shamanic Power Animal – my guide to the other realms.

I can't remember when I last saw a picture of a pelican and I've certainly never seen a video of one moving, hunting or calling for its mate. I had always thought of the pelican as a silly, half-mythological creature, ridiculous enough to be consigned to the Roald Dahl books of my childhood. Strange that a creature I know nothing about will be looking out for me as I travel across planes of existence.

He emerges from the water – I see the flapping feet of a water bird, a fringe of greyish-black on its folded wingtips. He has a graceless waddle but I'm transfixed.

I kneel down to him and we stare at each other for a long moment. I feel like I'm looking at someone I knew a very long time ago – like a preschool best friend or someone I met and swapped secrets and ice lollies with on a family holiday. But even as these thoughts enter my mind, I realise there is so much more to it. Beneath the curiosity, there is a deep recognition, like we've been inhabiting the same body for many years but have only just turned our heads to meet.

This is the 'oversoul' of the pelican species. Every creature must have one – the oversoul of the mole, the oversoul of the anglerfish. The more I look at the pelican before me – or is it Pelican with a capital P? – the more majestic I think he seems. His head held upright despite the weight of his beak, the fearsome angle of that bill and the solemn stare that makes me sit up a little straighter. He is a creature that demands respect.

The reason I'm here drifts softly over to me, thick and lethargic like the jungle air.

I ask Pelican, 'Do you have anything you want to tell me or show me?'

Pelican stares at me and a strange feeling comes over me. It is a dark sensation like I'm remembering someone that left me feeling cold and numb. It's a bad feeling and it pulls at my chest so hard that I have to hold my heart.

I hear a voice in my head and know it belongs to Pelican. *This will get better.*

I close my eyes, heart in hand, and want to cry. This feeling Pelican is showing me is one I know all too well. I remember the very first time I felt it, aged twelve, cooped up in a History class, moving slowly between watching the rain outside and ferociously doodling in the back of my exercise book. The feeling of depression was like a model ship had sunk inside my torso – it was the sudden drag of matter from somewhere around my sternum and into the pit of my stomach. There were many things that might have activated this feeling in me: maybe it was the rain, the threat of Thursday afternoon PE or the outburst of hormones that made a hypersensitive child even more aware of the small world she inhabited with its bullies and social ranking systems of secondary school. Ever since then, this feeling has appeared sporadically through my years, brought on by that nagging sensation that something about me just 'wasn't quite good enough'. I've never figured out which part of me that is, in fact, it is difficult to think much at all under the fug of depression, but it has always felt like there is something missing or like I'm just a bit too different to be able to make friends. Seeing the image of this spindly child with one sock pulled higher than the other makes me want to reach out and pull her close. I'd like to tell her that it's not so bad – your friends are incredible; you have a cat now! Although I know that in those moments it is virtually impossible to feel anything except the constant drip of dark water. Through my dreamy Lower World state, I think of the band of people around me in this room, each walking in a different world; I think of Pelican with his doleful eyes showing a depth of feeling and compassion as I clutch my chest.

With one sentence, this creature has made me feel more accepted than I have ever felt in my life. I'm so glad I came here today. I'm in the right place.

This will get better.

The drumming that has provided a backdrop to my entire journey picks up a rapid beat to make us aware that the journey is about to come to an end. I look at Pelican, who gives me a nod of acknowledgement that reaches my core, then I begin to rush back through the jungle and into the cave, back to my axis mundi.

The drumming stops entirely and I am lying on a church hall floor with a scarf over my eyes and the lights are gradually coming on around me. I scribble everything down in my diary as we've been encouraged to do.

We split into groups to discuss what we've seen. The majority of people have been able to find their Power Animal: wolves, lions, bears, a horse and a single butterfly. Lottie tells me about a powerful and striking tiger who circled her like it was assessing whether to bring Lottie into its tribe. All of these creatures, on paper at least, seem a lot more regal than my Pelican and when I tell people my Power Animal I say it with a grin.

When we return after lunch, I'm itching for my next journey. Why wouldn't I want to journey every second of the day?

Chris is looking just as flushed as I feel. There is a palpable excitement in the air that everyone is tuning into.

'Now, this journey is going to be a longer one. This time, you can ask your Power Animal for healing. This could be because you have a dodgy knee or it could be some emotional pain that you have stored up and want to release.

'Don't worry if your Power Animal decides to rip your head off and stuff you with cleansing smoke, or bury you, or maybe even burn you. This is all a part of shamanic healing – even if it might seem violent, it is always about removing the bad and replacing it with something good and restorative.'

I raise my eyebrows at Lottie and she grins savagely.

And so we begin our second trip.

As if my mind has flicked on a switch, I'm in my axis mundi. Pelican is there, practically dancing from foot to foot. I have a sense that he is excited to show me something although that bird gaze is unfathomable. We both slink into the crack in the side of the weathered rock and emerge from the cave into the Lower World . . . at least I think it's the Lower World. There are towering, thick-trunked trees that go back in precise diagonal rows, each one wound tightly with vines. The pattern of trees spreading out silently like a chessboard makes me uneasy; blurred with grey mist, I can't see the outlines of trees more than forty feet away from me. The place feels wrong, like I've taken the wrong path into Knockturn Alley. Bile rises in my throat.

This isn't where I'm supposed to be.

I look at Pelican with trepidation. Under his level gaze, I hear the words in my head, *You know what to do*.

I'm not sure I do, not one bit, but I know I need to leave this place and its dangerous energy.

I lean against one of the creepy trees, cautiously – is it going to eat me? The tree absorbs my body, the trunk bubbling around me until I am actually in the middle of the tree. Inside, it's hollow and I look up towards a light. Ahh, my mind tells me. This feels like the right portal to get to where I need to be. I'm glad Pelican had faith in me! I climb up the inside of the tree towards the brightness, my feet finding knots as rungs until I emerge at the very top above the canopy. The light here is startling after the dark strangeness of the world I've just come from. I'm in the heart of the tree's sprouting leaves; they remind me of palm fronds only much bigger and firmer, like an enormous succulent. There are a million trees around me, each with delicate white fruit hanging from its boughs.

I feel calm now, completely at ease; that Lower World sweetness seeping over me. I look to my right and Pelican is there, his lower jaw wobbling slightly as he moves his head. I fight the urge to hug him close in relief.

I will take you somewhere safe. Pelican's beak doesn't move but I hear the words as if they were whispered straight into my ear. Without a moment's hesitation, like I've been given an instruction, I climb onto Pelican's back, my front against the thick plumage of his back, and we are flying over the jungle towards the horizon.

I ask, 'Do you have anything you want to show me?'

The reply in my mind is so soft that I crane my head around to Pelican's face for a closer listen but I still can't catch it. Instead of speaking, Pelican lifts the left side of his upper beak, curling it like a lip to show the inside of his bill. I frown and look closer. The inside of his mouth is coated with thick, green moss. It looks deep enough to lose a hand in.

'What is this?' I ask.

Healing.

I reach out and put my hand inside, feeling waves of cool, healing energy coming from the moss. It reminds me of lying down in an ancient wood at the end of a day of hiking and feeling the forest absorb me into its ecosystem for a short time.

'Should I go deeper?' I am full of questions.

Pelican's beak opens a fraction more, then wider still. Soon, I can see the entire inside of the moss-carpeted bill. It is welcoming; enticing.

With that thought, I crawl inside.

I am minuscule in the damp greenery of Pelican's beak. There isn't just moss growing here, but an entire rainforest. I close my eyes and slump in a U-shape against the curve of the beak, my shoulders deep in vegetation. A small, dreamy part of me thinks, Tee hee, I'm inside a beak.

In my mind, Pelican's clear voice says, *Breathe in all the droplets of the rainforest.* On my next inhale, I sense the droplets from the leaves around me lifting to form a soft mist. They settle on my body and coat the inside of my nose. It is a deep, healing aloe balm. I can sense myself being healed, but I don't know why. Which part of me needs to heal?

I'm questioning this when Pelican's voice speaks authoritatively in my mind.

All will get better, you are in the right place.

It is such a simple message, encompassing many things, but his words appear before my eyes like they've been written in stone. It is a promise, an absolute certainty from the Lower World. I want to cry; I want to sob on my knees and tell him thank you. I want to do many things, celebrate, tell everyone, but then the mist comes.

It appears very gradually from deep in the rainforest, evaporating from the dense, shadowed leaves. A thin white mist is drifting towards me. It makes my cheeks dewy and bright as it settles around me.

Take it into you. Pelican's disembodied voice comes over the hiss of steam.

I know I am safe and slow in this dark womb space and Pelican's soft command is as smooth as liquid silver. I breathe in through my nose and inhale the mist. As soon as it hits the back of my throat, something happens.

I feel my body start to convulse.

My chest rises me up from the floor, before my body falls back down. But not just in the Lower World – my back smacks down on my Middle World yoga mat with force. What is happening to me? The mist is coursing through my body, brushing every digit and cell with a light-fingered touch. I feel it surging through me, lighting up the fine and delicate sinews around my joints and under my fingernails. My body jerks again, like a dam is being blown up inside me. But I don't feel scared. There is no panic. This feels like a necessary part of my healing process. It feels like a purification – the movement shaking pockets of black heaviness loose from my chest. I am totally in Pelican's hands, or wings . . . or mouth – things are pretty confusing right now.

But I know one thing: this energy is powerful.

I take a deep, releasing breath and the drumbeat changes. As if nothing at all has happened, my body starts to settle again into the comfort of Pelican's deep bill, completely held in its delicate, moss-filled curve.

I come back to the room and peel off the scarf from around my eyes. People are smiling, a serene inner glaze shielding their eyes from the church's strip lighting. With the rustle of blankets and pillows, everyone's shoulders shake with the force of documenting their findings in their notebooks.

Did everyone else just experience this? There don't seem to be any shoulder blades knocked out of place from anyone else's body-slamming. The room is a glowing bubble of contentment and mussy-haired dreamers.

On the way out, after thanking Chris profusely, Lottie and I are electric. Lottie's journey was equally as mesmerising; Tiger had ripped out her insides and filled her with gold. So much healing had taken place in that room today and I was holding the power of the Lower World inside me right now.

I am once again faced with the fact there is so much to learn about the world around me – and I'd just added two worlds on top of that. Today felt so natural, as if I had slowly extended my hand and grazed something that had been walking in parallel footsteps beside me all my life. My mind, so focused on the working world, a steady pay cheque and monotonous life admin, had dampened my senses. Shamanism is certainly not the witchcraft I know and love – far from it – but there are elements of it that make me wonder if witchcraft came into my life to guide me to this experience on this day, on this particular church hall floor. Shamanism is a part of all our histories and today has been a glimmer of something ancient. That deep appreciation of nature. The connection to Mother Earth. But also a connection to my past self who was feeling so lost, and to who I might become in the future. It's all there in front of me.

I think I might just have remembered something as old as time.

*

Some days, I don't feel like a witch.

I don't feel at home in my body; I don't feel like a powerful woman who is shining in her own skin. In fact, I feel dumpy and bloated, achy and so *so* old. I think back to all the athletic hikes I used to do in my early twenties, swinging myself over stiles like I was a training gymnast then running the last few steps to the top of the hill. These days, I mainly just feel tired. I look down at myself in the mirror and wince – those weak thighs that have barely taken a trip to the park this week, that stomach filled with processed food because I needed a sugar kick to get me through the afternoon. When this happens, I run through my head wondering what could be making me feel this way. I got a normal amount of sleep; I ate a whole bag of spinach this week so I can't give myself a lecture about iron. Maybe I just had too many crisps last night. As a last resort, I check the calendar – oh, look, there's a big-ass full moon in the sky.

I find it amazing how closely linked the female body is with the moon. I remember hearing a quote from comedian Sandi Toksvig about one of her anthropology classes at Cambridge. Her professor held up a picture of a bone with twenty-eight notches in it. The professor said, 'This is often considered to be man's first attempt at a calendar.' The female professor then went on to say, 'My question to you is this – what man needs to mark twenty-eight days? I would suggest to you that this is woman's first attempt at a calendar.' Women's cycles have often been overlooked in the male-dominated tomes of history – for Toksvig this was an eye-opening moment, and we must also ask ourselves the question, has the tinted glaze of men's writing been a driver in women's disconnect with their own bodies?

Many women turn to witchcraft or earth magick and, looking at it from this perspective, it isn't difficult to make the leap as to why that might be. Witchcraft and nature religions offer us a connection with the world and the monthly pattern of our menstrual cycles.

I've mentioned that the full moon can turn us all a bit crazy but she can actually affect us in many ways. For some people, they are full of energy, like the moon herself has reached down and touched them with sparkling fingertips; they want to dance and socialise. For other people, myself included, the full moon makes them want to sleep and sleep for three days straight. Research from the University of Basel found that during a full moon people have on average 30 per cent less deep sleep and 20 minutes less sleep every night.[18] I like to think the moon is shining down on me, giving me more power than I can handle right now, but setting me up for the month ahead. On the flip side, the new moon is meant to be a time of rest – in yoga, practitioners often say to only do slow, contemplative poses, focusing on meditation and a more introspective practice for the days around this time. The new moon is not blasting out the same amount of energy as it does when it is shining brightly across our cities and oceans, affording us an opportunity to drop inside our minds and be considered and reserved with our energy levels. Whatever the time of the month, I'm very aware of the moon's effects on my schedule.

One day shortly after Beltane, I get an email from my astrologer, Florence Devereux. I had contacted Flo for a natal chart reading not long before and was so impressed with the way she had skilfully navigated it. I'd scribbled notes down in my diary, so intent was I to learn everything there was about my connection with this universe. I tried to look back through these notes recently and realised I'd been a bit too enthusiastic because I couldn't read a single word I wrote.

I like to think I'm a dab hand at astrology, having spent hours, possibly weeks, of my time with my nose in the horoscope section of *Mizz* magazine or the slimline zodiac books that my mum picked up for me from a rotating stand at M&S. *Aries: A Look at the Year Ahead*. As a child, I couldn't get enough of it; inside, the book was divided into sections on Love, Money, Career. At age nine, I had zero experience of these things but I was very happy to find out that I was going to marry a Sagittarius. After seeing Flo for the first time, I realised that I knew nothing about astrology whatsoever; it is another world filled with people highly knowledgeable in the occult and who can discern your life's trajectory with a passing glance at your astrological birth chart.

To give a brief overview, your astrological natal chart is a snapshot of what was happening in the universe at the exact time of your birth. Many witches use astrology to figure out their place in the world, where their skills lie and, ultimately, what they will end up doing with their life. There has certainly been a renaissance of this skilled art over the past decade; if you don't know your sun, moon and rising signs, do you even know who you are anymore? If you're interested, I'm an Aries, Cancer, Leo. However, astrology has age-old roots and has been practised as a way of divining the future of individuals and events by many ancient cultures such as the Greeks, the Egyptians and the Babylonians.

This great art saw a lull in the western world from the sixteenth century onwards as the Enlightenment movement swept Europe. But in the modern world, why has astrology become so popular once again? Why has the phrase 'it's written in the stars' never been taken more literally? In her book *The Signs: Decode the Stars, Reframe Your Life*, author and astrologer Carolyne Faulkner says that when this tool is used 'to enhance self-awareness, it helps to navigate a much smoother path through our lives' allowing us to create 'deeper connection with the more authentic parts of ourselves'. For me, astrology has not only been a way to understand myself but also to seek connection with the wider world. Paths were destined to cross. That job interview paid off for a reason. You and I are *meant* to be here right now, sipping a cup of tea, legs curled under us with the soft tap of rain against the window. The idea of fatalism is tantalising in a world of performance and increasingly meaningless transactions.

I open Flo's email and find that it is about a course taking place next month. The course is in conjunction with a fertility specialist called Siri Kalla, based in Norway, and helps people to use the moon to understand their monthly cycles, and to harness this lunar power to manifest their goals. My eyes widen; this couldn't be any more up my street.

Anthropologists say that in ancient times, as well as our not-so-distant history, women would bleed naturally in synchronisation with the moon. A spike of oestrogen is triggered by more light in our skies, and the ripe full moon would fill the night with the glowing silver brightness needed to push our bodies into action.

I know that I'm totally out of sync with this. I bleed on the new moon and ovulate on the full moon – a product of a very modern society. The infiltration of street lamps around the cracks in our curtains and our ability to catch the night bus home at four o'clock in the morning rather than being curled up in our beds by nine o'clock in the evening means that many of us no longer live by the rhythmic ribbons of the moon's pull. I've been slightly unfortunate with my menstrual cycle and have had issues galore with it; pain that rockets down my thighs, heavy bleeding that has caused chronic anaemia and mood swings that I can only describe as prison-worthy. Many women experience this and it's difficult to say whether this is a time-old problem or something more recent, caused by our modern diets, mainly sedentary lifestyles and propensity to stay up into the early hours. Let's not mention the lack of research funding into endometriosis, PCOS (which both affect one in ten women in the UK alone) and migraines (experienced by 25 per cent of women compared to just 10 per cent of men) meaning that many more women than men suffer from severe and chronic pain with no miracle cures on the horizon. As I've got older and instinctively witchier, my connection between the body and Earth is something that feels more tangible. When our mental health improves, so does our physical health, so often linked with proximity to green space and nature. The Earth nourishes our wellness through birdsong and jigsaw patterns of sunshine across our faces. Our bodies were *made* to thrive on this Earth. We are innately connected with our planet and the vast Milky Way, and therefore with the universe itself.

That Flo's course has arrived so close to the primal festival of fertility spurs me on.

The course takes place over three days spaced out over a month, giving us a chance to track our cycles and document the phases of the moon through our windows. Over the course of just one month and really paying attention to the smaller cycles of the world – not just the macro turning of the seasons – I feel so much more in touch with the world and my own body. Now armed with new knowledge and connection, even when I'm brimming with pre-menstrual tears or I've got a hot-water bottle strapped around my middle, I close my eyes and remind myself this isn't forever. I will get myself in sync with the world's natural rhythms. I might not be there quite yet, but I am a woman of this Earth and a witch to boot. One day, I'll be bleeding and dancing at the same time.

Flo is one of those people who are effortlessly themselves – an artist, musician, a diviner of fate and an alchemist; she's at a level of cool that

I can only dream of. A modern mystic and an animated sage. Even over Zoom, I can see she moves with precision and chooses her words with care and a hint of seriousness.

I ask Flo about her first interactions with astrology and had thought it might be similar to my own experience of messing around with old magick books on my bedroom floor, but I'm open-mouthed at what she has to say.

'I have three brothers, so when I was nine or ten years old, my mum thought it was time for me to "spend time with some women". She knew this amazing free-spirited artist who lived north of Barcelona, so Mum sent me on some exchanges to Barcelona to spend time with her and her daughters. But when I arrived, in the typical fashion of a mystical artist to whom traditional Saturnian time doesn't really work, she had forgotten that her daughters would be at school while I was there. So she had this nine-year-old girl with her and wondered what on earth she was going to do with me.

'But actually, this turned out to be a godsend because she took me under her wing – she bought me my first set of paints and we developed this really strong artistic bond. She was like a mentor to me. As I got older, I went back nearly every summer and, when I was seventeen, she had become obsessed with astrology and taught me everything she knew. I remember seeing my birth chart for the first time – written out by hand on beautiful old paper – that was a real epiphany moment for me. The symbols and the actual configuration of my chart really spoke to me; it was something about the patterns and the actual way it looked on the page that made me sit up. From then on, I was secretly studying astrology even when everyone around me thought it was a load of BS. I read about the history of astrology under the table between classes in college. It felt like this private magical cave for a long time.'

I get a sense of her complete fascination. It's one I have felt many times over aspects of witchcraft. Astrology wasn't just a hobby for Flo. Studying the stars to see the hidden layers of the world also offered a lot of deeper meaning when things in the physical realm didn't offer up palatable answers.

'When I studied Environmental Philosophy and Ethics at university, that's when I became very interested in man's split from nature. What were the causes of that? And what were its implications? It was such an interesting period of my life but also a depressing one because I was reading so much about the climate crisis. This was something that wasn't really in the public eye so much at the time and there was no one there to share this ecological grief. I was really facing the hard statistics and the extinctions alone.

'It was when I had just finished my course and left university that I had a dream about my artist friend and about going to see her. I think I was looking for someone who could speak to me about a cosmology of interconnection – linking everything together: what I had learned, my emotions and my desire to move beyond the materialistic world that was destroying the planet. I felt that my mentor was someone who lived that – she really embodied that way of being, living outside the confines of the western world. So I went to be her apprentice and took a deep dive into astrology. It was a very magical experience.'

Flo gives astrology readings to clients all over the world from her home in London. I asked her why she thinks practices such as astrology, tarot and witchcraft are having such a resurgence, particularly among younger generations.

'I think that people are realising that our relationship to our environment is broken and are looking for alternative ways of being.

'We are living in a world where capitalism has failed, ultimately. I think this has created a new space where people are more open to seeing things in new ways, perhaps more mysterious ones. The world doesn't work in a logical way! So maybe there's more of an openness to this kind of thought now.

'We see tarot cards and crystals in a lot of mainstream stores now – it has become very accessible and visible, whereas this wouldn't necessarily have been the case for other generations. The counterculture from the twentieth century, like the spirituality of hippies seen in the late fifties and early sixties, has been commodified. It's that old saying, "Counterculture over the counter". Neoliberalism has a real knack for taking something that's counterculture and putting it on the marketplace.'

What did I say? Sage. I find a lot of truth in what Flo is saying. We are living in a time when there is free access to a lot of information and we are force-fed it from the moment we wake up and tap our phones to life. Of course, it makes sense that we are looking for another layer of meaning beneath the obvious. The mystery behind searching for information just doesn't exist anymore now that we have all the facts literally at our fingertips, so we are seeking that mystery for ourselves. Flo sees our relationship with this more esoteric way of thinking as coming from a range of factors.

'It's a combination of the environmental crisis, Instagram, feminism, neoliberalism, our more fluid ways of seeing the world as a generation and probably all being a bit *desperate* that have given rise to this movement.'

The modern rebirth of witchcraft feels like more of a complex web than I had considered before. Perhaps our renewed interest in the occult is far more than just the drip-drip effect of witches in the media and the rise of feminism helping women and marginalised people to harness their power over the past few decades. For me, the love of the outdoors and my admiration for the Halliwell sisters made my witchy thoughts balloon into my very real interest in the craft. But could the intensity of the media onslaught and the systems of the modern world we live in that praise fact and logic above all else actually be pushing us towards the darker, more mysterious things in life? Who wouldn't want to be a witch in such a black and white world?

*

As May comes to a close and the days are sunny more often than not, I take a book to the park where I sit on a bench and take a deep breath. It's very difficult for me to believe that just a couple of months ago I couldn't leave my bed, legs tangled in dusty sheets, not wanting to open the window. My mind feels awake, perhaps more than it's ever been. I'm used to equating the idea of 'awakeness' to 'busyness'. If I'm 'doing' stuff then I am validated; my day is full, therefore I am productive and making the most of my time.

But now, I am not 'busy'. I'm quiet and recovering. My days are filled with this purpose and my mind has space to be filled with thoughts rather than a list of actions.

It's . . . uncomfortable at first. I'm definitely not used to this feeling of stillness. Is anyone?

As I sit in the park overlooking the playing field, I can almost feel the synapses between my neurons replenishing themselves, fizzing like sherbet.

I could attribute my recovery to a number of things: a surplus of vitamin D, wearing yellow, a few daily sun salutations. Yes, time off from the world of work has helped to speed up the process but my reconnection with the spiritual world found through witchcraft and my newfound love of Shamanism feels like a thrumming gold cord, vibrating with a steady beat like a skin drum. It is holding me upright, making me stand tall. It is helping me remember who I am.

Feeling better in myself has freed up a section of my head that was clouded with black cobwebs before. I am ready to connect. I *am* connecting. Not just with nature but with actual living, heart-beating people too.

Over the past month, I have seen a real difference in my mental health. Being outside of the office and not having to manage the mask of my professional self has allowed me the headspace to come back to *me*. I am dipping my toe into the ancient art of living simply in a world that tells us we must sift through the complications to find our life's purpose.

LITHA

When I was about twelve years old, I asked my parents for a herb garden. In the teenage fiction series I liked to devour, the main character had one so, obviously, this was the mark of a true witch. One Saturday afternoon, I picked up a copy of Ann Moura's *Grimoire for the Green Witch* from the wonderful treasure trove that was Borders before skipping off to the garden centre to pick out herbs for my new project. I chose thyme, rosemary, chamomile and parsley before digging them into a row in the little planter on top of our guinea pig hutch. I was so proud of them; there they were battling rain and shine. I shouted my mum over when the rosemary began sprouting delicate purple flowers. I'm not sure she was as invested as I was.

Looking back, I ask myself, what would a twelve-year-old want with some thyme? I didn't cook anything – I wasn't yet allowed to operate the hob – and thyme is traditionally used for prosperity magick but the only things I bought with my birthday money were magazines and more books on witchcraft. In all honesty, I barely used those herbs for rituals in my bedroom, but I loved to go outside on a warm summer evening and crush a leaf between my fingers. Thyme, for me, had the earthy scent of woodlands about it, like I might get lost on a long walk and wake up in that smell, nestled among it. I didn't yet have any scents in my nasal repertoire to compare to chamomile except maybe marshmallow, but now, when I drink cups of it as a much older person, I always think back to sniffing chamomile flowers beneath my fingers in that little planter.

Herb lore is a fascinating subject and there is a magick in growing things and tending to them, helping them ride the weathered waves of the seasons. I forgot this for many years but when I remembered and plunged my hands into wet soil for the first time in fifteen years, I think my mind was called home.

*

'What are we putting here?' I pointed.

'Cabbage?'

'And here?'

'The apple tree.'

'And here?'

'I was thinking that could be the wildflower meadow.'

'Really?' I squealed.

Early June is in full bloom and the fresh heat means squeezing into last year's shorts and hoping Will doesn't notice I've eaten the last Magnum. We are down at our allotment – a recent development that we are still grappling with. We stand with our hands on our hips, surveying our new land. When I had first thought about putting our names down for an allotment, I assumed we'd be taking on a raised bed of carrots and maybe a patch of potatoes. We've been given a plot that's the same size as our whole flat.

Will has drawn up a plan on a Post-it Note and we squint down at it in the bright sunlight. We've done the preliminary work, the digging and turning over the soil with a shiny new spade. It was tough work and Will has put a lot more graft into it than I have – I prefer pointing at where the flowers should go to shifting manure – and the place looks neat, ordered and ready for a tangle of greenery.

Older, wiser and more experienced gardeners from other allotment plots have been giving us tips on what to plant, when and where. But Will has decided our allotment will be an intercontinental plot. Whenever Will and I go away somewhere – Portugal, Croatia, Malta – we have gathered seeds; a bus ticket folds up into a great makeshift seed packet. We have no idea what 99 per cent of our spoils are, but if something looks pretty, we promise we will try to grow it at home someday. Now that we have our own space, filled with fruit and veg from the plot's previous owner, it is time to make good on our promise. Alongside the usual additions to a vegetable garden, we set to work planting weird and wonderful things and hoping for the best.

I applied for the allotment as soon as Will and I moved in together. My boxes were barely unpacked, but I had a new library card and was now writing an impassioned note to the council's online chatbot about what we could do with an allotment. It was for Will primarily – I hadn't gardened for many years after 'helping out' my grandparents by mowing the lawn in wonky lines – as he loved to garden and had filled the flat with pots and trays overflowing with geraniums, ornamental peppers and wild strawberries we'd picked from alongside the canal.

It was nearly two years before we heard anything more about the allotment but I pestered someone at the council and, within days, we were trundling along the canal in our gardening gear, looking like we'd just been rejected by the city, to start work on our new plot.

After that, most weekends were spent at the allotment. Turning, planting, snipping. Our little escape from city living. We grew more confident and I rediscovered a latent love of herbs and green witchery. Physically shattered from a day digging raised beds, I enjoyed delving into my books to find out what I could do with the borage that had popped up at the edge of our allotment. I liked chopping down nettles and using them to make teas and pesto, building up the blood with their vital vitamins and stinging my wrists as I tried to stuff them in a Bag For Life. So many wild plants that people don't give a second glance at can nourish the body and give us more nutrients than we could ever absorb in a single day. But some plants, although medicinally sound, are also bound in folklore and superstition. Pop some rosemary under your pillow to welcome in good dreams and keep evil spirits at bay. Attract the love of your life with a bulb of fennel. Don't pick the delicate pink-white cuckoo flower, or you might get taken off in a cloud of angry fairies! Growing plants and making them into teas or vinegars to help with healing is one of the great draws of witchcraft on my soul. Plants are truly magickal.

Of course, working with herbs and potions isn't just reserved for the witches among us. Up until very recently, before the condiment aisle existed in Sainsbury's, many people – mainly women – would have picked their own herbs and known exactly where to find them. Knowing your lovage from your nightshades was crucial. The rich pot of knowledge on the non-medicinal uses of herbs spread across the globe and has been passed down into the hands of witches so that we know *exactly* what herb to give your best friend's ex-boyfriend to keep him 500 miles away.

But sometimes it's just good to grow nice things and eat them for dinner.

We have inherited some strawberry plants – *so many* strawberry plants – and they take up half the allotment, but the temptation of bowlfuls of glistening fruit come July makes us keep every single one of them. Each wide white strawberry flower fills me with excitement. It's tough work but our allotment now has carrots, marrows, tomatoes, rhubarb, chard, rosemary, garlic and leeks. In the summer, this place will be thick with the buzzing of pollinators that have dropped in for a bite to eat.

I look over at Will with his mud-flecked forearms and his brow furrowed in concentration as he listens to his little orange wind-up radio and plants sunflowers. I'm happy and content in our little sunny life together; just the two of us and our calico monstrosity in our second-floor flat, making pasta sauce and growing green things.

*

You hear about 'cat ladies' all the time. They have scraggy perms, chipped teapots and wee-stained slippers; maybe they hurl a tabby or two at strangers like the old woman in *The Simpsons*. I never classed myself among them until I had to give up my cat.

In ye olden days, any animal seen hanging around a suspicious-looking woman – or maybe even any woman at all – could have been her 'familiar', a demon come to keep her company, or maybe it was the Devil himself disguised as a black dog or a wild hare. Over the centuries, cats have become synonymous with witches, being just as 'mysterious' and hard to discern. Look at a cat and she could be planning her next napping spot or plotting to claw your jugular while you sleep.

Linnet could well be a demon in a black and ginger tuxedo.

'You've got to let her sniff you first,' I say, 'then you can give her head a scratch, but only her head; she doesn't like her back stroked. And she scratches the door if you leave it closed so don't even think about it.

And she likes to drink water out of human glasses. Oh, and her enemy is the Hoover.'

'I've had cats before, Jenn.'

'But Linnet is . . . different.'

I'm hovering in the doorway at my friend Chris's place. Linnet is trying to get into his wardrobe, as she is wont to do. I'm hoping that she'll come to my calls willingly when it's time for me to go so I can look like a good mother.

'She'll be fine!' he says,

I'm going on holiday. Just a week away with my parents, Will, Caroline and Adam, but I feel like an awful person. Linnet thinks we are terrible parents for leaving her for an entire week and will probably be traumatised for several years. She is ignoring me while rubbing her entire body around the door frames and gazing up at her auntie and uncle with round aventurine-coloured eyes.

Chris and Kara are in their pyjamas and are ready to chase my cat around their flat with squeaky mice on sticks and scrunched-up tinfoil but I can't help but think there are several million things they need to know about my small furry child that will keep her alive for the next seven days.

Linnet is more than a cat to me. She's my pal, my confidante and witch's familiar. On my way back to the tram, I cry.

*

In the past month, I've done something that has changed the course of my witchcraft-filled year, something which threads my stomach into knots like I have something dark to confess.

I've returned to the office.

A new job in a new place filled with new and shiny people. Part of me is enjoying swapping stories, sharing restaurant recommendations and giggling over a brew as we turn on our computers each day. I've made some amazing new friends, even after only being in my new environment for a few weeks. However, there is a part of me that feels shaky and a little unlike myself after several months away from the world. Every day is something new and I'm still discovering hidden corridors and how to use the mammoth printer in the basement. I'm nervous. Nervous that I went back too soon. I had no other choice, of course; my savings were being depleted every day – a girl has to eat – and I was starting to get restless for conversation and to be able to bounce ideas off other people. As much as I love the freelance lifestyle, cats have a limited lexical range and I do like to chatter on. My mood seems fine and I haven't slipped back into the darker thoughts I had before Yule, but I am monitoring it and making sure I stay on the Wheel so I don't lose my focus on natural rhythms and Pagan practices. Now is the perfect time to take a holiday and refresh my head.

Pembrokeshire feels like a return. The last time I was down here, I was twelve years old and just starting out on my journey into witchcraft. Still a child, and a shy, quiet one at that. But being twelve brings certain pressures and, in my world of magazines, weeknight TV and trying to tame my unruly eyebrows, I was looking to find an identity. My innocence was evaporating and I was searching for knowledge about the world as well as a way to cope with all the changes that come with being a pre-teen; my body was morphing into something new and the people at school were learning a whole new vocabulary with which to be nasty human beings. Perhaps it was amongst the crystals and incense of Pembrokeshire gift shops and the wild caves of the coast that I started to see myself and feel a calm sense of purpose descend. I recognised something within witchcraft that spoke to the curious part of my soul.

This is the perfect place to set the scene for a new witch: Stone Age forts, standing stones, hidden caves only reachable at low tide. The rolling hills, gannet squawks and the craggy cliff sides filled with a fluffy pink wildflower called 'thrift' are such a vital part of my spiritual path now. I find it strange and yet wonderful that I have reconnected with that Pembrokeshire beach so recently in my witchcraft journey this year and here I am again in this tiny spook of the British Isles with the breeze rolling in cool off the sea. I'm breathy with excitement as I get out of my parents' car. It feels like a well-needed retreat after readjusting to office life.

The Welsh landscapes were once filled with Celtic peoples. For those of you living in the UK, it's not hard to discover a Celtic monument close to your door. England, Scotland, Wales and Ireland are full of hidden monoliths or standing stones. You only have to open an OS map and you'll quite often see *Stone Circle* written in gothic cursive among the carefully laid-out squares and winding pathways. While we all know the theories and mystery surrounding places like Stonehenge and Avebury, these particular stones, so similar to others across the country and in Europe, would have been a very real part of lives in the Stone Age. Whenever I am among the sacred stones once frequented by the nameless many who lived off the land, my mind is often filled with colour as I think back through the many ages. I picture skirts and scarves in deep blues, reds and yellows, rainbow *cluties* tied to every tree, people laughing with full baskets of wildflowers for burning and tankards of mead to keep the merriness flowing.

It's a romantic image, but when we see these grey stones against the bleakness of the British countryside, it can be easy to forget how important such places once were. I like to keep them alive in my head.

This year, I feel blessed to be in beautiful Pembrokeshire at the height of Midsummer – the modern Pagan festival of Litha (*'LEE-tha'*). With the rolling light of late spring, it could be Midsummer every day right now. Swallows loop-the-loop across the fields and blackbirds sing late into the golden-pink evenings. This year has been particularly baking and I push aside the fears of global heating to focus on the feeling of the sun melting my hair around my shoulders. Right now, I am happy almost every day, flying high. OK, we all have our Ben & Jerry's and Bridget Jones days, but my mental health hasn't been this good in years. But I know through experience (too much experience) that my mood has the ability to plummet without warning. However, right now, I'm chattering away like a swallow. No depression could ever affect me here.

By the time we arrive on the first day, it's late afternoon. We are staying just outside a little fishing village on the west coast but, instead of exploring, everyone else seems content to break out the snacks, unpack and sit around in the cottage. After the long drive down with the threat of childhood car sickness rearing its ugly head, I decide to head down to the beach. From the cottage, the village lies only ten minutes away through thick woodland. As I forge ahead, my legs snag on sprigs of red campion and I'm covered in splashes from the top layer of mud after a day's worth of rain. Everything is so overgrown, filled with sudden sounds as rain slips loose from where it is cradled by high branches. The walk to the little fishing village feels much-needed. I dodge a wodge of hogweed and make the descent into Little Haven. Outside the pubs, empty barrels are stacked and ready to be collected and a dog snoozes in the shade next to a steel water bowl; slanted white-washed houses have dark, misted windows and the cry of gulls is inescapable. A ramp down to the beach will bring in boats laden with fish late in the morning or send out the lifeboats when the sea rises up with flicked wingtips.

We used to come here when we were kids – wet suits, body boards, although we never squealed as the waves hit us – we were serious kids, always wanting to join the older teens and daredevil dads out beyond the surf. I got swept out once, the pull of the sea like a goddess's hand on my ankle, tethering me to the spot like I had to pass a test for her to let me back to shore.

The village frames the bay and the tide is in. I only have a few memories of this exact place but they are all filled with sunlight and long dreamless sleeps from playing and walking all day in the fresh air. Back in the early noughties, on one of the last nights in our nearby cottage, my family and I climbed up to the highest peak to watch the sunset. The tide was in then too and was a rippling blue-gold like the cape of an emperor in the sun's glow. I remember looking out over the bay where the sun was dipping and my mum gasped. She said, 'Your eyes! They're so green,' and I – thirteen and unused to compliments on anything other than my schoolwork – smiled in the transformative blaze of the sun.

Now, I walk up the same path to where the sun is setting once more. I watch the yellow glow on the horizon, the softness of those cloud stacks, and smile softly to the sea.

*

The summer solstice, which usually falls on a day between 20 and 22 June, is the time of year when we celebrate the lighter side of life. Slip on your shades and head down to the beach – have a drink, dance around, soak in that summer sunshine. Similar to the reputation of Beltane, an old Swedish proverb says, 'Midsummer Night is not long but it sets many cradles rocking.'

As with many of the festivals, this day is ripe with traditions and folklore. The summer solstice is a sacred time for the oak tree, a tree long associated with strength and spirituality. One of my favourite Pagan writers, Glennie Kindred, writes that, at this time of the year, the oak can be seen 'as the doorway into the inner realms and the new dark cycle of the year that is about to begin'. Midsummer is, of course, a celebration of the light as we bask in the glory of the longest days of the year. The Northern Hemisphere is tilted as close to the sun as it gets all year, meaning the nights are quick and eager to turn back into the next summer day, but it is also the tipping point – Midsummer Day has the most hours of light, and the day after begins our slow descent into autumn.

Modern Pagans call this Sabbat 'Litha', from an old Anglo-Saxon word for 'June', which has been adopted to mean just the festival of Midsummer in recent years. In times long past, ancient Celtic tribes would dance and feast on the longest day of the year, believing their singing and laughter could banish evil spirits that might blight the coming harvest. Some folklore says this time of year is ruled over by the Oak King, the tree of summer, after his long battle with the tree of winter – the Holly King. When the winter solstice arrives, the Oak returns his crown to the Holly in their eternal seasonal dance. Many people head down to Stonehenge, which has long had an association with this festival. The stones within the structure of Stonehenge are arranged so that Midsummer can truly shine there: on this day, the sun rises precisely behind the Heel Stone to the northeast of the circle so that its rays shine directly into the centre of the stones. While Stonehenge itself is closed off to visitors now and one can only see it from afar to prevent further damage to this ancient monument, it's one of my life's missions to watch the sunrise in this ancient place.

Litha is not just another festival, however – this turn of the Wheel welcomes in a new aspect of the goddess and a whole new type of energy.

At this time of year, we welcome Rhiannon, the pregnant mother goddess of summer. She is the epitome of Mother Nature. In late June, the Northern Hemisphere is as verdant and alive as it gets; many chicks are about to fly their nest and Rhiannon is keeping her own child safe in her belly. In folklore, she is pregnant with the autumn's harvest and, at the height of summer, she is as round as the full moon.

I don't think many other goddesses can evoke such a sense of calm in us. She is serene, an assured ruler, maturing from the childlike goddess Brigid into someone with a sense of certainty around her as if she knows that everything will be just fine. I like to think that she's being pampered by all the other gods and goddesses in Celtic lore, being treated like a queen as she carries her baby and the future harvest of so many people.

Among the golden beaches of Pembrokeshire feels like the best place to mark this incredible time of year. There are still a few more days to go until the festival of Litha itself but tonight is an esbat, a full moon, so there's still plenty of celebrating to be had, and yet . . .

I'm inside, playing silly card games and eating a home-cooked meal with my family. Not exactly the most Pagan of celebrations. Today was a long trip and I'm just plain tired. Sometimes the festivities just have to wait. Just before bed, I yelp, 'Wait, I need somewhere to charge my crystal!' Adam laughs but then realises I'm serious and falls deathly silent. I put a chunk of clear quartz in the conservatory and wait for it to be cleansed by the moon's full white stare. It takes me an age to get to sleep; my head is jangling with full moon energy, and a fiery Sagittarius moon at that. I imagine energy pinging from every corner of the room, crystalline light that makes just as much noise as a Blackpool pinball machine. For someone who practically worships the moon, she doesn't do me many favours. My head is full of every thought there ever was in the world. Sleep finally crunches into gear at around one o'clock in the morning.

Crash. Clang.

Mum is in the kitchen making breakfast at 7.20 a.m. *On holiday.* Is she not as painfully aware of the full moon as I am? No, apparently not. Although it seems like everyone in my family has been up since five o'clock, has already been out for a run and has read four books each by this time. I think back to all those early morning birdwatching trips I used to take and wince. Am I entirely incompetent these days?

Nope, just the full moon.

Caroline feels drained too. I always suspected it about her; she's a sensitive soul and seems to be influenced by the moon as well. When I picture her, I think of a slightly curled hand inside her chest, curved to shield her heart from the evil in the world. I think of her as an innocent (and not just because she's my little sister, although I still picture her as a curly-haired thirteen-year-old) and a fellow HSP – although I'm sure she'd punch me in the arm to hear that.

After several hours of complaining over sleep deprivation (I'm very good at moaning when I'm tired), we finally set off. Mum, Dad, Will and I do a walk at a small National Trust-owned estuary to see some wading birds but there aren't many battling today's drizzle. The forest surrounding the estuary is lush and the rain makes every scent come alive; last year's softened pinecones and the crush of feathery-white cow parsley. I wish that we could spend longer there but it's time to move on to the next beauty spot. What Welsh holiday would be complete without a castle or two?

Castell Caeriw is a ruin but a spectacular one. Surrounded by a white river, the fortress was once home to Princess Nest, whose husband was Gerald de Windsor. She had *twenty-one* children and a very interesting life by all accounts in the late eleventh century. As I walk the moss-slick floors of the ruin, I picture her there with her long hair twisted into an elaborate braid and hidden under a kerchief; perhaps she is leaning to steady herself on a door frame, as heavily pregnant as the goddess Rhiannon. It is so difficult to imagine these draughty stone fortresses inhabited by anyone other than soldiers, sticking their narrow bows through the slit windows, threatening to rain down arrows on an unexpected visitor, but this place was the home of many families rich and poor, all going about their domestic lives; peeling potatoes into a pewter bucket, telling their children to finish their greens, trailing a bit of yarn along the floor for the kitchen tabby to chase. I think of the ancient practices that Princess Nest might have observed. Did she follow the servants out onto the green each May Day and dance around the maypole with the rest of them? Maybe she made a corn dolly in September with the final wheatsheaf of the season – also known as the *caseg fedi* or the 'harvest mare'[19] – to make sure that next year's harvest was just as bountiful. Did she weave symbols of fertility and happiness into her cloth? I hope that she found joy in the small ancient practices of the area, tying her and everyone around her to the land.

By now, the rain has become torrential and we are all fighting to stay undercover in the leaky ruin. We split off to explore our own areas of the castle, some of which are much drier than others. I climb the north-west tower stairs, a whole section of the castle that has had its roof blasted off. My raincoat is powerless here. Despite the damp, this room feels still, a very different energy from the rest of the castle. It's as if this cavernous room (or what's left of it) was a place of tranquillity for many who owned it before. Perhaps Nest came here to take a breather

— goddess knows, she needed it with all that spawn. It would be a good spot to relax too; the view over the solid thrust of the river below makes me feel like I'm the owner of an ark, placidly floating on a silver sea after a storm. I lean out of the window, folding at the waist, and take a long breath in. Two swallows zip across the water. They flip and swoop low over the white expanse.

Afterwards, I buy some mead in the castle gift shop. Few parts of the world warrant a medieval piss-up and I feel the need to honour a time-old tradition while in deepest Wales. Shame about the rain.

Around about this time the year before, I was stretched out in a field with one of my closest friends, Em. I was wearing a long yellow skirt and a mustard-coloured bandana around my head and Em was dressed in white — we were like two Californian hippies in the summer of love. Her sun-kissed, blonde-bobbed hair fanned out on the grass around her like a goddess's halo, her chin raised up to the light. In my fifteen-plus years of practising witchcraft, it has rained on Midsummer's Day more than half of the time. I remember once squatting among the half-finished go-karts and bin-bags of books in Lottie's garage when we were fourteen doing our Litha ritual out of the rain. Have I mentioned how glamorous witchcraft can be? But lying in the field next to Em with the straps of our tops pulled down to avoid tan-lines and our cauldron burning just a few inches away makes me swoon, just how Litha was meant to be. It was the perfect summer's day.

I'm keeping my fingers crossed that the summer goddess is dancing in my favour again this year when Litha strikes later this week.

*

On Tuesday I walk down the coast on my own towards St Bride's, the next village along, and see three whitethroats, a handsome pair of bullfinches, a singing linnet and some very young goldfinches. It's been so long since I've seen whitethroats that I let out a gasp of pleasure! The angular shape of their bodies and their bug eyes really are captivating. I feel like nature is waking all my senses; I'm shaking off the sleepy veil of the moon as I buzz about the long, overgrown country lanes of Wales. Red campion sticks out from the ferns at the side of the road – a flower favoured by fairies in folklore. The plant's hairy leaves and bulbous bottoms make them look somewhere between an animal and an instrument, but they are topped with the gentlest red-purple flowers. These delicate petals become easily frayed by the wind and the rain, so I'm relieved for them that they have found refuge in the hedgerows of South Wales, protected from summer storms.

In May and June, my Green Witch senses always start tingling. The names of wildflowers fly thick and fast through my mind and I find myself able to spot the tiniest bloom from a few metres away, ready to give a loud, 'Ooh!' We live in a culture where it's all too common to see bouquets of flowers in our local supermarkets. While daffodils proliferate on the shelves in their native early spring, most of the cut flowers we see are grown in a hothouse, out of season. This is another way that we live out of sync with the seasons. I love having a vase of flowers livening up our windowsill but it really worried me recently when I found out that we shouldn't be putting store-bought flowers in the compost bin; they're filled with chemicals to preserve them for longer!

There are so many beautiful seasonal flowers here along this hedgerow and I try to drink them in. In the spring, we see the time-old floral progression of snowdrop, crocus, wood anemone, lesser celandine, primrose, daffodil, cowslip, bluebell, before the summer flowers pull out all the stops to join the show: herb Robert and red campion in June and July before the dusky pink-purples of dog rose, devil's bit scabious and willowherb steal the show in August. These flowers really are the natural wonders of the world.

Many witches and herbalists use plants and flowers to empower their rituals, but also to heal people and prevent illness in the first place. As someone who had a wildflower ID guide strapped to their hand for the majority of their twenties, plants and wildflowers seem incredible to me – a source of unbridled joy when you come across them in a patch of woodland, filled with healing nutrients for all kinds of ailments, and they are also a life-sustaining delicacy for bees and other pollinators. Witches and herbalists must therefore learn to strike a balance between taking enough medicine to help the sick or empower a ritual and leaving enough behind for wildlife to thrive.

We have so much power. We can snap off a twig from a tree because it got in the way of a photo; we could pitch a tent in the woods and crush the entrance to an insect's home or burn their food as we light a cosy campfire. Being Pagan means living in harmony with nature's cycles so I'll say it here and I'll say it now, I'm a firm believer that we can all help nature by:

- Re-naturalising our gardens! Roll up the Astroturf and let the wild stuff flow.
- Growing flowers in our gardens and appreciating them outside. Cutting down healthy flowers just to look at them inside for a few days feels like a crime.
- Growing native flowers if you can – the wildlife in your area (our beloved bees and other pollinators) has evolved over millennia in tandem with the cycles of local flora. Feed the bees their favourite food and they will thank you for it! On the

allotment, Will and I will be swapping out dahlias for a swathe of cornflowers next year.

We are at a point in history where we have the power to actively move away from a culture that tells us to 'take take take' from the world's resources. In a world where we have believed it is our birthright to take what we can and throw away what we don't need, be the one who gives back to nature or leaves it alone to let it flourish without the touch of human hand.

To be among the Welsh wildflowers and the busy humming of insects, like all those many thousands of summers gone before us, makes me feel slightly dreamy and ageless. Nature is orchestrating this symphony of colour and scent for the sheer joy of it and I am just *here* witnessing it and being a part of their display. It's quite a shock when a red Renault Clio careens around the bend up ahead of me and I have to hop dutifully out of the way.

The holiday zooms by in the form of golden beaches and ice cream. Satnav cursing and mud slicks. Sunburn and Tupperware sandwiches. My chest feels wide open – my heart chakra absorbs the timeless patterns of sea and tree roots. I am filled with wonder by every bird I see. It's like I'm seeing them after emerging from a deep amnesia that has lasted years – Persephone arising from the underworld and rubbing her eyes after months of darkness. Birdsong seems both new and familiar. I'd forgotten how birdwatching filled my summers when I first took the hobby up – aged nineteen and pasty with spending far too much time indoors reading vampire novels in bed. Birdwatching got me out of my room, out of my head and into the wild places. It awoke the part of me that wanted to rejoin the natural world.

The next day is scorching and we take a small boat over to a green dot in the Irish Sea called Skomer Island. In birdwatching circles across the country, Skomer is a dream location and I've wanted to come here for almost a decade.

For an island that's only three square kilometres, there's a lot going on. Managed by the Wildlife Trusts, Skomer Island is home to one of the largest Manx shearwater populations in the world, and other seabirds like gannets, guillemots and fulmars can be seen diving from its clifftops. But they're not the stars of the show.

Puffins; puffins are everywhere! Everywhere you turn, a cluster of puffins sits looking slightly befuddled, each one facing in a slightly different direction, as if they've lost their train of conversation and have decided to go looking for new friends elsewhere. The world has some very ridiculous-looking birds and I'm very glad about it! Puffins are perhaps one of the silliest – after pelicans – with their sad little eyes, tiny wings and red-and-yellow-striped clown beaks. I burst into a smile every time I see one.

Being surrounded by this density of birds is a little overwhelming like my entire body is thrumming with joy. Being able to spend this much time back in nature has recharged my mind and I wonder about the people who might have visited this place in the past, with its Viking name and Iron Age forts. The ancient voyagers who stopped off on the island looking for new lands, food, booty or maybe just shelter for the evening. It feels good to walk the same paths that have been trodden by those people of the past who will have seen the same incredible birds and drunk in the sea air like they'd never be able to get enough of it. Here on Skomer, clumps of bulbous white sea campion look like they have escaped from under the water and the whir of the gulls calling almost feels like the rhythmic pulse of a drum, lulling me into a lucid dream. Yes, Pembrokeshire, you're healing me. I'll stop on this cliff with my hands on my hips and drink in the ocean, every last saline drop.

We return from the boat crispy from the sun and smiling from ear to ear.

20–22 June

Midsummer falls on the second to last day before returning to normal life. After many hours of sunshine that have addled my brain so that I feel like I've taken a trip to a shamanic world, I'm ready to pick up a tambourine and dance around the campfire this Midsummer. However, I don't think Will, my parents, Adam or Caroline would let me live that spectacle down. Instead, I ask the group if we can take a trip.

I want to see my beach.

I'm reticent to say which beach this is. It's *my* beach – didn't I just tell you that? But I know it's not mine at all. No piece of land belongs to anyone, especially a rock formation on the south Pembrokeshire coast far away from my home, but part of me has lived there for a very long time.

This is the place I've dreamed about for seventeen years. I've travelled here in my memory and in my unconscious whenever I've been upset or wanting answers or sometimes just to hear the sound of the waves. Part of me is expecting to see Pelican poking his head out from behind a boulder here today.

It takes forty-five minutes to drive there and by the time Will and I get dropped off, it's raining – what did I say about Midsummer?

There is a sandy hill down to the beach; one wrong foot and you're tumbling down like a sack of mackerel. But we keep our composure and as we walk I try to slow time with my mind, taking in each step on this sacred ground.

Having never seen a picture of this place except for the focused lens of my mind's eye, the beach looks almost exactly as I remember it and I shake my head in disbelief. A far-out rock in the expanse of sea draws the eye, making children dream of swimming out to it and finding treasure there. It spirals out of the waves like a trident. To the right of the bay stands a vast hunk of rock; a towering cliff face that casts some of the beach in shadow. Head past this and you will find a secret cove – a circular patch of sand, barnacled rocks. I immediately gravitate there, drawn to it by energy and memory.

As I get closer, I'm overwhelmed by the heavy sounds of this place as the rain hits the sea and makes it roar. The cliff face shields us from the crash of the loudest waves but the beach is a flurry of noise: gulls with their spiralling calls, the whir of wind under our hoods and the weight of several tonnes of water trying to break the cycle of the tides and flood itself onto the beach.

The awe I felt as a pre-teen is still there.

'I'll leave you to it,' Will says and minutes later I see him scrambling halfway up the cliff face like a teenager. I'm left alone and my brain begins the process of trying to remember every square metre in front of me so that I firm this place up even further in my memory. I scan shells, pebbles, rock pools – this visit, while not once in a lifetime – needs to last me another fifteen years.

The cove is exactly how I remember it. All those dreaming moments spent here, eyes half-closed, remembering the pulling rasp of the waves and feeling the sun on my face through the power of my mind.

The reality is that I will never know why this place has spoken to me more deeply than any other location. Perhaps my ancestors once touched down here and said, 'It's nice, that.' Maybe I was a Welsh fisherman in a previous life. Maybe it's just that as a twelve-year-old kid on the verge of adolescence, this place was filled with beauty and mystery, playfulness and something ancient.

We don't have long here so I sit and draw a circle in the sand with my finger. I close my eyes and feel the force of this place; the many millions of waves that have glanced their hands over these rocks, the slow-motion movements of crustaceans under the sea line. Despite the rain, it is still Midsummer – the festival of Litha – and a time of focusing on the golden things in life. I think of all the things that bring me light: my health, my community, my writing. I thank the Goddess for all these beautiful things – my wonderful family, friends and soon-to-be husband. I couldn't be more grateful to have my health back. *Thank you, thank you,* I murmur to Rhiannon and wonder if she can hear me over the crashing waves.

I thank her for this small piece of land, for the moments of joy it has brought me over the years. This place will always be my gateway – my portal to other worlds, my doorway from childhood to adolescence. Maybe we all have somewhere like this. When you close your eyes, where does your mind go? Where do you feel most at peace?

The land is calling to us to remember how we used to live; how we used to hold hands with the Earth whenever we picked its berries or laid our head between the roots of the trees to sleep. Our not-so-distant ancestors knew more about the seasons and the messages given to us by the elements than we could ever understand. We have forgotten those old ways, but they do not need to stay lost forever.

I put my hands on the sand and my pulse mingles with the beat of the waves.

I remember, I remember, I remember.

I get up to find Will and start the impossible task of getting wet sand off my bum.

*

We get back to Manchester at around four o'clock in the afternoon a couple of days later. Linnet stalks around the flat, sniffing the TV stand and door handles in case a fluffier or nicer cat has claimed her territory while she's been on holiday. She doesn't seem to hate me but I did just let her stick her face in the Dreamie bag.

Will immediately heads to the allotment and twenty minutes later my phone buzzes.

'PO-TA-TOES!'

A WhatsApp picture comes through – a full bucket of earthy potatoes, bubbling over the edge. I squeal. Midsummer has brought our allotment to life while we've been gone and will keep us rooted to the earth as we continue our trip around the Wheel so close to the city centre.

That night, the potatoes taste like butter and soil and heaven.

LAMMAS

If I close my eyes, late July always takes me back to wandering through the fields in my home village, the sun glazing the tops of the wheat and sweet grain popping into my hand with a deft squeeze of the fingers. Here, a blackbird is frozen on top of a hedgerow with an early blackberry poised in its beak. He waits for me to leave the path before throwing back his head and choking down his spoils.

Abundant summer is in full swing and I've come back home to visit my grandma and parents. This time of year triggers so many memories, all of them languid, filled with paperbacks and mostly involving large quantities of Vienetta.

When I first moved back home to Merseyside after uni, finding myself clunkily readjusting to village life after four years in the city, I used to walk in loops down the pavements shaded by suburban trees. I'd tread the well-known streets and then the lesser-known ones. Finally, as summer heated up to the max, I wanted to get away from the cars, the pushchairs and bored school kids who hoped there was more to life than hay fever for six whole weeks. I made my way out into the fields, to the places I had never been before.

Pex Hill, out towards Cronton, Merseyside, is within walking distance of my childhood home and gives a stunning view of the Mersey Estuary. I've come out here today for old time's sake. On a clear day, you see right out past the vast steel structure of Runcorn Bridge and Liverpool's Radio City Tower to the purple Welsh hills. It is the highest viewpoint for miles around; a disused fifteenth-century quarry carved into the hillside that has now morphed into a wildlife haven. Pex Hill is a strange mixture of oak woodland and heath and the place certainly has a colourful history: a local story says that a Cronton lass called Peg Pusey was enticed up to the ancient heathland of Pex Hill by her lover and killed. Now her ghost is said to haunt the hill. Oh, these cheery halcyon days.

While my home village might never have played host to a famed coven or seen faeries dancing down by the brook, I do love a good ghost story.

I've been helping Grandma in the garden all day – strimming the hedges, mowing the lawn and pruning petunias – the mud all over my knees and calves acting as sunscreen like I'm a fat, happy pig. You have to walk up a long, winding road to find Pex Hill, switching sides constantly as the pavement disappears and cars fly out of thin air. The only motor I can hear now is a tractor overturning earth in the field next door and the driver waves at me as he flings scraps of mud out from underneath him. The cornfields on either side of me make a *pinging* noise, the hard kernels of corn cracking under the late July heat. Beetles and crickets flee as I pass by, little *whooshes* of sound as they spring to safety, and a young sparrow with fresh black lines etched into its feathers loiters on the path, unfazed, as I approach then scuttles into the corn. I am bitten to shreds by this point – insects seem to think I'm the Messiah and I refuse to wear anything but shorts as soon as June hits.

When I arrive at the base of the hill, I am plunged into the coolness of woodland. The abrupt change of landscape as you enter the shade of the gnarled oak trees jars the senses; from the scorching, unshielded sunshine to the leafy cover of Pex Hill, you might as well have been transported 400 miles.

I feel a sudden rush of gratitude for shade.

Once undercover, my walk slows. The trees are old here, older than any living human, and they are murmuring with stories from many lifetimes.

I think about my own life's course and where this year has brought me. This year has been one of way-finding and I've been practising witchcraft more and more, spending as much time outside as I possibly can. My deep tan is a testament to this. I've been reading about Shamanism and the messages fly thick and fast between Lottie, myself and the wonderful group whom I met in Speke at the Introduction to Shamanism day. We've affectionately named ourselves the 'Scouse Tribe' and we've been meeting via Zoom every Wednesday night to journey together and explore other worlds from the comfort of our living room floors. Thinking back to where I was at the start of the year and the goals I set myself, I don't think the 'me' now would recognise the pallid woman I was back then, lurking like a ghoul in the corner of the bedroom. I'm not going to lie, I'm still processing the experiences that brought me to that dark point in my life – the crush of concrete and the intrusive thoughts I used to get about how I could never fit into this world. The displaced witch. In comparison, the woman walking under the trees right now is *glowing*.

But there is a lot of unprocessed trauma there. Perhaps this is a prerequisite of the modern world. In my research, I haven't come across any policy changes designed to make it easier for workers or anyone planning for the future we were told we could have if we 'just put the hours in'. The strains and pressures of normality have not eased up in the few meagre months I was away. I can feel myself fretting over unreplied-to emails and stress eating when a badly concealed fight breaks out in the board room. As someone who is highly sensitive, I'm sick of being told to grow a thicker skin or to build my resilience. I'm still finding it difficult to understand why the working world would need this fierce characteristic to be a baseline requirement for working with others if we're all trying to reach the same goal.

Softness and sensitivity hold very little space in a skyscraper office.

I'm not entirely sure I've found my place in this busy world yet, even after eight months of soul searching, but I have found a group of people where I can laugh and talk about my beliefs freely and not be put in the stocks. I feel lighter and my walks in nature have made my thoughts creative and refilled my head with a sense of wonder. These might not be the qualities you'd find on every job spec but they make me happier than I've been in years.

While I might not have all the answers just yet, I've come far from my starting point on the Wheel and there is a lot to celebrate.

The incoming Pagan festival of Lammas (*'LAH-mus'*), or Lughnasadh (*'LOO-nah-sah'*), on 1 August, is all about abundance and fruition. For our ancestors, this would have been a time of great toil but also one of incredible reward – the long hours in the hot fields with nothing but a scythe and the steady drip of sweat scorching the ground would finally give way to a harvest you could take home wrapped in cloth or toppling from a woven basket. It was something to be proud of and enjoyed with a mug of the finest ale in the village, the backbreaking work somehow forgotten for an evening or two. While the Irish Gaelic derivation of this festival 'Lughnasadh' literally means 'in honour of Lugh' the Celtic sun god, the Anglo-Saxon term 'Lammas' means 'loaf mass', bringing the festival back down to earth and showing its connection to the harvest. Any Pagan will tell you that Lammas is the time of fancy bread-baking, and the whole late summer period is dripping with ancient folk customs about assuaging any troublesome harvest spirits to bring even more bountiful bushels the next year.

In her book *The Magical Year: Seasonal Celebrations to Honour Nature's Ever-turning Wheel*, Danu Forest – Druid and Celtic witchcraft practitioner – looks deeper into the links between toil and abundance at this time of year:

> *Lughnasadh has an even older Gaelic name: Bron Trogain, meaning 'the sorrows (or sacrifice) of the earth' – a term connected with the labour pains of childbirth, and suggesting that the life-giving abundance of nature was honoured at this time together with the precious agricultural skills that transform this abundance into crops and livestock.*

This links the festival to the pregnant Celtic goddess Rhiannon, birthing the harvest and living through the pain of it so that we can all have enough food to last the winter. For Pagans and witches in the modern-day world, we can take metaphors and meaning like this from these old Celtic tales, honouring hard work and reaping its rewards, and transfer them to our twenty-first-century lives. Now, the vast majority of people don't earn their living through farming, but the principles of Lammas are still in place. We can still take stock of all the things in our lives that feed us and keep us warm, whether that's physically or emotionally.

It's a good time to assess your achievements: What kind of energy have you been collecting this year? How have you worked on yourself? How are you nourishing your friendships?

What have you done that's made you proud?

As I've said, there is a lot to celebrate right now and my strides feel confident, strong, in the dappled sunshine.

Finally, after an hour or so with my thoughts on Pex Hill, I leave the blissful shade of the trees and the distant notes of hunting buzzards to make my way back down to the fields. I seem to have been walking a very long time when I realise I'm not back on the path I arrived on. I can see the hill but . . . wait a second, it's right in front of me. Did I just follow a ginormous crop circle? I look from left to right – there doesn't seem to be another way out of this field. Why can't I find a path that doesn't involve trudging through hip-height corn?

I stand still, baking slowly, searing from the shoulders down. My feet crackle in the dry straw. I have to admit it – I think I'm lost. Google Maps is no help whatsoever to someone at midday who doesn't know which way they're facing and has an atrocious sense of direction. A pair of wood pigeons walk in front of me, the dowager empresses of the farmland. They seem to know where they're going but I've made the mistake of following wild animals before and ended up in some pretty hairy parts of the world. A loose coil of panic tingles in my stomach. There is no real scent in the air. I take a sniff anyway like I'm going to be called home by the smell of freshly baked sourdough. I turn right down a footpath that I don't remember passing on the way down and . . .

OK, I really am lost in my home town. Home *village* even. I didn't know this was physically possible but this is a year of firsts after all. I make my way down this newly appeared path, surveying the land before me with waving cornstalks in every direction. In the distance, I see Tower College, the Hogwarts-esque private school that was the intense rival to my state education – its tower flourishes with smug victory from a copse of trees ahead. I know I'm aiming roughly for this but my path is taking me around the edge of the field away from the tower.

I'm used to getting lost in the countryside and I even relish it but it's uncomfortable to be lost somewhere I thought I knew so well.

A strange little feeling starts to irritate the edges of my brain. It starts with a flurry of panic. What if I overheat and pass out before I can get home? What if my phone dies and I can't call anyone for help? What if I just drop down dead here?

The feeling quickly morphs into anger.

'Oh my god, you are so *stupid*. How could you let this happen?'

The dark, tangling sensation rests at the front of my forehead and makes me clench my teeth, my fists and my thighs like I'm ready to spring, coiled like a snake hidden in the long grass, shrinking from the eagle overhead.

It's a familiar feeling and it's not one that sits comfortably in my skin.

It's something that I felt every day last year. The frustrated feeling that my agency has been taken away and that I'm not good enough for the task at hand. 'Of *course* I got myself in this situation – it's such a Jenn thing to do.' These thoughts usually go hand in hand with feeling lost and far away from my witchy, nature-loving self.

I recognise this as a twinge of my past self, one that I thought I was doing well to get away from. My stomach drops in acknowledgement. Maybe I've not quite conquered those old feelings yet. Perhaps I've been so focused on turning through the Wheel that I haven't sat still to listen to the thoughts that I needed to deal with first.

As a typical Aries, I *hate* being wrong.

By the time I get back to my grandma's house, I'm dehydrated, even muddier than I was when I set off and confused about where I'm going.

*

Let's talk about panic attacks.

There's something about the phrase that makes me wince. The term doesn't sit well with me. 'Panic' just isn't the right word.

Unbeknownst to me until very recently, I think I've been experiencing panic attacks since I was about fourteen years old. Why didn't I know this? The name.

A panic attack isn't always about huffing into a paper bag, head between your legs and sniffing smelling salts as the name suggests. It is a sinking feeling of dread, a dark, churning, oily sensation in your chest. For the twenty minutes it takes for the panic attack to unfold, the whole world feels like it's crashing in around you. It is a tectonic tremor that knocks loose thoughts of catastrophe:

'Everyone will hate me if I don't show up today; I'll have to quit my job.'

'People are looking at me. They don't want me here. Run, RUN!'

'If I don't get this work done, my boss will shout at me and I'll have to kill myself.'

It doesn't matter how small and inconsequential the action might seem – a missed deadline, tripping over your words in a presentation – your body is telling you that the worst is happening and it is preparing you for an avalanche. Every ounce of adrenaline your body can produce is causing you to pant, grab your possessions and leg it out the door.

A panic attack is a full-body experience and it is exhausting; it can sometimes take days, even weeks, to recover from. Maybe you have had them yourself. Two per cent of people – that's one in every school year group, maybe three or four people in your workplace – have a documented panic disorder, but some of the dark feelings I've had while experiencing a panic attack have been labelled as depression instead. So, maybe more people are experiencing these attacks but just not being taught how to recognise them.

In the world we live in, we've been taught from a young age that traditionally masculine traits are what will make us succeed: intelligence is measured logically through tick-box tests, the loudest voice in the room tends to win the debate and we are told to be cruel to fight our way to the top. The world is dog eat dog – fast and hard.

But what about those of us who are soft and slow?

I don't mean slow-minded, struggling to put two and two together; the kind of slow I'm talking about is listening to birdsong before our alarm, taking our time to get ready in the morning, closing our eyes as we breathe in the steam from our first cup of tea of the day. We meditate, we stretch, we take time to cook nourishing meals for our body and rub in oil to keep it supple and full of vitality. The concept of 'slow living' has become popular in recent years, with the internet awash with mindfulness tips and ways to enjoy the simple pleasures in life. As well as this, more and more people are looking to live off-grid with tiny eco houses, hand-stitched clothes and 'growing your own'. This backlash against fast-paced twenty-first-century life feels like a swoon-worthy dream, at least to the hundreds of thousands of people who like and share the videos. And how could it not appeal?

But these ways of life are hardly practical for the vast majority of us – the workers, the providers. If we all waltzed off in our caravans, who would be left to answer those emails?

For those of us who do not exhibit the hard, fast traits in a world where our merits are measured by how productive and hyper-masculine we are, how can we find a place where we belong?

These masculine traits that dominate the world with the crack of a belt are ruled by the left-hand side of the brain. However, the creative, slower, more artistic side of the brain – the right – is chronically underused. If we do not exercise these traits and sink into that slower way of life that our right brain thrives on, we are living discordantly with the self in our daily lives and not nourishing 50 per cent of our own bodies. We all have these sides of us, but if we do try to flex our right brains, more often than not, we are called lazy, idealistic *Guardian* readers, a critique often accompanied with the rolling of eyes. But this rigid attitude is the cause of our society's mental health epidemic.

So, what is the answer? How do we start living in harmony with our witchy selves to fulfil the life we've been given on this Earth and to keep our brains happy and healthy? The answer doesn't necessarily come from us as individuals, but the organisations we work for who need to understand that the people that work for them are human, with both masculine and feminine traits. We can't be expected to work flat out until we drop every day and there to be no consequences to our mental and physical health. A societal shift is needed and the values we have grown up with must be dispelled. Balance is everything; something seen in cultures across the world. In Ancient Chinese philosophy, the yin yang symbol represents balance in more forms than one. Traditionally, the symbol shows us that there is light in the shadows and darkness in the light, but the symbol represents all duality on Earth – hot and cold, wet and dry, masculine and feminine, busy and slow.

When I say this, I'm not just speaking to women and witches but to everyone: we need to reclaim the part of us that we have been taught to hide, the segment that we've been told will not serve us well in this patriarchal society. The soft, nourishing yin – the feminine – within us all needs a big hug.

Call it self-care, call it a digital detox, call it what you will, but switching off our phones and the bright shiny colours of modern life has been proven to improve our wellbeing. The laptops we use to work at night emit over 33,000 per cent more light intensity than the full moon, so it's no wonder our circadian rhythms are all out of whack![20] By switching off our devices and tuning into our bodies that we've been taught to ignore, we can start to shift the biases we've been told about the world.

But what will it take for our society to prioritise mental health?

*

Lammas, you are yellow, orange and foxglove-pink.

Down at the allotment, it's been another busy day. Our bare legs are dusty, tanned and smudged as we stretch out in the shade. There's not a lot of space for lying down amidst the wild tangles of raspberry bushes but, from my view of the world on the narrow path, I can see the chard over-spilling onto the flags, our strawberries under their leafy nests and the woodpigeons sounding out their awe in the pear tree overhanging our little plot of land. Pear trees are traditionally the helpers and healers of small children; right now, I feel like a child of the Earth sprawled out with my mucky toes splayed wide and my arms shielding my eyes from the sky.

I can hardly put into words how proud I feel of our allotment and the hard work we've put into it. Despite the busyness of our lives, we still find time to cycle down here almost every day to care for the land. Will is the pro with a plan in his mind and a garden fork in his hand – I tend to rock up with a trowel and look at him expectantly for guidance.

Gardening is something I thought I'd be a dab hand at but it turns out nature has a mind of its own and tries to make it tricky for you to bend it to your will. Who knew?

Right now, we have a greenhouse full of ripe tomatoes, our potato patch is booming and we have five marrows lying in wait below their prickly canopy, as well as carrots, leeks, runner beans and broccoli. In the shadows between the rosemary and rhubarb is a patch of mystery bulbs we planted last winter that have yet to flower. I check them for signs of their grand reveal each day. Every day we come away with a bag of vegetables and a little bubble of pride.

'Will, maybe I could do a spell for the allotment.'

'Oh yeah?'

'I've heard of these spell jars. You bury them to protect an area from harm. Maybe I could keep away the slugs.'

'I'd prefer it if you picked up a spade but . . .'

'You fill them with pins, old scraps of metal and anything nasty to shock the even nastier spirits and make them leave you alone. Oh, you wee in them too.'

'Jenn, I'm not having your wee jars here. Why don't you go dig a hole?'

I don't hear the rest, already plotting out how I'm going to help our allotment thrive even more than it already does, and my mind wanders to my evening Lammas ritual. Tonight I'll be giving thanks in true Lammas fashion.

I stand and put my hands on my hips, shorts rolled up as high as they will go. Will's blond head is bobbing up and down as he weeds the potato patch. I think to myself in a small voice, *I think this is the happiest I have ever been.*

Today, we have another pot of tomatoes to take home. I've perfected the art of chutney making since our tomato crop has gone haywire and is shooting out fruit at an unfathomable rate.

Of course, our ancestors in Britain would not have had access to tomatoes, but their gardens would not have looked too different to ours. Peas, leeks, parsnips, cabbage, carrots – that sounds like a good soup right there. They would also have had access to beautiful flavours such as garlic, lovage, fennel and watercress to spice up all those root vegetables. Even though I might be growing things that would have been deemed very exotic in the medieval period, I still feel the connection here on my little plot of earth.

I feel Mother Earth under my feet and let her hold me. She is with me today on Lammas and she is raising me up to the sun with both arms. I'm shining. I'm humming with the vibrations of the earth underneath my nails and caked into the creases of my knees.

And I'm ready for my Sabbat ritual.

1 August

Back at home later that afternoon, if I close my eyes, I can smell the freshly baked bread that Pagans across the world are making in honour of this harvest festival. However, tonight we will have a dark super moon – a powerful new moon with enough energy behind it to blast real change into the ether. After the wobble I had the other day, I'm ready to shock some energy into my life. If I'm honest, it's scared me. I've been no fun over the past week; something buzzes dirtily around my breastbone, nervous that I've lost some of the progress I had been making over the course of the year. OK, maybe it was only a minor setback but to be reminded of all the feelings I'd had the year before . . . I feel unclean somehow.

Time to use magick to get back on track.

I place four crystals – red jasper, blue agate, new jade and carnelian – at the compass points, light a white pillar candle and sit in my circle with my hands resting on my knees.

I call to Her.

I remember first reading about Rhiannon in a book I picked up in a Welsh gift shop – perhaps down in Pembrokeshire as a pre-teen when I was lapping up knowledge like a greedy kitten. In the book, she wore a bright, ornate cloak and was surrounded by birds while she rode on horseback across the land. She is straight from the pages of *The Mabinogion*. Within this book, deities and legendary figures were often interchangeable, with Rhiannon seen as a real human woman who married Pwyll Pen Annfwn, King of Dyvet in the west of Wales, and went through many hardships relating to her firstborn son. The romanticised image of Rhiannon in fine regalia, at one with the natural world, doesn't come across as strongly in this original tale, but Rhiannon has other roles to play.

As a goddess, she is akin to the Greek Demeter, an Earth Mother, a fertility goddess. She is also depicted as riding a white horse, the Welsh equivalent of the Gallic horse goddess, Epona. In Berkshire, England, people take part in the White Horse Festival as the season is tipping over into autumn and pay homage to the goddess and this rich symbol of fertility. Rhiannon is soft, full of rounded edges and draped cloth, but she is wise and regal too. She is the queen of the faeries and often rides on the back of her white horse to the Otherworld. We also know her in popular culture where Stevie Nicks told us that 'dreams unwind, love is a state of mind' in Fleetwood Mac's 'Rhiannon'.

Now, on the festival of Lammas, the time of Rhiannon is at its peak. Cross-legged and robed on my study floor, I take in a deep breath of her energy. I'm cocooned in it, as if I could stretch out my arms and feel the inner side of a crackling seedpod all around me. She is helping me grow.

'Oh Rhiannon, I welcome you into my circle.'

And there, without a beat of hesitation, she is in front of me.

The woman before me is tall and elegant with a rounded belly, almost ready to pop with Lammas harvest, wrapped in shawls and beautiful trailing sleeves. She exudes power from her freckled cheeks with just a hint of blush behind them. She is as real in front of me as Brigid was all those months ago but it doesn't stop my jaw dropping.

The first thing she does is plant a firm kiss on my lips.

For a few moments, I can't speak. It is like being in the presence of a queen, one that likes to snog her subjects. Not that I'm complaining.

I giggle to myself.

My plan for this evening is to give thanks for everything I have, and welcome in the abundance of Lammas and the powerful new moon. But the circle is throbbing around me, lusty and hot with August sweat. I'm lost in this energy. I could dance! I could run around like a maniac! Ever since I rekindled my love of witchcraft, the elements and the Goddess have been coming to me more readily like they were just waiting behind the door for me to call their name and tonight I'm giddy with the magick that is now so easily at my fingertips. Rhiannon is smiling down at me. How can this be happening? How can she really be so close? Could it be the celebratory mead I've swigged or am I just deranged? I'd like to hope the answer is neither of these things.

Standing up, shaky with dehydration from the summer heat, I start to speak out loud, visualising everything good I have in my life. I look right into Rhiannon's light brown eyes.

'Thank you for my wonderful friends and the people in my life whom I love.'

Rhiannon nods.

'Thank you for making me healthy.'

She nods again.

I hesitate before I speak next.

'Thank you for helping me love myself.'

She looks at me, suddenly seeming far too tall for my little room. I'm five foot nine but this woman is a giant. I feel like a child with mud still under my toenails in my little circle. I'll admit it. The panic attack has shaken me more than I'd let myself acknowledge. I've been trying so hard to be in tune with the world this year after a few years of being out of sync but the feelings I had in that cornfield touched my core and knocked me back a few months to the lost person I'd been last year.

I want to get back to how I was at the start of summer.

'I love myself again,' I say with conviction, repeating it again and again in the orange light of the setting sun. I thank the Goddess with my hands on my chest and hope to bring that love back round again.

Rhiannon looks at me then touches my left shoulder. She closes her eyes then the room starts to blur. A white energy floods the circle and rises up in a dome around me, coating the space with burning hot snow.

Honestly, nothing surprises me anymore so I just go with it.

While this could be frightening, the white light is actually peaceful, smeared into the air around me like icing with a spatula and seeping through the pores of my bare tanned arms. Rhiannon is trying to calm me down and I feel another loose spring of gratitude uncoil inside me.

There is energy crackling in my fingers like a pleasant kind of nerve damage. I want to keep it for myself but instead, I throw it out into the universe with my arms flying above me. *Here, take my gratitude! Take it all and multiply it.*

I sit with the energy for a long, long time, eyes squeezed shut and fighting back the tears of wonder that always come. When I open my eyes, I'm sobbing my heart out and Rhiannon is gone, just a fizzing static left in the air.

I close the circle, blow out the candle and immediately put my forehead and hands to the floor, grounding down and feeling the energy flow out into the earth. It pours into the foundations of the building, through the steel girders, and finds the little fists of worms nestling below, staying cool from the heat. I'm so dizzy with Goddess energy and mead that I giggle into the laminate.

Afterwards, I eat a huge doughy calzone that takes me twenty-five minutes to finish. I'm very grateful for this beautiful Pagan excuse to carb-load.

*

Gratitude. While we're on the subject, if I'm going to give thanks for any one thing in my life and never take it for granted again, it is my health.

I have always engaged in holistic and alternative therapies, having studied aromatherapy and massage when I was seventeen and going to my first yoga class aged fifteen. They were a way to soothe my soul and jar me out of my thoughts. Now, if ever I'm having a bad day, I try to find a massage as quickly as possible to force my shoulders down from around my ears. Or I'll book onto the nearest yoga session and face-plant the mat until I'm feeling perkier.

Right now, I want to honour my body, which I have always tried to keep strong through birdwatching hikes and too many sun salutations. Now, after experiencing the effects of my recent panic attack, I am slowly regaining my strength but it is taking some time. It was like someone had just whacked me in the chest with a cauldron lid, and I still prod myself nervously to check for bruising. I wonder whether I'll ever be able to go a full year without having a panic attack. Surely there must be a way to iron this out? With this in mind, I call my favourite massage therapist in the whole world.

Sarah is a holistic pro. Not only does she have her own massage company – NU.U Therapy in Manchester – she does reflexology, Reiki, facials and is a trained yoga teacher. I don't know how she does it with her tiny ballerina frame, but man, that girl is strong (and talented to boot)! Not only that, she's a typical Gemini and talks a mile a minute, which often has me snorting into the massage table.

Today, we chat non-stop during the massage because there's always a new herb to discuss or a podcast to dissect. She is passionate about herbalism so every meet-up turns into a witchfest. I love how I always come out of a massage from Sarah with my aches and pains dissolved and my mind pinging with creative ideas.

But I have a confession. I've come here with an ulterior motive today – a niggling sensation at the back of my head is after some career advice . . .

I've always felt an alignment with Sarah. Finding someone in your community is like watching a glowing ball of light bob across the room in your direction. You know when a person in your life just 'gets it' because of the blossoming warm palm of light that happens in your chest – a complete recognition. It's a rare feeling, one that I feel when I'm around my Scouse Tribe. But being in a job like Sarah's means coming into physical contact with a lot of people; how does an empathic person deal with these energies on a daily basis? I'm under no illusions that being a holistic practitioner is an easy gig.

Sarah says, 'I think that to find true connection with those around you – and to stay sane while living in a city – you first need to align with your inner being. You have to centre yourself and ask what are the little things and the practices that align with you? What fills you with energy?'

I've always had Sarah down as a very centred and wise person. I ask her what connects her with herself and the world around us and she tells me: nature, sunshine, looking at the stars, being close to the beach and sea, smelling flowers, breathwork, inner work, music, feel-good food, herbs, meeting with friends and family, flow and movement in the body. I couldn't resonate more with this list.

These little things are so important in keeping us stable and in our own bodies in a hectic world. Holistic practices tend to have a lot of mindfulness techniques woven into them to help us stay present in our skin and rooted in the world instead of in our heads. Sarah calls them a 'natural prescription' in a world where we are forced to live so externally that it's like we are having out-of-body experiences on a daily basis. This, of course, has a problematic effect on the body and our health as a whole. I've often found that fellow empaths tend to be drawn to alternative and complementary therapies as they have a strong feeling that they've been put on this Earth to help people and to heal themselves. I wonder whether this is what drew Sarah to holistic therapies in the first place.

'It actually didn't cross my mind to become a therapist until I hit my twenties. I studied Afro-musicology in my last year of university and wrote about how music enhances experiences through culture and festivals and how frequencies affect the brain. The idea that music and sound can improve our health and wellbeing scientifically as well as emotionally really resonated with me. I travelled to Egypt during Easter break in my third year where I learned about aromatherapy – how oils are made and what the benefits are – and this really sparked my interest.

After university I wanted to find something that included music and aromatherapy, and holistic massage therapy includes both. So I picked up a course a few months after I graduated to study complementary therapies including massage, aromatherapy and reflexology. It wasn't something I intended to do at all but I believe the universe brought me to it.'

This feeling of being drawn to something that wasn't on your initial path feels familiar. Life throws obstacles our way and we deal with them in ways that help us grow. I know that Sarah has always had a unique perspective on life. For her, yoga and meditation helped her stay mindful and calm when she had experienced some terrifying paranormal events in her life, after having seen spirits since she was a small child.

'Growing up, I always felt a presence that was really hard to accept for a while. It made me feel scared or that I had something wrong with me. As I replayed these experiences in my head or talked about them with others, I had to explore other ways of looking at the world and this helped me find acceptance of who I was and what I could see. Now that I've found acceptance and enlightenment through yoga, meditation and spirituality, I feel like the spirit world is something I could reach out to safely, and when I pray I feel safe to connect to my ancestors for some guidance. I believe this world is more than what we see and the more we accept that in ourselves, the more we come to trust our instincts. I also believe in vibrational connection, and vibrational connections cannot be faked or mistaken. When you allow yourself to expand your senses, your mind and body, it is so powerful. That is why it is practised all over the world. All these experiences have led me towards holistic living and to help others too.'

Sarah's path feels quite similar to my own only I have never fully trained to be a holistic practitioner. It's one of those things that has kept popping up over the years; I'll see an opportunity to complete a massage qualification or a reflexology course but I've always been crazy-busy with work and picking up extra freelance writing in the evenings. It just hasn't been the right time.

But these wonderful experiences of massage, Reiki and even somatic breathwork have really helped to keep me grounded in times where I was so frantic I thought that if I let go of my bedframe I might whir away like a spinning top.

Lying on the table today, I start to wonder if I could be a holistic therapist. To help others as I've been helped. Isn't that what a village witch would have done? Could I use holistic therapies as part of my own spiritual journey?

Muscles delightfully prodded and poked, I wonder, not for the first time in my life, if I need to re-examine my skillset.

*

What would happen if I went 'Full Witch'?

The idea isn't even that crazy. Many people are professional healers, tarot readers and herbalists. However, these kinds of professions have always been a fleeting dream for me; my inner critic telling me that I'd never be able to earn enough money and that I couldn't possibly be as good as all those shiny, sparkly practitioners online. For as long as I can remember I've seen writing as my path in life, priding myself on my use of the semi-colon. The practical side of my brain hasn't had that much chance to flex itself as I can hardly hang a picture frame and living in the flat means there is little peace and quiet to sit down and learn a new skill, what with the constant onslaught of traffic and Linnet screaming to be fed.

But what if I took the time to reorder my life and prioritise the thing that brings me most joy? Would the world implode? Would my friends abandon me?

I know the reality is that they'd all be supportive and maybe even queue out the door for a monthly Reiki session. But there's something holding me back – I seem to have a negative answer for all the questions that arise in my mind: 'It's not a proper job, is it?', 'People will make fun of you', 'You don't even know your twelve times table; how could you run your own business?'

However, if I did decide to do this, I wouldn't be shunned by society. More people than ever are embracing holistic practices as a direct response to our hectic lives. I could bring people together in weekly rituals, I could teach people about the moon cycles and the craft that makes me feel so proud to call myself a witch again. The world needs its prescribed dose of Paganism. Right now, in the early twenty-first century, I could walk down the street straddling a broomstick, screaming, 'Fly, my pretties – fly!' and it probably wouldn't even raise an eyebrow. Either that or I've been in Manchester for too long. Of course, if you were living in sixteenth-century Europe and were a bit of a weirdo, girl, were you in for a treat. The Pendle Witches lived in the shadow of the looming hill that would soon symbolise their dark demise, but they were just a handful of the many outsiders who have been persecuted for the sin of witchcraft over time. I realise how lucky I am to live in this century; a thought that doesn't come round to me that often.

If I went 'Full Witch' . . . I think everything would be just fine, but perhaps there's still a part of me that's worried history will repeat itself.

The world has a precarious relationship with witches. It's the whole Wicked Witch of the West versus Glinda the Good thing, time and time again throughout history. 'Dangerous women' who smile baring all their teeth and don't bow their heads to show prim and proper modesty have been demonised since the beginning of recorded time. So long as you're casting sweet little charms in your back bedroom to give your child a good night's sleep – what an angel you are! Crystal tinkerers and general do-gooders have always been fairly accepted when it comes to the mystical realms but step outside your box and there will be more than a sharp rap on the knuckles waiting for you. A witch who flexes her power – who commands the skies and shouts above the waves – is rising above her station and needs a little bonfire under her petticoat to teach her a lesson. Being a witch is and always has been a feminist issue.

We all know at least the basics of the Salem Witch Trials, maybe even the witch hysteria that swept Southern and Central Europe during the reign of Elizabeth I, and, of course, there was the brutality of James I's witch hunt obsession during the early 1600s. These times, etched deep with superstition and capital punishment, were not sunny highlights on the timeline of witches and many hundreds of people were burnt at the stake or hung for little more than a mumble under their breath. This was also happening startlingly recently; Janet Horne[21] was the last person to be executed for witchcraft in the British Isles in 1727 and Helen Duncan of Perthshire, Scotland, was the last person to be imprisoned under the Witchcraft Act of 1735, in . . . wait for it . . . 1944.

The fear of the unknown wrestles with the notion of personal power and an eerie knowledge of Mother Earth's remedies. In his 1911 book *A History of Witchcraft in England from 1558 to 1718,* Wallace Notestein speaks of the 'cunning women' that were fixtures in almost every village and small town in the early 1500s. These women were seen as 'good witches', even though they practised the 'forbidden arts'. Of course, these cunning folk were not just women and were often well respected as healers and seers in the tight-knit community.

I came across a quote from the fantastic and seemingly ageless historian Ronald Hutton in *Cunning Folk* magazine recently. When asked the question, 'Are we going through a period of re-enchantment?', the professor of History at the University of Bristol said:

> *I think we are — largely because the two forces which have most vigorously operated against an interest in magic over the years — orthodox Christianity and the enlightenment rationalist sceptic attack — have both moderated in recent years. I think there's a general recognition of the world as more complex and mysterious than seemed to be the official message in the early twentieth century. I also think there's an excitement and appeal about magic, now that people are less afraid of it. When people are less afraid of being bewitched or suffering evil magic, there's much greater freedom to look at the positive benefits of magic and explore it as a personal path.*[22]

Our ancestors lived in tune with the land, but witches took it one step further.

I feel more in touch with the past. I don't exactly repel modern technology, I've spent just as long on the phone to IT as the next person, but I know the difference between a day of being outside and one strapped to a screen indoors. Putting my hands on turned earth at the allotment is a world away from the frantic and frazzled feeling I have after a day of pings and buzzes coming from my computer monitor.

Maybe modern witches want to banish themselves away to the edge of the village too. Live on the fringes with our herbs and our tea and our 700 cats. But perhaps now more than ever there is a renewed role for the cunning wise woman in our society; someone to guide us when we're lost and help us use the powers of nature to heal our broken hearts. All stereotypes and warty hags aside, maybe she could exist once more, living on the peripheries where she is connected with the trees and the bees, a lifeline to the wild world beyond.

And besides, we'd have way more fun in the woods.

I feel that now, more than ever, is the time to bring witchcraft into every aspect of my life; not just to heal myself but to help others too. Being a witch isn't only about lighting a few candles and wearing some rose quartz — it's a lifestyle and a set of beliefs with a deep-patterned history that spreads over all areas of my life like a warm, guiding palm.

I've made my decision: I'm going to fully embrace my inner witch.

*

Swallows, what would summer be without you?

Every year in April, thousands of people across the country await the return of the swallow. We cross our fingers that they make it unscathed on the treacherous journey from Central Africa, over the Mediterranean Sea, and all the way to our suburbs. Once the swallows are here, the swifts will soon follow and then spring is well and truly underway.

You will have seen strings of swallows chattering on phone wires, their voices as synonymous with summer afternoons as a scone with jam or the sweet smell of cut grass. Their red faces, white bibs and pronged tails have been a fixture in our lives for millennia, so it's not hard to find them in folklore and myth across the world.

Swallow migration was not understood until the nineteenth century – how could such a small bird possibly travel so far? So, many people used to believe that swallows hibernated in the UK, burying themselves deep into the riverbanks until spring came.

Many farming communities in Britain believed that disturbing a swallow's nest would mean a farmer's cow would stop giving milk.[23] They have also been known as 'the bird of freedom', based on their Hebrew name (*deror*) meaning liberty.

This sense of freedom comes across in their acrobatic flight. Few birds in the world have such a dramatic, pirouetting dance. They are an absolute joy to watch. One of the most magical moments in my life happened on a summer's afternoon in August. I'm walking my usual route from Clayton Vale through the graveyard and up the hill back to Philip's Park. This uphill stretch is a wide, open meadow. As summer first sparks into being, it fills with bright, lusty poppies, bursts of ragged robin and ethereal sprigs of cow parsley. In August, the meadow smells like heaven with huge swathes of white-gold meadowsweet interspersed with bright flashes of devil's bit scabious. It is a place to slow down your walk and just breathe in.

I'm about a third of the way up the hill when a swallow dances in front of me; a navy-coloured butterfly with a forked tail, fluttering and darting. It clicks and chitters in the air like super-speed Morse code. There is no one else around and for a second I wish there was someone there to share my grin but then I realise this is a moment between the swallow and me.

It laps around me as I continue my walk, like casting its own witch's circle or asking me if I want to play. I do! I do want to play! I twirl around in the meadow and the swallow encircles me again.

Or does it? Another has appeared!

The two identical swallows wrap infinity symbols around each other and me and I feel like I am part of an intricate ballet. It is only mid-afternoon, the air is clear, not filled with insects for swallows to snap up. They are dancing for the sheer joy of it and I'm so glad they have chosen me to play with!

It is only when I reach the shade of the trees that they let up, twisting away from me in a helix of chattering song. I feel like a magical creature from another realm has given me a secret message.

No witchcraft required, just the pure magic of nature.

*

Returning to an office after a prolonged time at home with so much access to nature is a tricky experience. I'm back in the swing of it because it's what I'm used to. I love my colleagues and have become a proud member of the secret office WhatsApp chat. Such privilege. The office is rarely quiet, always one conversation or another going on, with the usual clacking of keys and the hum of the fans dispelling the summer heat. Yes, it's what I'm used to but this time around, things feel different. After several months of recalibration, I'm now questioning the processes: Why is this person a manager when they would obviously squash ants? Are we really all going to work through our lunch breaks today? OK, that's cool. Could this meeting have been an email? (Yes, yes it could.) There is an expectation to sit still, tense our stomach muscles, sit up straight. Put your bag under the table, don't let your coat trail on the floor, watch an online training module.

What would happen if I cartwheeled my arms right now? What if I bent double laughing?

I think back to what our ancestors would have been doing not that long ago. The farmers in my bloodline would be bundling hay. The rhythmic pulse of the scythe on dry grass. The gentle thud and tumble of vegetables into a burlap sack. Bulging willow baskets creaking with pasties, pies and fresh flowers. I think of these soft susurrations and I feel calm instantly.

My mind turns to my own basket – the skills I have in my arsenal. I could certainly not be a farmer as I have the upper-body strength of a gerbil. I'll leave that one to the professionals and stick with my small allotment. I'm a writer by trade and prefer the creative side of things to the corporate, which doesn't always inspire head hunters. I've got a lot of different articles and magazines under my belt – I love the process of putting a magazine together; the flatplanning process of mapping out exactly what will go on which page, writing the articles, sourcing the images and seeing it right through to publication. It's a very satisfying process but there aren't many editorial jobs available outside the M25.

What else do I have that I could use to shape my life? I'm not (yet) blessed with a hedge fund or a winning Lotto ticket so can't take time out of the world of work forever. I know that I have always wanted to help people with whatever I do and have gravitated towards jobs in the charity sector, and since my conversation with Sarah on the massage table . . . I've been having some thoughts. Now, with a new perspective on the world, how can I help people in my own way?

Could I really be a professional witch?

Maybe. I mean, it's not the craziest idea I've ever had.

Witches have a lot of skills peeking out from under their pointed hats. We are the sensitive folk of the world who love to listen, to help, provide ointments, and can teach you how to slow down your breathing when you're in a tizz. Witches brew healing teas and always know which flower you need to put a spring in your step. Personally, I'm already trained in Reiki – what if I could use the coming months to top up my skill set and become a full-time holistic practitioner?

In the office, I twiddle my pen between my fingers. Lammas has taken hold of me. I have an idea ripening in my head.

7

MABON

I notice a red tinge on the eye-shaped leaves of a cherry tree in the park and shake my head. Nope, this isn't happening – it is still August. Although only just. The leaves' edges turn up into a ruffled frill as if each one is adopting a Victorian gown of mourning; all these trees are looking pretty sorry for themselves. A week later, autumn sweeps through the streets like the air has been caught in the wake of a steam train, grasped by something much darker and more powerful than the trundling summer days.

I listen to the pips and swoops of starling song. They are revelling in this new clear and cooler air, allowing their voices to travel in long, haunting kazoo notes. Commuters on the way to the tram stop are still in short sleeves and are solemn-faced at their lack of layers as they trudge down the street – the worst decision they'll make all day. Here in the graveyard, the long sleeves are back out and I couldn't be cosier in my yoga pants and Will's oversized grey jumper.

But I've said it before and I'll say it again, I don't like winter.

Winter is not coming, you say. Autumn isn't even here yet. I hear you and I don't believe you. These first few crisp days of autumn are the things I have come to dread, perhaps tied up in that old 'back to school' fear. While I still have the urge to nip out to Rymans and refresh my stationery cupboard as September approaches, my gut is rumbling around like I have stage fright. Of course, it's still summer. But no light comes through the tree canopy in my sitting spot below the graveyard elm tree where I performed my Beltane ritual earlier in the year. Dry leaves unfurl around me on the ground with a cracking sound like the drop of a careful footstep. It makes me start every time and I look around either side of the tree trunk in panic. The sun is high and by midday the air will have shred its crispness but Mabon (*'MAH-bon'*), the autumn equinox, is three weeks away and it shows.

I've felt it coming for over a week now, that slow, steady *plink plink* of darkness hitting the horizon, minutes earlier each day. Soon it will be out with the SAD lamp. I feel that post-summertime sadness trickling in, no longer energised by the effects of light triggering my normal circadian rhythms. After the euphoria of Litha and the green days of August, something darker has begun taking root. I see the swallows gushing through the air in exuberant flight as they fill their tiny bellies with enough gnats and flies to carry them across land and sea to the Sahara. They won't be here for much longer. Winter is so close, that time of quiet streets where a footstep can echo a mile away and your breath pours out around you in a fountain to reveal your body's secrets.

On our allotment, fallen raspberries are turning to mulch on the soil. We have cut the chunky stems of our sunflowers to collect the seeds and dry them out in the shed over winter, their sunny heads tossed on the compost heap.

I have had the most incredible year rediscovering witchcraft and the ancestral practices of the land around me and I am not ready to lose the vitality I have found in my newfound appreciation of the world. My lightened months have meant hawthorn blossoms, curious deer and the heat of the sun shining on my hair. But from now onwards, the chill in the air and the dense morning dew that doesn't leave the lawn for hours make me want to curl in on myself like a smooth pebble, tossed back to the earth.

I am entering a mourning state, even though I know the ethereal beauty that the autumn equinox can bring.

I sit crossed-legged at the base of the tree, the roots forming the perfect chair. A wren almost obscures the sounds of the traffic on the nearby road. I'm burning an orange- and cinnamon-scented candle, meant to evoke Christmas puddings and nights in by the fire, but the smell brings out the sweet note in the autumn leaves. I breathe into it.

As I sit under my elm tree, I inhale deeply and say to the flame, 'I welcome in all opportunity.'

Now in September, almost a year after I started my witchcraft mission, I find the path before me easier to see, the guidance comes quicker and my intuition is like a set of sturdy reigns that steers my gut. My knowledge of witchcraft has rebuilt itself – all I need now is a crooked, cobwebby bookcase to house it all. I've been doing some thinking about my Lammas realisations and am ready to welcome in change; I want to gain new holistic qualifications, I want to push my life forward.

But there is still a part of me that is scared – nervous about the feelings that autumn has historically brought. My August panic attack unnerved me and I've been experiencing more of them ever since. I desperately want to forge on but there is a part of me that's hesitant. Scared.

I hope more than anything that the upcoming Sabbat can bring back some stability into my life.

MABON

*

Mabon is almost here. Cauldrons out – witch season is coming.

The autumn equinox, or Mabon, on or around 22 September marks the first official day of the season – one of only two special days of the year when the length of day and night is perfectly balanced. Mabon begins our turn into a darker world where the starry nights are longer and less easy to shake off, with the days seeming harder to face now that the lightness of summer has faded away. This time of the year is one I feel wary of. Depression always seems to strike harder in the colder months when there are more shadows to spot out of the corner of your eye. But I know now that I really need to face the darkness of winter head on if I'm really going to change my ways and break the old cycles I am so used to.

There is, of course, another equinox in the calendar year but, contrary to the new life and bright lights of fertile Ostara, Mabon offers an invitation into dark introspection. Mabon wants us to close down and look inside as we begin the descent into the cold, dark months.

But, is that the true purpose of Mabon? Must we totally surrender to autumn's shadow? Of all the spokes on the Wheel of the Year, Mabon is perhaps the one that speaks most to both the light and dark in us; the masculine and feminine; the face we present to the world and the one we try to hide. It is a celebration of the world's equilibrium. We even enter the star sign of Libra on 23 September – the ultimate sign of balance.

Ostara, the flipside of the autumn equinox, does not focus on balance in the same way, even though it is also a perfect mixture of the dark and light. The spring (or vernal) equinox is a time of rebirth and new energy – the dawn chorus tells us that every day of the season –

there is no time for darkness here. Ostara shifts our focus away from the contemplation of winter, telling us to let our worries go. Having ignored this sense of balance in spring, excited for the renewal of the world, Mabon can feel like a tricky festival for some. It is the one chance we are given each year to reflect on both our darkness and our light – even when we don't want to.

Mabon can be filled with hope – it is the main harvest of the year, bringing a full belly and a time that many of the dreams and manifestations we have worked on throughout the year can come to fruition as we harness the last of summer's drive and perfectionism. However, Mabon can also be a time of fear – a failed harvest would have meant a dangerous winter for many communities across the globe not so long ago; shorter days would mean the need for more protection against the creatures of the night, and the darkened skies make everything seem that little bit bleaker than they would have done in the Midsummer sunshine. Even though we don't necessarily live hand to mouth in the twenty-first century and we all have a bedside lamp to brighten the corners of our room, we do have other, more modern hopes and fears to combat at this time of year. For me, seasonal affective disorder brings fear that comes in strings of anxiety and panic attacks that lead to trails of half-mad thoughts which can stop me functioning for days at a time: *you're an imposter, you're no good at your job, you need to quit, but I can't because I need money to live, I'd be a disappointment to my family, I guess I'll have to fall off the face of the Earth then, bye.* During these months, these feelings can seem all the starker once the glory and frills of summer have been stripped away. Maybe my problem with winter is that there are fewer distractions, fewer hits of beauty and light, and more of myself to contend with. In the dark, there is nothing external left to look at – the only thing left to see is ourselves.

Mabon is a gift to us. It's a time to explore, squirm, get uncomfortable and feel joyful in our revelations. It is a time to examine those old anxieties that are woven into the fabric of our ancient selves.

I've been guilty of almost skipping over the autumn equinox in my practice in the past, with the pull of Samhain, the Witches' New Year, almost too much to resist. When the shops start filling with jack-o'-lanterns and glow-in-the-dark fangs, I'm drawn to the orange light like a spectral Halloween moth. But Mabon's message of equilibrium and the search for more than just lightness in our lives is a valuable lesson to listen to.

Many things can help us – witch or not – to balance out the dark and light by reminding us what feelings to stay in touch with at this time. Journaling, meditation, divination techniques like tarot or rune casting can help us take a closer look at our shadowy thoughts, the scary things we don't like to talk about with our friends. This time of year when the world begins to slowly die and prepare itself for renewal can often bring up morbid feelings in us, but it is important to find balance right now; reminding ourselves of our positive and light qualities as well as the darker, more dangerous behaviours we engage in as a way to really tap into the energy of this time of year.

Maybe autumn is 'our season' for a reason. Perhaps as witches we're more willing to accept and welcome the darker side of life. As the traditional renegades and outcasts of society, are we more open to different ways of thinking about the world, other people and ourselves? Being different allows us an opportunity to delve inside ourselves and ask the questions that society doesn't want the answers to.

While we may not wish to embrace our demons and the skeletons in our closets with open arms, Mabon is the time to acknowledge them, while also focusing on the positive work we've put in place to overcome and take ownership of them. I've experienced a lot this year and have come a long way in terms of personal resilience. I hope, with this recent black crackling mood, that I have enough resources to get me through the winter without falling too deeply again. I look at the trees in the park every day, saddened they will lose part of their identity over the coming months to preserve their energy. I wonder if they are looking forward to the autumn equinox or not.

But before Mabon comes, I have a journey to take.

*

My head is fizzing daily. Anxiety flames in streaks across my nerves and I wake up at four o'clock in the morning every day, my head churning through paper coils of 'to do' lists. I feel like I'm living a double life; my office self with the perky grin and the cooped-up city-dweller shaking and stammering through meetings containing more than two people.

September is a shock to the system. One morning I step outside and I am greeted by the smell of earth on the wind – a sign that the leaves are turning. Autumn is here.

Without hesitating, I pick up the phone to Laurie and arrange for Linnet and I to head over the next week. After the floods of late 2015, Laurie moved from our old flat in Lancaster overlooking the River Lune to a tiny tucked-away village in the Forest of Bowland. It's somewhere that takes a good while to locate on the map and only has two buses a day. For me, it feels like the perfect escape. But for some reason, even with the promise of this retreat, my anxiety remains sky-high. Losing the beauty of summer feels like losing a close friend. It is a little death and my body doesn't feel ready for it. Does being a summer person make me less of a witch?

I really need to work through this fear of the winter and stasis.

During Mabon season I'm constantly reminded of it and it makes me twitchy. Surely as a witch, attuned to the seasons, I need to be able to sit within the darker times of the year? Night-time skies, dark corners and stormy nights, surely this is witch territory? I've been working hard to conquer my fear, but it doesn't stop the nervousness rising in my chest as I now meet this time of year face on.

When I arrive at Laurie's in the pouring rain, emerging from high-hedged country lanes, I tumble into the little cottage and immediately fall asleep. The fatigue is back with a vengeance that scares me. I only wish I could have one final blast of summer to keep me going through September. The next morning, Laurie and I sit on his living room floor with our backs propped against the sofas, covered in blankets. Linnet is snuffling behind the sofa for the ghost of last night's Dreamies. But even this cuteness isn't enough of a distraction.

'Can we go to a stone circle?' I ask Laurie.

'Of course, but I don't think there are any around here. How far are we willing to drive?'

'But there are loads, look.' I spread out the Yorkshire Dales OS map in front of us and point. Stone circles, cairns and prehistoric settlements blossom from under my finger. That's a beautiful thing about this part of the world and the South Lakes – our Pagan heritage emanates from the rocks and crags around us.

Stone circles have rolled into being all across Britain's wilderness. And it's not just the major players that hold ancient power. I've not been to Stonehenge or Avebury in about ten years – a family holiday to the Cotswolds and Gloucester with some witchy-themed daytrips. A photo of me with a late-noughties haircut and an English Heritage tape recorder shows me listening to Jeremy Irons read me the Neolithic history of the henge. Dates, facts, speculations. Many people drift past me with folded arms, waiting for the stones to impress them. Some among them must be like me, waiting for the stones to accept them — make them feel part of a homecoming.

I hear a few comments as I wander along a quadrant of the circular path.

'It's so clever really, isn't it? How they lined it up to match where the sun rises. Do you think they knew they were doing it or was it just coincidence?'

'Do you think I can get Auntie Linda a snow globe in the gift shop?'

People go to Stonehenge because they're intrigued by the mystery, to protest the A303 bypass, or perhaps just need a stop-off on the way from Kent to Cornwall. When people talk about Stonehenge, there is little reverence for the astrological wonders that would have been celebrated there.

I'm not an expert on stone circles, nor do I profess to understand the 'real meaning' behind Wiltshire's biggest tourist destination, but I have spent a fair amount of time visiting sacred circles, in fair and foul weather.

*

Laurie and I are halfway through a fifteen-kilometre climb up Barbon Low Fell. Barbon is just a few miles north of Kirkby Lonsdale, a small town binding together the county lines of Yorkshire, Cumbria and Lancashire. It's an overcast day and the rain has threatened us several times, but we are striding out with the promise of a wood-burning fire back at the cottage.

This stone circle is nowhere in sight.

'It says it's here. Right here.' I point to a small hillock and wonder if this is it, all the stones rolled away by teenagers or muscular foxes.

'I don't know . . .' says Laurie with the tone of someone who knows exactly how to read maps. 'It says it's in that field over there.'

I wrinkle my nose. No, Laurie, you are obviously wrong.

Laurie hops over a stone wall into a private field and I'm immediately alert watching for ruddy farmers with shotguns popping up from the bushes. I take this second alone to take a deep breath.

'Jenn!'

I jump over the wall with much less grace and there it bloody is.

While I'd expected to find a small hollow filled with cowpats or the remnants of last night's barbeques, there before me is a wide fully intact stone circle. The low stones shine almost white in places, their surfaces weathered away.

'All that we need now is a full moon and a hare,' Laurie says.

We turn round and, as if on cue, a hare darts out from a crop of tufted grass and over the wall. I'm beginning to think that Laurie is a witch too.

Each stone in the circle has a different shape and size; some rough and craggy with the layers of limestone worn away at different rates to create jagged fissures, but some are green and rounded, protected from the elements by a coat of moss.

Researching this little miracle later on, I find that this stone circle has no name. There are no signposts to say 'Major Historical Talking Point – This Way'. It is a nameless, largely forgotten circle in between two sheepfolds and private, walled oak woodland. Part of me is enraged that a place of such beauty could see maybe a dozen visitors a year, but the idea of secret stones gathering moss, lying in wait for those who will truly treasure them, makes me feel like I've just been part of history. In the Mesolithic era, stone circles like these would have been gathering places for those who worshipped the sun and the moon, regularly used and woven into the magick of the everyday. Stories would have been told here with people, young and old, rapt on the old man spilling tales of buried gold, sleeping dragons and gigantic gods making thunder in the sky. At least that's one theory on stone circles, or maybe you're more of the 'brought here by aliens' mindset.

Laurie walks away to look for more hares but I stay in the stone circle. The wind blows streamers of hair across my face. This is a rugged place, with the grey sky only roughening its edges further. However, the people who carried these stones here many thousands of years ago must have seen some beauty in it.

I feel demoralised and so, so tired. This isn't how I wanted to be so close to the end of my full circle around the Wheel. Where is my sense of adventure? Why am I feeling like this? If the Goddess wanted to find me and help me right now, I'd like to think that standing in a stone circle would be like lighting the warning beacons of Gondor. Please find me! Please send me a sign!

I look over at Laurie and see he is mesmerised by something in a tree. A typical birdwatching stance. I feel like I have a few minutes to do what I want to do until the bird flies away.

Working clockwise, I hold my hand onto each stone, passing a white light from my palm and into the rock. It's a faint light, I'm not capable of great magickal feats right now, but it is a show of appreciation for the circle here, the people who created it and the animals who call this place their home.

A shimmer of vibration runs through the circle now. I want to show my deep gratitude for the natural world and all the beautiful things we have created in it. Maybe this circle has housed coven meetings, maybe people have sung here. It might seem like a bleak and lonely place out here but these stones are singing quietly back at me, always here to remind us of the Earth's propensity to heal.

*

Lottie and I drive through the A roads of North Wales. The beauty of Colwyn Bay is twinkling along the coastline in the late summer sun revealing Puffin Island hovering off the east coast of Anglesey. The Menai Bridge over the strait is so short that we're not even sure we've entered an island at all. I've been to Anglesey twice before: once on a school trip where a few of us tried to play strip poker on the bus so the less said about that the better, and once with my dad to visit RSPB South Stack on the west of the island. I saw my first puffin on that trip, a gorgeous sunny day during university not long after I'd got my very first pair of binoculars. Today is just as beautiful but the only birds I see are the gulls twisting over the bridge and a trickle of young pheasants that block our path at every turn in the country road. They run straight ahead of the car in single file, looking back over their feathery shoulders every twenty seconds. We crawl along the road behind them giggling and making videos on our phones.

I'm still not feeling great. Inside me is a shudder of coldness that is the lingering effect of depression — seasonal or otherwise. In the rare missed beats of mine and Lottie's conversation, the feeling comes back and I have to gaze at the bright blue horizon to bring me back to this beautiful day and the weekend of Shamanism ahead.

We arrive at Tyddyn Môn Farm just after seven o'clock in the evening and have a few minutes to compose ourselves and throw our bags in our twin room before we go to meet the group. The house is modern and light, originally designed as a place where people with physical and learning challenges can come to spend time in the great outdoors and feed the animals on the thirty-three-acre farm. For us, it offers the perfect place to escape reality, which I intend to do thoroughly.

We have come away on a shamanic retreat with Chris and the whole of our 'Scouse Tribe'; a long weekend in the area of an ancient Druid training ground. Anglesey was long the stronghold of the Druids. When we think of Druids we might conjure up images of the long-robed figures at Stonehenge, travelling bards telling tales around a fire in Celtic Britain and the whispers of ancient blood sacrifice at stone altars. Now, Druids have a less fearsome reputation and, over the past fifty years since the laws on magickal practices changed, Druidry has risen once more to become a prominent spiritual path within the bracket of Paganism. Practitioners share quite similar beliefs to some witches in that they see nature as the divine and perform their rites outside where possible. Inspired by Celtic legends, song and stories, the Druids are incredible storytellers and look to use their creativity to evoke awareness of the beauty of nature and the spiritual aspects of life. It is a peaceful path and one that could be on the cards for a little Green Witch like me someday.

Anglesey is covered in standing stones – the megaliths and menhirs of the island – a testament to the Druid's strong presence here and how ritual would have shaped their everyday lives. While this Druidic land has had many names, the Romans wrote about 'Mona', which was turned into the modern-day Welsh name for Anglesey, 'Ynys Môn', in the great libraries of Alexandria as far back as CE 150. The island was named after Mona or Modron, a Welsh earth and mother goddess, who is said to be the 'Mother of Wales'.

I find it interesting that in Welsh mythology Modron was the mother of the Welsh hero 'Mabon', so is very apt that we have come to be close to this patch of Welsh earth so close to the festival of Mabon. Beyond the rural SPAR shops and tractors, I hope I can catch a glimpse of true magick.

We're greeted by Chris and a hug with plenty of squealing. She's 'made up' that so many people came. I can feel my latent Scouse coming through already.

Lottie and I head upstairs into the open-plan kitchen and sitting room. When the door opens, my eyes widen. There are at least twenty people already inside, with the promise of more people coming tomorrow and later tonight. The number of bodies in the room is genuinely a surprise as there are people I've never met before from outside the tribe, but I'm happy for Chris that so many people have been drawn to her teaching. Most people are Scousers, coming from all over Liverpool and the Wirral. Since I left Merseyside at eighteen, my residual Scouse tends to come out when I'm excited or during long car rides to nature reserves with my dad. Watching a movie becomes seeing a 'filum' and my gym kit becomes a 'trackie'.

Together we eat a gorgeous, freshly cooked meal and listen to the tales of everyone's journeys. Some people have come from as far as the West of Scotland and Suffolk, making our own trip seem pretty piddling in comparison. Many have never practised Shamanism before but there is a sense in the air that the people in this room are tuned into the hidden workings of the world. I will later find out they are some of the most empathetic and spiritual people I've met. As we talk, I catch wisps of stray energy, let loose in bursts of anxious conversation or with the excited flourish of a hand. There is an ease to the way people are with each other, perhaps because they are so used to having to hide their true natures among subscribers to the modern world. Now, allowed the freedom, our barriers are down and I find the density of the energy in the room a shock to the system. I feel my own energy dancing on the surface of my skin in flutterings and pangs like I've suddenly forgotten how to regulate my emotions and my patterns of speech. My anxiety of the last month is showing through; maybe other people can sense it. My sense of self has been shaken by the sinking dip of depression I have just experienced and my childhood shyness and stutter overtake me. At this dinner table of friendly jostlings and delicious food, my fists are tightly balled in my lap. I feel frustrated with myself that I could be in such a reassuring place and still allow myself to be this on edge.

I hope that when my nerves calm down I can start to feel this hub of ancient Druid knowledge for what it really is and connect with the earth around us.

I'm almost relieved when it's time to go to bed.

21–22 September

The morning after, I awake to the near-darkness that only hotels bring. In the bliss of blackout blinds, I'm disorientated. I shove on some trackie bottoms and head out into the mist of the morning. The long car journey and yesterday's jumpiness have left me with the urge to get out and feel the solid earth jolting my feet. I find myself on Google Maps then aim my torso towards the beach.

The morning feels crisp as the last tendrils of September mist unwind from the long thistles and teasels in the grass. My feet hit compacted mud, which allows me to bounce all the way down to the beach along a hidden path. It weaves in and around itself, rustling with wildlife, and I'm delighted to spy a red squirrel on my way. That's some Druidic magick right there. I feel strong as the sea air hits me, as I emerge from the hedgerows and onto the beach. It's way before nine and there are a few dog walkers out but the bay is silent except for my sped-up breath and the Velcro crackle of water pulling on the sand. To my right, the dark shape of mainland Wales hold the bay in the crook of its arm. The tide is going out and newly laid shells are glistening against the sand, my vision rainbow-warping in the low light.

It's easy to see why Chris chose this place for us to shift between worlds.

I'm so frustrated that my heart won't step up a notch in this place so filled with the lulling sounds of the womb; the different swirls of water feeling themselves, the pebbles and the small scuttling crabs. My head feels like the ticking clock of a bomb detonator, frantic, wary and attached to something that terrifies me. I watch the waves for a while and try to still the dark wave within my chest. My insides feel like they're trapped inside a sinking ship, tossed across black waters. However, by the time I head back, I have a new sense of stillness.

Almost.

Back at the house, we start the day with an Art Therapy session where our wonderful tutor, Marie, gives us the chance to use art to neutralise the right and left hemispheres of our brains. In a bright conservatory room, Marie explains that we live in a society that is left-brain dominated, as the left side of our brain is pinpoint-focused on logic, rationality and structure. If we are to access and embody the fullest beings we can possibly be, we need to begin to exercise the right brain; the fleshy store of all our emotions, our creative ideas and our wonder. While I haven't picked up a paintbrush since my disappointing C in GCSE Art, I begin to paint using my right hand – my non-dominant side – and feel the frustration of a child who cannot hold something steady. Our tutor explains about the left and right hemispheres of the brain and how we can tap into repressed memories by using our non-dominant hand to perform art and to shock us out of our usual mindset.

It is such a beautiful way to explore other perspectives and the class turns into a thoughtful discussion about the binaries within society. If only art had been taught this way in high school! The session is eye-opening and more emotional than I had anticipated.

Throughout the day, we forage, eat, and talk about the principles of Shamanism. Some of my favourite things. Yet my nerves are still all over the place. I'm trying to relax and have brought out a thick piece of clear quartz to rest between my thumb and forefinger, stroking it over with my thumb-tip again and again. Lottie bends her head to me and asks, 'Everything OK?' I feel like I'm firefighting the jangling energy all around me, making me abandon my usual defences, but I nod all the same.

When it comes to our first shamanic journey of the weekend, I'm shot. Fighting off a panic attack really does take it out of you. As I fight the urge to run for the rolling Welsh hills, Chris leads the session and we lie on our yoga mats inside a large tent with our blankets pulled up to our chins. It's a setting I've been comfortable with dozens of times before, having visited Chris and Shamanism many times over the past few months, but this time my mind stays firmly in the room, rooted in my babbling nerves. I won't be journeying today and I feel the same exasperation well up inside me like a spluttering tap.

Afterwards, there are a few hours before dinner and people head back to the house with the setting sun brushing their faces a vibrant orange. I hover by the entrance to the tent; there is a rapid, irregular electricity thrumming through me, knocking nausea about in my gut. I need to get out into nature and ground myself.

When I arrive at the beach again, the sun is lowering behind the sea in the slow, languid fashion of late-summer evenings. I take the coastal path to the next cove along from the beach close to Tyddyn Môn. As I walk, the blackberries here are packed in tight red fists, yet to unfurl their juices. Tattered sprigs of meadowsweet cling on reminding me it is still summer despite the pulling chill of autumn. There are even the remains of this spring's honeysuckle.

As I walk, calm descends over me like washing my face with a warm, wet flannel. The act of moving at my own pace balances me out. The festival of Mabon, with its levelling force of equal day and night and the even-weighted scales of Libra, has come to settle me. The beach spreads out in front of me — low tide — so I can see the land and sky in equal expanses. Half earth, half air. A small smile pushes up the corners of my lips; I need to listen to the world around me right now, put my ear to the ground and listen to the words she's speaking that will bring my shaky head back to still water.

This cove is quieter than the first with a vast divider of pebbles between myself and the sea. The sand is darker here but the stones are pure white, with some speckled chestnut like the eggs of ancient sea monsters. A small white conch and two stones have found their way into my bag already. The sea is the deep iridescent blue of labradorite and, as I look around, I don't see a single speck of human evidence here except a tiny distant lighthouse. It seems to know no worry; it is calm, erect and completely itself. Under its gaze, I am the only person sitting in this age-old curve of the sea with salt on my lips and the sun warming the skin through my jeans.

I pull my hood up against a sudden coolness. Closing my eyes, I begin to stretch out my senses to feel the world around me, ready to look at something other than the inside of my own head. On my left-hand side, ever so slightly behind me, I feel Pelican's presence. He stands just inches away from my left shoulder. The deeper I get inside my meditative mind, the stronger I can see him. The white feathers make me long for his physical presence, for the downy, gentle touch of him that I feel so closely in the Lower World. Even though Pelican is ageless, genderless, I get a strong sense of 'him' and when I haven't journeyed for this long . . . I miss him.

I get the feeling he is saying, *It'll be OK. You're doing just fine.*

Calmer though I am, I stay until the beach shakes me loose with the chill of the air.

*

Saturday arrives and I'm a different person. A good night's sleep has grabbed my anxiety by the nose and flung it out the window into the sea. Today brings more art, mediation, an introduction to Taoism and incredible food. I could get used to being fed like this.

It's the most perfect retreat day. We chatter on and turn our faces to the sunshine. Later on, we have another shamanic session and when it's time for a journey – fingers crossed deep in my palms – I manage to meet Pelican after a few minutes of trying. In the evening, we sit around a campfire as a group and Lottie sings us a beautiful folk song, sending a shiver down my spine.

She and I stop by a farm gate on our way back to the main house and look up at the sky. It is so incredibly clear that I can see the powder puff of the Milky Way. Constellations seem to glow five times as bright here, with no city light to rein them in. They rule over the sky, showing us the stories of cultures past. I hear the distant Scouse speech patterns of our friends and tribe going to bed and everything just feels right.

I sigh. 'I'm so glad we came here.'

I look over at my dear friend with tears in my eyes.

*

On the final day, we perform a water ritual as a group, letting things go into the sea that no longer serve us. When we reach the sea, I touch my hands to the gentle lap of the tide and let it pull out my nerves. I let the overthinking, the palpitations and the weird physical symptoms I get in times of stress go into the waves.

Contentment hums in the air. It's been a beautiful weekend and Chris wants to finish off our time together with one last journey. The sun has completely set now, leaving the farm in total darkness, and we are all lying on the kitchen floor on our yoga mats with blankets pulled up around our ears. There's a palpable excitement buzzing through the room. This is the last time that most of us will see each other for a while, but we have come to know each other's rhythms in this short space of time.

Chris says, 'With this journey, you can ask your guides anything you want – for any help or guidance you need.'

What guidance do I need right now? I am coming towards the end of my journey around the Wheel of the Year, but what will come next? I decide to look to the future with this shamanic journey.

Marie picks up the drum and everything fades away.

I meet Pelican at my axis mundi and we jump around, hugging one another. We are so close that I find myself licking the spaces between his feathers – preening him like he is my own child. My hair feels wild and free as we dance our way inside the cave. There is so much movement and happiness in us both.

I let Pelican know my intention for this journey. 'I wish to connect with the universe and let it guide me to what I should do next.'

In my mind, the quest feels so large and vague that I have no idea what will be in store for me this time.

We come through the cave and I know immediately that I am in the Upper World. The expansive mountains show me an Alpine world shrouded in white cloud that I have only been to a handful of times in my journeys. This space is more ethereal than the earthy Lower World and I get the sense that Pelican and I are hovering a few inches off the ground, floating in this heavenly realm. I tentatively step out behind Pelican as he guides me towards the largest mountain. We seem to walk forever in maybe five seconds, then we are in front of a large dark archway about the size of a five-storey building. Pelican seems to be waiting for something but I didn't come here for a tour of the architecture and wonder if we should be moving on. Just then the figure of a woman emerges from beneath the archway. She is dressed in something I vaguely recognise as traditional Chinese ritual wear; a long gown embroidered with pinks and silvers and a heavy sash sits around her waist. The woman's hair is intricately twisted around a tall headdress. I look at Pelican apprehensively. Is she here to talk to me? I have no knowledge of Chinese myth and legend so wonder what this could possibly have to do with me. I stay where I am, unsure as to whether to proceed. The woman walks forward through the Upper World mist and I see that she is smiling. Her clasped hands do not seem dangerous and I make my way over to meet her.

I try to make out her name but know this is hard among the ethereal matter of the Upper World, but the way she walks and the energy spiralling around her mark her as someone very important.

We follow her.

The three of us come to a circle of stone chairs surrounding a deep well filled with blue-purple liquid. In my body, I know that the depth of the well goes on forever and ever. I take a seat in one of the stone chairs, empty of any council meeting that might take place there. The woman scoops out a cup of the well's liquid and holds it to my lips to drink. She says it is the 'Pit of Ages' and will give me knowledge of the universe. This is the reason I am here so I drink hungrily, but as I do so . . . something is happening to my body.

I look down to find that my neck and ribcage have burnt away so that I am just a central spine hovering on my hips and legs. In place of where my lungs should be there is a whole swirling universe made up of colourful planets and glowing stardust. I stare down in amazement.

The woman says, 'You can be everywhere at once, on infinite planes. While you can't fully comprehend the universe's expanse, you must understand that you have the power to be everywhere.'

I think about this for a moment, wondering how that could ever be helpful. Why would I want to be in different places at one time? But perhaps she is trying to tell me something else. When I look up at the woman over the universe in my torso, she is smiling, motherly and nurturing.

My brain whirs with possibilities.

'Do I have some higher purpose in the Middle World?' I ask.

She nods, smiling still, and says, 'I'll show you.'

We stand together and my body is whole again. We walk to a slow-flowing river, maybe fifteen feet across, and get in. The woman holds me, floating me like my own life-support system. Pelican bobs close by to us and between the pair of them I feel completely safe, loved and cared for. The woman begins to rub flower petals onto my skin and braid my hair with small yellow flowers she picks from the river's edge. I feel like a goddess but as I look at the woman, I know she is the real Goddess here.

We continue to float down the gentle current until we reach a circular open pool. The Goddess drifts away from me slightly and, in my relaxed state, I let my limbs starfish out. In my vision I see myself from above, a pale figure in a red dress, stretched out over a pentagram sunken into the pool and shining silver below me. It glows around me. I am the pentagram, I am the five-pointed star.

The Goddess speaks softly in my ear. 'You need to show people the magnificence of the pentacle.'

I close my eyes and smile. I feel the energy of this place; the cool, dripping stone around me sprouting moss and mallow, the Goddess standing in the shallows and Pelican having the time of his life paddling in circles. I didn't think I could ever be this peaceful.

But there is an abrupt awakening. The Goddess takes a knife and slits open the insides of my arms all the way up to my armpits. We are on the river bank and the blood spurts out of me. Pelican is dancing in the blood, opening his mouth to catch the red mass, splashing his feet in it. I am wide-eyed with panic but trust that this is the Upper World's intention.

The blood flow stops and Pelican opens his mouth. The Goddess reaches inside Pelican's gaping beak and pulls out a pink-veined white orb. She presses the orb into my womb space and I feel the orb's light filling my body, pulsing electricity in white flashes reaching all through my veins and into my fingertips. I am filled with light and purpose.

Pelican curls into me, making me safe and calm. From far away in the Middle World I hear the drumbeat start to change. It is time to go back. I thank the Goddess and Pelican and begin to make my way back into the other realm, ready to embody my life's purpose.

There is silence across the room. The kitchen is still vibrating with the resonating sound of the drum's beat. Everything I've just seen is still with me under my eyelids and if I open my eyes it might dissolve into the normality of the kitchen's pots and pans, the everyday appliances of modern life. I don't want to lose all the beauty of the Upper World, the

Goddess in the river and the joy I felt at finding my purpose for being in this Middle World reality.

And, of course, I have to go back to that reality.

When I open my eyes, it's as if something has shifted inside the room. Everyone's face is serene like they've just travelled to heaven and back. As we scribble down our journeys in our notebooks furiously, the sound of the dripping kitchen tap seems like an alien noise. Maybe I'm still hovering between realities.

From speaking to the rest of the tribe later on, I know that many of us in that room experienced powerful journeys that evening, ones that will stay with us forever. Lottie is sitting bolt upright, her bright orange hair on end with the zapping electricity of the room and her eyes bright. A few people share their journeys with the group and it becomes so apparent that we have tapped into something ancient here today. As we write, I stay quiet, my eyes glazed with stories, cocooned in my blanket, a new version of myself.

*

Things feel different from this point on.

Sleep means putting aside wonder and slipping back into the body. It feels like such a trivial action when your head contains knowledge of other worlds.

In the morning, Lottie and I stay at the farm making friends with the pigs and some suspicious-looking geese until the last possible second before we wind ourselves into her little Nissan Micra. Our thoughts and shared experiences are so tied to this place, why would we want to leave?

When I arrive back in Manchester, the edges of the buildings seem blurred, dulled almost against the smog. Anglesey might be a million miles from here. I feel like Anglesey gave me a glimpse of a possible future, one where I was striding along the beach, fully embodying my true self. In this possible future that the Goddess said I was destined for, I am telling people about witchcraft, the 'magnificence of the pentacle'. I am writing in a room filled with the energy of past rituals and the residual touch of the Goddess herself. Now, back home, I realise there are still changes I need to make in my life. My heart dips as I see now how far there is to go on my journey with the magickal parts of the world; I am still very newly returned to witchcraft and have a lot to learn. But maybe my path is meandering like the course of the river in my shamanic vision, and I'll be floating over the water with flowers in my hair for many more months until I come into full bloom.

There is a new resolve in my stomach. The retreat has given me a beautiful gift, a direction and a driving force. Emboldened by the beauty of this weekend, I decide to take the next steps in my plan.

SAMHAIN

The Wheel turns, and here we are again once more.

There'll be no trick or treaters this year. Living in a flat which once came attached to expensive marketing brochures stating 'luxury accommodation close to the vibrant city centre', I am used to the fact that no tiny vampires or zombies will knock on my second-floor front door.

When we were little, Mum would decorate the hall for trick or treaters. You'd open the front door and be greeted by a cloud of cobwebs, cardboard cut-outs of witches and pumpkin bowls of Black Jacks and Fruit Salads. We'd always get excited and buy our Halloween chocolate early and scoff it all two weeks before, so we'd probably end up buying three batches of sweets. On the night itself, kids would come from all over the neighbourhood to sneak Mum's intricately decorated fairy cakes, all covered with ghosts and ghouls. Halloween was a big affair in our home, even before my witchy days began. Even the lovely old lady across the road knew it and saved all the best Halloween sweets for us. I liked the excitement in the air, the early fireworks and, most of all, the sugar rush.

But this year, things would be different.

Things have been different since the retreat. Going into the weekend, I had felt like the scared little girl I had been on the first day of high school. I came home a High Priestess, filled with new knowledge. I have stepped into my power. I welcome it and feel the pulse of it greet me every morning as I wake up and stretch my arms to the autumn sun.

How can I describe this power? I think I always felt a little lost; worried that if I took the wrong path I'd end up running frantically to find my way again for the rest of my life. For what feels like the first time in my life, I feel *sure*. Sure within my body and my mind. I have a path to follow. My confidence is growing. In light of my recent trip, I have bought a car – a car! Seventeen-year-old me would have her jaw on the floor. No more being reliant on other people to ferry me here and there, I can go where I want, when I want, and the feeling makes me hold my head high. Getting over this old phobia is so uplifting. It seems like a small step, but I feel like this wave of confidence is propelling me into a new phase of my life. The next turn of the Wheel.

This year I have decided to spend Samhain in Glastonbury, a place of ancient power and knowledge. It feels like the perfect way to celebrate this culmination of a year's hard spiritual work. But I won't be alone. If there's one thing I've learned this year, it's the importance of friendship and connection, and how finding your people can help you grow.

April and I have known each other for years, since we were both nattering intensely across the office printer and our fourth cup of coffee at the RSPB. To find a nature nerd as a companion is one thing, but for her to be a secret witch is a major plus. I can imagine that if we lived in the same town we'd be witching it up in the Peak District every weekend, but it's a fair trek between Manchester and Cambridge. I've always thought April is a stunner – one of those shiny lights in my life – with her dark hair showing her Maltese heritage and her infectious laugh leaving me bent double every time we chat.

As far as I'm aware, neither April nor I are big into the rave scene, so Glastonbury might seem like a bizarre choice for our annual get-together. But Glastonbury has the highest Pagan population outside London. This wonderful phenomenon isn't just down to the already existing witchcraft community there (although I would move there in a heartbeat – please adopt me, Glastonians), dozens of 'witchy' shops and the leaflets advertising shamanic soul retrieval and angel Reiki on every street corner. The area has a history of witch persecution[24] dating back to the Middle Ages, but hasn't every quaint and cosy English village hanged a couple of crones in its time? Roberta Gilchrist, professor of Archaeology at the University of Reading, has called Glastonbury a 'living sacred landscape',[25] so wrapped up is it with Arthurian legend, ancient myths and the thriving spiritual New Age community that inhabits it. Unlike the Stonehenges and static monuments of the world, Glastonbury is very much alive and blends old forms of spirituality with the new. It is a place where people have come on religious and spiritual pilgrimage for many hundreds of years, drawn to it as a source of power. But why would this be so?

Ley lines, the invisible lines of deep spiritual power that wrap around the Earth like elastic bands, are potent sources of energy. Glastonbury lies at the epicentre of two converging ley lines – the St Michael's and the St Margaret's line, the bringing together of the male and female. The St Michael's line is perhaps the country's most famous line, running through sites such as Avebury Stone Circle, St

Michael's Mount and, of course, Glastonbury Tor. But if ley lines leave you cold, the stories of King Arthur linked with this place might get you going.

Every day for months, April and I had been messaging each other saying, 'NEARLY TIME'.

This Halloween is calling me back. The past year has been a year-long fight with my instincts. I've battled with my mental health and struggled to find peace in a world so geared towards making us feel like failures. I have truly gripped on to the person I have wanted to be for so long. In the spaces that witchcraft affords, whether that's in my small circle with the Goddess's gaze upon me and her hand below me or out in the vast expanse of nature, I feel whole again. When I am filled with magick and the breath of wild places, I feel confident, bursting with joy. It is like the Goddess is giving me a taste of what life could be like if I rejected the modern day and lived in my truth. While I know that I can't just switch off my laptop and chuck it in the sea, I am ready to take the steps that will allow me to live in a space that I can fill with the things that bring me joy.

Witchcraft has brought me a wonderful group of people who share my understanding of the world around us, who look out for the small signs of change within nature and make sense of the world by sitting quietly and listening.

It's been a long time coming and I've taken so many twists and turns to get to this point, but I feel like I've reminded myself of who I am. If truth be told, I have found myself and I never want to let her go.

This Halloween is a fresh start, a rare occasion, one that I am about to grasp with both hands.

*

If Halloween were a person, I'd have written her a love letter and set up a boom box outside her window. I've fallen in love with this holiday and the things it has done for my soul. Halloween was the start of my journey last year, the time the seed of questioning was planted in my mind. Now, full circle from where my journey began, I'm ready to write her a sonnet and get all doe-eyed over her.

My obsession with Halloween, however, goes back a long way. For me, whenever I see a street of fallen leaves, I'm immediately taken back home to walking the short stretch of road to my grandparents' house after school. The golden leaves were swept up the sandstone walls lining the street, so that the road looked like a shining tunnel. When I was little I was told not to trudge through the leaves where they were densest for fear of standing in dog dirt, but I didn't pay any attention as I crunched, ankle-deep, into the colours. This would be just before Halloween when the November rains have yet to strike, and each leaf is crisp, buoyant; the wind picks up a flurry of them like a storm of fiery butterflies. Sometimes, a black cat would perch on the wall next to the primary school and I'd try to stroke her before any of the other kids saw, making sure I had the first share. At this time of year, cherub-faced hedgehogs peered out from posters reminding us to check our bonfires for slow, spiky balls and there was gingerbread in the shape of ghosts in the window of the local bakery.

Even the late-blooming trees have orange caps in late October, but most are a deep ochre. Puffball mushrooms hunker broodily in the park and fierce, orange stagshorn fungus sprouts from the sides of dark stumps. A shiver runs down my spine – oh, I love it!

Of course, this period brings back memories of dressing in stripy tights and black eyeliner; *Nightmare Before Christmas* quotes and horror films that my fifteen-year-old brain was not prepared for. Being a teenage witch automatically makes Halloween your favourite holiday and helps you get creative with the backcombing and hairspray.

This is the big one. Halloween, in my opinion, is even better than Christmas and, for many witches, it is the most important time of all. When I was a teenager (probably dressed in a long lace skirt and something with skulls on it), I riffled to the back pages of my teenage magazine to find 'spells' I could perform on the spookiest night of the year. I stayed up until midnight to look over my shoulder into a mirror so I could see my one true love. But as the years have gone by, I've seen both the light and the dark sides of this powerful Sabbat.

Halloween, or Samhain, is perhaps the most well-known Pagan holiday of them all. Every year, the whispers across witches' circles utter, 'The veil is thinning, do you feel it?' This thin boundary between worlds – this one and the next, or dividing our realm and that of the spiritual or divine – which is usually so clear cut. All around the world we see different cultures either celebrating and honouring their dead, or using charms to scare them away. Samhain was traditionally a Celtic festival and was seen as a time when it was easier to make divine prophecies about the year ahead. Without the distractions of technology, many spiritual people would be able to (and still can) feel the different quality of the ether on days like Samhain. Like the pull of the full moon, powerful festivals such as this one can have a profound mental and physical effect on the sensitive HSPs of the world.

Celts honoured their dead on this day, knowing that their passed loved ones could hear their voices across the airy boundary between the worlds. However, ghosts and ghouls were seen as a very real part of life and people would carve terrifying faces into turnips and light candles inside the hollowed gourd and put them outside their doors.

The ghostly shadows cast on the street could frighten away evil spirits, much the same as the tradition of hanging a mirror next to your doorway so evil spirits would be scared by their own reflection and leave the household alone. Celtic peoples may be shocked, or delighted, at our skilful carving of modern-day jack-o'-lanterns, who knows? However you view the dead, the supernatural abounds at this time.

Scaremongering traditions aside, Samhain is a time of great power, of harnessing the divine. Those who have worked with spirits, elementals and the powers of the earth, or who are naturally more intuitive and psychic, may feel things more intensely during the month of October. Have you been getting visions and prophetic dreams this month? Well, you're probably exercising your natural psychic abilities; we all have them, but most of us supress them in childhood or ignore them as we get older. Learning to embrace these gifts is what Halloween is all about.

But how does one actually feel the thinning of the veil? I have seen many instances of spectral behaviour in my life, but never so much as around the time of Halloween. That flickering in the corner of your vision, the candle that keeps snuffing out even though there's plenty of wax still left in the pot. I used to have a friend who, after the death of her grandmother, would see the lights and TV flickering. When asked whether it was her, the lights would snap off then on again. Although probably meant to be reassuring, this phantom Morse code didn't make it easy to drop off at night when I visited her house for sleepovers.

In Shamanism, some beliefs about the afterlife differ – within animism, when we die we return to the universe, the great tree of being. The ghosts (also called the unquiet dead) to be found still roaming the Earth are only the essences of very recently deceased people, existing in confusion about their deaths.

I'm still not 100 per cent sure what I believe about death, but I have seen a hell of a lot of ghosts in my time.

There are other ways you can tell the veil is thinning that don't involve a shiver down your spine. You may find that your mind is in overdrive with vivid images, complex storylines and 'messages' coming through. If you are finding this, make sure to keep a notebook by the bed so you can scribble down any wording from your dreams. Things might make a bit more sense in the light of day. Your psychic senses could also be off-the-charts and you might even get some telepathic abilities; be sure to freak out your best friend by telling her exactly what she's thinking. While all these veil-thinning 'symptoms' may have your browser history looking *pretty* weird right now, it is completely normal to be feeling these things.

For those of us who are more sensitive to the supernatural happenings of this world, we might always be in tune with the tingling sensation we get when we open the door to the attic. I was chatting recently with a friend who told me about the most terrifying experiences she'd had with the paranormal since she was a child. We laughed and chatted about all the weird shit we'd seen over the years – the white orbs floating on the landing, the shadowy outline in our bedroom doorway – like it was as normal as popping down to the shops for a bag of Maltesers.

I was thinking about this and my witchy online community; we talk about the unseen without batting an eyelid. With this in mind, I decided to ask a few 'normies' about their own experiences with the paranormal. Is it usual for preteens to be seeing the supernatural every other week?

Apparently, the answer is no.

*

This time of year always brings witches out into the open. We peek out from under our capes and go in search of one another. It's like a calling from beyond the veil.

There is something very different about practising magick and performing rituals with other witches opposed to just with your cat. I have been asked to join two covens in my life; these group experiences have ranged from calmly sitting in a brightly lit room on plastic village hall chairs and drumming together in rooms filled with incense to something very wild and different altogether.

I was asked to join a coven for their Samhain celebrations in the woods one year as a 'try out' session. Was I a good fit for the group? Was I willing to dance around and get my ankles dirty or was I going to shy away under the tree canopy? The answer, of course, was that I was very willing, but nothing prepared me for what was about to come.

It was after dark and I had managed to navigate the train and bus that got me there in my long black dress without arousing too much suspicion. It was Halloween after all.

When I met my host at the entrance to the wood, I don't think I was quite ready for what I was about to see. He was dressed in a costume made up of a long black robe topped off with a deer skull and antlers. I must have looked alarmed because he took it off while we walked to the clearing where the campfire was glowing. The High Priest was dressed as a depiction of the Horned God, but backlit from the nearby streetlamps he might have just stepped out of a horror film.

The clearing was filled with just ten of us and there was a palpable buzz of excitement in the air that verged on hunger. We were all in black, a sombre colour to honour our ancestors who had gone through the veil before us and, in the violent flicker of lanterns placed around us in a circle, we were lit orange and black like a Halloween window display.

I'm not going to lie, I was a little spooked. Being out so long after the sun had set, with the quiver of night-time animals quaking the crisp fallen leaves around us, my senses were on high alert. We were in a wood where anyone could find us and jump out from behind the trees. But the group had a strong energy; charged, potent and ready to raise some magick.

Alongside the coven's High Priest, the High Priestess was also wearing ceremonial garb; a long gown and a metal crown affixed with the triple moon, the symbol of the Goddess, which caught the firelight. We chatted for a while and set up our snacks, the campfire growing and making the underside of the branches glow, skin-like, in the blaze. I felt quiet suddenly, intimidated by the dark and the palpable feeling that these people meant business. We were ready to begin.

We stood in a circle and listened as the High Priestess began a low chant. Within this world of magick circles, carved symbols and breathy dances, everyone has a different way of conducting a ceremony. There is no right way to align yourself with the Earth; it understands every language and every form of praise. We stood and listened, replying in unison when there was a space for us to speak.

When she finished, we welcomed the Goddess into the circle to work with us on this Samhain night. Although this Goddess had a different name, it was still my Goddess and I still felt her presence in our circle.

Then, we raised some energy.

Walking in a circle, murmuring a low song, we moved clockwise around the fire. Our chant grew louder and our feet moved quicker under the black sky until we were a blur. Our breathing was hot and heavy against the cold air. We were ageless, pillars of energy, the blood gushing in our cheeks and, as we danced, I watched the fire colour our bare legs a ruddy, primal shade of red.

While I have sat and given the covens' offers a lot of thought, ultimately I said no. Joining a coven requires a lot of time and dedication to your fellow members – many covens meet on the esbats as well as the Sabbats and other occasions, keen to experience the intense bond that ritual work can bring – and, unfortunately, this isn't something I have been able to give while stuck in my routine of busyness for so long. However, practising magick with others is something that I believe everyone should experience every once in a while – the thrill of flushed faces and the combined energy flowing through the space is immeasurable – and I'm hoping that through my journey around the Wheel I can learn to find more time to dance with like-minded people in the woods.

*

April and I arrive in Glastonbury on a drizzly afternoon.

Glastonbury is bowed low under the weight of autumn clouds. The rain has been relentless for days; on the way down I navigate through sheets of spray from the passing lorries, unable to see the road for five seconds at a time. It is a baptism of fire for a new driver and I resist the urge to scrunch up my eyes as I fly through the tsunami of storm water.

Now that we're here in this quaint countryside town, I feel so far removed from the churning of tyres and the concrete. The place is strewn with relics from an older way of life. Sixteenth-century cottages line the streets and one pub looks like something straight out of Shakespeare's London. People in brightly coloured clothing duck in and out of the buildings, smiling and waving merrily to one another. I feel like we've just crashed the biggest hippie reunion in the world.

This is not somewhere I had ever imagined coming, never having been someone who likes a Jägerbomb and booming house music at 4.30 a.m. I had been close to this place a few times on the motorway, on the way to a Cornish beach or to visit Tintagel, the 'birthplace' of King Arthur. Glastonbury has even stronger ties with Arthurian legend but my parents perhaps shared my views on Jägermeister and decided to give it a miss.

Around us, people are hugging trees, clogging the entrances of shops with incense spilling from under their doors, and I pass people openly talking about their witchy Halloween celebrations. If I'd arrived twenty years ago I'd say I'd just stepped into Diagon Alley. I can't imagine there are many places like Glastonbury that exist in the world, but I think everywhere should be a little bit like it.

31 October

I had a picture of the day ahead in mind: do some 'Glastonbury things', hoard some crystals and stumble in on a secret coven meeting and immediately get absorbed into a mysterious meet-up.

When April and I finally decide to leave the house on Samhain morning, after two hours of back-to-back *Buffy* and toast as thick as *The Goblet of Fire*, we head for the Tor. It is pouring with rain, sticking our hair to our cheeks – everyone else is still wisely eating breakfast in a cosy café, but the foolhardy nature lovers that we are means we will brave the weather at all costs. We're both wearing macs, probably not the witchiest of gear, but I've snuck my *vesica piscis* necklace on underneath my jumper.

Brown signs for the Chalice Well catch our eye so we make a quick detour to lap up the holy well.

Nobody else is here as we enter the gates and find ourselves in a small circular garden. 'If this is it, I'll be so pissed off,' I mutter to April, out of earshot of the ticket booth.

The Chalice Well's red waters have been drawing pilgrims from across the world for thousands of years. The iron-rich waters had once been overseen by the Druids in this area and they are seen as sacred blood of the Earth. Drink them and be filled with the world's blessing.

As we walk around the gardens at a snail's pace, I notice it in the air. Stop.

What is that?

Everywhere we go feels like a force field. I feel like I'm pulling myself through frogspawn just following the carefully kept path. I look over at April and she looks like she's in a trance, bending down to examine the bright flowers that overhang the pools of water around us then standing back up slowly. Has time suddenly slowed down here? The power rolling off the ginormous yew trees in this space is ancient. It almost ripples before my eyes. So is the magick of 10,000 years' worth of sacred pilgrimage.

I turn a corner, past the torrent of red, iron-fuelled water coming over the stones, so reminiscent of feminine energy, and find myself struck dumb. The *vesica piscis* – it's everywhere! My hand flies to my throat. The two overlapped circles within a larger ring are on everything, the floor, the covering of the holy well, carved into the stones around us. This symbol of duality and connectedness – the power of both feminine and masculine in one – is raised up on an altar, decorated in Samhain colours and filled with the deep feelings of dedication and care. This is a symbol I've carried with me throughout my whole journey of the

Wheel of the Year and here it is, blazing in front of me surrounded by candles and flowers. Without a second thought, I break down in tears, knowing I was meant to come to this place. I was supposed to complete my journey here.

All I can do is flop down on the stones around the holy well, overwhelmed with the incredible command of this place.

I am surrounded by yew trees. These trees have long been thought to hold potent power; I remember going to see the Fortingall Yew – the oldest tree in Britain (and possibly Europe) – in Scotland a few years back and experiencing the power rolling off it. Feeling the life force of a non-human being can be unnerving. It is very different from just stepping into the much-needed shade of a tree; the radiating power coming from every branch, creating an orbit that pulls you in and weighs on your shoulders. It is both enticing and ominous. However, at the Chalice Well, the pressure of the old trees here is a huge protective force, like I am being given a hug from a giant.

I think of all the people who have experienced this here before me. Part of me, the sullen teenager with her arms crossed during prayers in Monday morning assembly, feels unsettled knowing that for many hundreds of years this place would have been visited by Christian pilgrims, those who feared or perhaps hated the 'old ways' and their Pagan ancestral practices. The place is rich in symbolism and Christians have said that the Chalice Well is the place where Joseph of Arimathea placed the chalice that held the drops of Christ's blood at the Crucifixion. In Philip Carr-Gomm and Richard Heygate's *The Book of English Magic*, the authors suggest that the Holy Grail was buried below Glastonbury Tor and the Chalice Well's waters sprung up from it. The Holy Grail was the object of King Arthur's quests, with the remains of King Arthur and Guinevere's 'grave' found in 1190 close by after the destruction of Glastonbury Abbey, with Glastonbury also said to be the final resting place of the Holy Grail.

Christianity abounds with masculine symbols in its rather successful attempt to erase the divine feminine, and it therefore feels strange that this holy well, so rich with feminine symbolism, has been a Christian stronghold for so long. However, in more recent years, this place has become frequented by witches and spiritual people wanting to get in touch with their heritage and listen to what the sacred flow of the water is trying to tell them; I feel like this place has been neutralised by the footfall of women, their lighter tread and their veined hands touching every portion of the earth here to give their thanks to the earth goddess.

April and I leave reluctantly.

Afterwards, we almost get blown off Glastonbury Tor, witnessing people arrive in the doorway of St Michael's Tower only to be swept right through to the other side. We trundle around the shops, brushing our fingers lightly over second-hand books and crystals ranging from the size of a fingernail to that of a rhino fetus. Goths, hippies and Wiccan High Priestesses walk the street with the general air of merriment like we're all off to a firework display. It's like the first chapter of Harry Potter where Voldemort disappears and all the wizards come out to play.

We work our way down the list of other 'Glastonbury things' we wanted to do, but my mind is still on this morning.

'What do you want to do now?' I ask.

'Ummm, back to the Chalice Well?'

We shouldn't have let our Glastonbury experience peak too soon.

We get in the much, much longer line back at the well and head straight to the *vesica piscis* pool in the main garden. The sun is shining across the wet cobblestones around the pool, making the whole place glow. At this time of day, there is no chance at all of getting close to the well itself. Long-haired men and women sit crossed-legged on the stone ledges around it, eyes closed, hands in the earth symbol over their yonis. Some have guitars. It's an odd mix of serene meditation and peacocking display. I feel completely blessed to have arrived so early this morning and spent time in this sacred place without the buzz of tourists and pilgrims.

We sit away from all of this and think about our new moon ritual that evening.

It's been a few months since I've done a new moon ritual, the pressures of my new job mounting and biting into my evenings, but after the shamanic retreat I have a new resolve.

I take a final glance into the red waters of the well and know what I will ask for this evening.

After a year of searching for answers and trying to find a way to live well in a society that doesn't prioritise our health and happiness, I am ready to embrace my new way of being and live my life in a way that brings me joy.

*

Oh, hi again, Cerridwen. How are you doing?

Yes, it's crone time again. Throw your hands in the air and say hello to your inner Morticia. Of course, I'm sad to see Rhiannon go and I'll miss summer with a fierceness that lasts all winter, but Cerridwen feels like *my* Goddess. She's the one that I relate to over any other form of deity.

Why? you might ask. My handful of early grey hairs have yet to spread their web over my head and I only make a small *oof* noise when I'm getting myself out of a chair.

However, I feel very 'Cerridwen' when I'm in a bath shadowed by candle flickers on a dark evening. I am Cerridwen when I walk alone in the woods. I embody her when I set my face sternly and tell someone exactly what I think. What I love about her is that she *doesn't care*.

Cerridwen thrives in the darker months and owns it. She is *done*. She doesn't care if you're in your Pikachu onesie at two in the afternoon. She doesn't care that you used the phrase 'as per my last email'. She doesn't care who lives and who dies. Cerridwen does her own thing and she is a celebrator of all things dark. I should know; I've felt her energy very closely.

I've mentioned before that Cerridwen isn't the cutesy Grandma archetype from Little Red Riding Hood. She is the witch from Hansel and Gretel – she is the hag with a sick sense of humour and she will let you bargain for your life if you have something better to offer her. Last year on Halloween, before my calming lavender-scented bath, I dug out my old Sisters of Mercy CDs and had a good old goth dance during my ritual. I danced so hard in my circle that I almost slipped into a trance. Through my half-closed eyes, I could see Cerridwen standing in the darkened corner of the room. Her stone-grey hair was under a cowl and she leaned heavily on a staff as she watched me with hunger.

'This is for you!' I muttered into the dark.

She didn't move. She's not one to give her approval easily.

The music sped up and so did my movements, my arms hovering around my body like dragonfly wings. At that point in my life things weren't going so well, and I was dancing as if to shock all the pain out of my system for good.

'This dance is for you,' I said. 'I am ready for change. I am your servant.'

The words left me before I knew what I was saying, but this grabbed

Cerridwen's attention. She nodded in her corner and I felt her energy all around me; stalking and prowling in a circle like she was a wolf of the ancient woods that might once have stood here. She was assessing me. Testing my mettle. Was I good enough to meet her standards?

I was to spend the next year serving the Goddess, practising witchcraft and not being scared to tell people about my beliefs.

In the space of a single year, all three forms of the Goddess have appeared to me. They have been fleeting visitors in my world, but they have looked at me with a steady gaze. We have drunk each other in in acknowledgement.

But tonight is Samhain once more, dedicated to Cerridwen and her powers of transformation and darkness. I embrace her tonight.

*

It's a cloudless night, showing the moon's absence and making the sky look like a lonely place to be.

Inside our warm and tidy Airbnb, with its view of the river, we're going to make some magick.

We light the tea lights we've packed in our rucksacks, opening all the windows wide so as not to invoke my old enemy: the smoke alarm. The cold air streams in, pricking goosebumps on our skin. The black sky is a dilated pupil watching over our work.

April and I are standing with our arms up to the sky in the middle of our circle. The energy ripples around us in a murmur, trying to pull our new moon wishes from our throats.

'You ready?' I ask her.

She grins. 'Let's do it.'

I begin. 'Hail to the guardians of the Watchtowers of the North, by the powers of Earth and stability. We invoke thee.'

My voice has a different timbre when I speak to the spirits and the Earth. It's like I come out of myself, out of my small mouth and human voice box, embodying something else entirely. One by one I invoke the elements, turning round in a circle to each of the compass points.

I stand bolt upright, my eyes half rolled back in my head as I feel each element enter the space. I'm listening intently to my voice bouncing off the walls back to me, I can scarcely believe this is my voice; this resounding sound with so much command. This voice that hardly used to speak up in a meeting, which wouldn't volunteer to 'go first' in class. Leading a circle brings out the best in me.

'Great Goddess, Cerridwen, I welcome you into our circle tonight. Fill us up with your knowledge and power on this new moon.' April joins me now to chorus, 'We invoke thee, we invoke thee, we invoke thee.'

A gust of wind suddenly hits my face through the open window and I grin. A crone-like grin with all my teeth.

I reach my head back, throat held high to the Goddess. Cerridwen, my secret love. Brigid and Rhiannon don't hold a candle to her wisdom. I can feel her energy in the room with us. She is in every dark corner, every flickering shadow of candlelight.

The ceremony is to be quite a simple one. April and I take turns in holding the athame's point into the air above us. We say the things we wish to invite into our lives.

'I am confident.'

'I am wealthy.'

'Opportunities have opened up for me.'

Then we press the athame into our chests, allowing the energy of the elements and the Goddess to flow through us. The statements we say are in the present tense like they are already happening to us right here and now. The athame's wooden handle feels safe and smooth in my fist. I think back to our day at the Chalice Well and the ripples of energy I felt there.

I inhale deeply, feeling two sets of eyes on my face. 'I have become who I am meant to be.'

In my mind's eye, Cerridwen smiles in her wily way as I let the energy flow through my chest.

*

I'm driving back north, back to my life. Back to my laptop and Excel spreadsheets. Back to food shops and cat litter trays. The road is the same, the flurry of lorry spray half-covers my little Mazda just as it did on my way down south. The perils of a UK autumn getaway. I'm still shaky on the road – the little newbie driver in her four-gear automatic – but somehow I am different.

Thanks, Cerridwen.

Back in Manchester, Linnet greets me with a sleepy 'purp' from her blankie on the arm of the sofa. She looks at me, then double takes. 'Surely you'd left me forever, Mother?' Will and I haul my stuff upstairs, my bags now five times heavier with hefty new crystals. My study window is filled with plants, candles and the witchy relics I've collected over fifteen years in the business, hiding the northern downpour beyond. It rained in Glastonbury, but Manchester must be one of the rainiest cities in the world. The Seattle of England's North West. The next few days of November bring storms, meaning intense hygge, boxset marathons and trying but failing to scoop Linnet onto my lap. Right now, it would be easy to get swept downhill with the autumn leaves clogging up the drains and slip into post-Glastonbury blues. The weather could ruffle up those darker feelings I so associate with winter, but this time things won't be the same as they have been these past few years.

I am breaking the cycle.

I remind myself that the world is renewing itself, rotting the fallen leaves down into the fertile mulch we need for the coming spring.

The tree roots must shrink down and preserve their energy; a well-deserved rest after the beautiful displays they've given us all year around.

Small animals are slow, heavy balls of sleep right now, completely unfindable in their frozen hidey-holes. Winter is coming; the great time of settling down.

All that is green and filled with life will return once more. There is no need for winter to be a time of sadness.

In the weeks that follow, the adjustments that I've been making all year, the meditation, the rituals, the conscious effort to get out into nature and nurture the new friendships I've made in the worlds of witchcraft and Shamanism, all fall into place for me. These things have become so much a part of my life that I only need pick up the phone and I can speak to some wonderful person about the upcoming solstice, about the prickly feeling I had in a certain room, like I was being watched by a spirit, or the properties of carnelian. I really have found my people.

I've found myself too. My power is strong. That shy little street urchin of last year would rub her eyes in disbelief at who I am today – and let her! I've come a long way. I have power running in my veins these days. Not only do I feel mentally stronger, I feel like I've been guided to grow and help other people to heal.

The Earth spins on its axis; a slow, lifelong pirouette of learning.

Maybe I'm not exactly where I need to be just yet, but I'm learning every day and I'm close to the top of the mountain. My path this year has taken me through many hallways, and I am now ready to step out of the door and tell the world, 'I'm here.'

The coming Yule will draw us back into the circular dance. We will spin and twirl again and again through the snow, the April showers, the summer sunshine and the gusts of autumn leaves.

The Wheel turns and our old selves burn away. We are constantly renewed by the cycles of life and as we move around the circle, our inner magick will be set loose – it is long overdue.

AFTERWORD

Things are moving on as they always do, with the momentum of a dandelion seed caught in the wind.

A few months later, I am still embracing change. The promise of spring shifts the fleece of winter to reveal a glissando of willow warbler song and an army of straight-backed purple crocuses. Will, Linnet and I sit in our new house close to the countryside, watching the world away from the city sirens. In my pantry, I am storing seeds I collected from our allotment last year and we are ready to start work on the raised beds, making sure we have a herb garden in place for when the world renews itself.

When I open the window, I hear no sound at all. All is peaceful here.

I have had a year of relearning how to be in the wild places of Britain and how to feel the subtle sensations carried on the air – both the magickal and the natural. It's taken some time but I know now which furrow I should be following. My dark days come and go, sometimes unexpectedly. But this time, unlike 'the before times', it is different; there is hope. Things never feel hopeless when you have a quiver of tools at your disposal that you have worked hard to gather; I have all that teenage knowledge from reading about herbs I had never even seen before, the meditations that took me to other worlds, meeting fellow witches who would shape my practice and guide me to the person I am today. I have restored my age-old intuition. Shamanism, witchcraft and my appreciation of all things green and growing have brought me closer to my authentic self. I have surrounded myself with knowledge and I remind myself of it every day with small and magickal things – the *vesica piscis* around my neck, the bundle of sage drying above my kitchen window and the moon rising and falling over my new and surprising garden.

I am building the life I want to create for myself and my little family of three. Very soon, I plan to keep Linnet in Dreamies with writing and Reiki, putting the nine-to-five life to rest forever. I can feel it. I sometimes think back to my Upper World journey with the light blooming out from underneath my dress in the river. It feels like the moment when everything clicked into place – when the Wheel of the Year stopped turning for a few seconds to say, 'Look, this is it! This will change everything.'

When Beltane comes around, I intend to lie in our garden in the shade of the apple tree and watch the blossom focusing and unfocusing the clouds above me. Perhaps Linnet will join me, perhaps she'll be snuffling around the hedges, finding new hidey-holes and eating leaves that turn her white bib lurid green. I would gladly lie here feeling the alternate patterns of May heat and breeze on my skin, letting the chill of a sudden wind make the fine hairs on my forearms shiver like pale grass.

Brigid is welcome in my garden, she is welcome in my home. I will throw open the doors and windows to her. I will let her eager white light in, dancing and fragile as blossom. But for now, I can only watch the winter rain patter on my flowerbeds and wait. The snow sometimes falls and creates a soft cover for the world, telling it to sleep on for just a few more days. Cerridwen commands the nearby trees and tells them to stay naked until the Wheel turns once more.

Always turning, always forging on. Nature won't let us sit still for a minute.

Winter, which was once my least favourite season, now feels like a gateway to even deeper learning – a time I could (possibly, maybe) even grow to love.

I think of all those times I have resisted change in my life, letting the anxiety take over. The strange physical symptoms I felt, pointing to adrenal fatigue, anxiety and burn-out, sometimes rear their heads these days but very rarely. This last year was not about completely healing myself – although I have taken the steps to do so – it was about finding answers to the questions that kept arising for me.

And, what have I learned from this year?

From my conversations with friends and fellow witches, I find it so much easier to understand how we need to live if we are going to thrive as a society whose leaders do not prioritise our wellbeing and the wonders of nature. I know now that to live with our ears to the ground would make this a very different planet Earth. Still, we live in a world that is not shaped by nature and the deeply feminine practices of nurture and care; ours is a hierarchical one that perpetuates the myth of human supremacy. Nature is subordinate in the eyes of our governments because it uses zero currency. Witches, wildlife lovers and those who appreciate nature as much more than just a pretty view continue to understand the need for connection to the wild and pour their energy into it. This gives me so much hope for our future.

I have a lot of optimism about this world. Witches are leading their own quiet revolution; respiritualising themselves and rewilding their gardens. New environmental wins happen every day. Over the past year, we have seen a flurry of reports from influential government advisors stating the importance of returning to nature and what it will mean for our economy and the lives of future generations. These reports in isolation are unlikely to achieve major change but they have received major backing from the press and key environmental charities. At the time of writing this, there are still no legal en masse protections for the environment in the UK, but I have faith that as people use their voices to become louder and big businesses begin to shift towards net zero, our ways will slowly change.

Who knows, maybe we have the power to inject a little magick back into the world.

I hope that reading this has stirred your inner cauldron, ignited your balefire or maybe you were already taking steps to connect with the elements and the magickal world. The witchcraft community may look spooky with our long dark hair and bare muddy feet but we don't bite; we just know a few curses.

We are all bound to the fabric of this world. Every single one of us. So reach out with both hands to the mossy Earth, magickal person, and grasp it.

REFERENCES

1   Multitasking in the workplace can lead to negative emotions,
     University of Houston, 11 May 2020, www.sciencedaily.com.

2   The 2020 UK Workplace Stress Survey, www.perkbox.com.

3   The problem isn't remote working – it's clinging to office-
     based practices, Alexia Cambon, 21 June 2021, www.
     theguardian.com.

4   Urbanisation worldwide, Knowledge For Policy, European
     Commission.

5   Yes, witches are real. I know because I am one, Pam Grossman,
     30 May 2019, www.time.com.

6   Monsters, men and magic: why feminists turned to witchcraft
     to oppose Trump, Sady Doyle, 7 August 2019, www.
     theguardian.com.

7   Cerridwen, dark goddess of transformation, inspiration
     and knowledge, Judith Shaw, 30 October 2014, www.
     feminismandreligion.com.

8   *History of Lancashire*, Thomas Baines, 1867.

9   'Out in the Dark', Edward Thomas (1878–1917).

10   Construction nears on major A303 upgrade in Somerset, Highways England, 20 July 2021, www.gov.uk.

11   Liverpool loses World Heritage status as Stonehenge decision looms, Benjamin Paessler, 22 July 2021, www.salisburyjournal. co.uk.

12   Nature-based solutions to the climate emergency, The IGNITION project, 27 August 2020, www.ukgbc.org.

13   Green stimulus plan could create 1.2m UK jobs in two years, research finds, Tommy Greeve, 20 April 2021, www. theguardian.com.

14   Green social prescribing funding boost for Greater Manchester Mental Health? 1 February 2021, www.gmhsc.org.

15   *Earth Rites: Fertility Practices in Pre-industrial Britain*, Janet and Colin Bord, 1982.

16   'Clock-O'-Clay', John Clare (1793–1864).

17   Halloween clothing & costumes survey, 2019, fairylandtrust. org.

18   Evidence that the lunar cycle influences human sleep, *Current Biology*, volume 25, issue 15, 5 August 2013, www.cell.com.

19   Cynhaeaf: customs, practices and folklore associated with the traditional harvest in Wales, Alan Robert Phillips, 2016, repository.uctsd.ac.uk.

20   How blue light affects mental health, Christine Dearmont, mhanational.org.

21   Actual name disputed.

22   The Re-Enchantment Issue, September 2020, *Cunning Folk*.

23   Take on nature: I meditate upon a swallow's flight, Stephen Colton, 23 April 2016, www.irishnews.com.

REFERENCES

24   Dark Somerset: the witches of Somerset, Laura Lineham, 6
       December 2018, www.somersetlive.co.uk.

25   What makes Glastonbury to mystical? Simon Ingram, 27 June
       2019, www.nationalgeographic.co.uk.

FURTHER READING

Books

Some books that have helped me along my path through the years:

Hedge Witch: A Guide to Solitary Witchcraft by Rae Beth

Treadwell's Book of Plant Magic by Christina Oakley Harrington

Pagan Paths: A Guide to Wicca, Druidry, Asatru, Shamanism and Other Pagan Practices by Peter Jennings

Grimoire of the Green Witch by Ann Moura

The Great Cosmic Mother: Rediscovering the Religion of the Earth by Monica Sjöö and Barbara Mor

Natural Magic by Doreen Valiente

The Rebirth of Witchcraft by Doreen Valiente

The Magical Year: Seasonal Celebrations to Honour Nature's Ever-turning Wheel by Danu Forest

Walking With Trees by Glennie Kindred

Instagram

For more information about witchcraft and spiritual practices, you can follow us on Instagram:

FURTHER READING

Jennifer Lane – @thegreenwitchwriter

Florence Devereux, Astrologer – @astrologyforthecurious

Sarah at NU.U Therapy – @nuutherapy

Ambrosia Hawthorne – @wildgoddessmagick

Witchology Magazine – @witchologymag

For more information about shamanic healing, speak to Christine Holt, shamanic practitioner, at https://therapeuticshamanichealing.co.uk/

To find out more about Treadwell's Bookshop and online events visit https://www.treadwells-london.com/

ACKNOWLEDGEMENTS

There are so many of you that need a shout out here – I'm so lucky to know all you beautiful people:

Thank you to my mum and dad, who took me on all those long car journeys to stone circles and up to Pendle so I could gaze longingly at witchy things. Sorry about all the incense. To Jocelyn Raine, Laurie Cookson, Caroline Lane, Adam Hamer and Charlotte Varela for all the nature walks and for listening to me talk about birds literally ALL the time.

To the beloved witchy and writerly women in my life: Em Jones, April McIntyre, Lottie Blake and Nicola Semple, who keep my life magickal and read these pages before anyone else. And to the fabulous Scouse Tribe – especially Annie, Karen and Chris – who make the world a spellbinding place. I want to say, this book was edited during the lockdowns of 2020 and 2021, as I continued to deepen my practice. I was able to spend more time in nature, of course, but it wasn't always easy to meet with witchcraft and shamanic practitioners and it can be difficult to feel the magickal bonds of the witchcraft community from afar. I believe I would have been able to take part in more group

ACKNOWLEDGEMENTS

rituals and events and woven them in had this book been written at a different time. However, these wonderful women helped me to keep my witchcraft and writing momentum going. Always there to offer support in the form of Zoom drinks and tarot sessions, they were part of the spell that continued to keep my anxiety at bay.

To my incredible agent Charlotte Atyeo for her continued support throughout this process and for always knowing this was going to be magickal. Thank you to Hannah and Charlotte at September Publishing for giving me the amazing opportunity to write about my passion.

To Jim Martin at Bloomsbury Wildlife for starting me off on this journey.

A huge thank you to Ambrosia, Sarah and Flo for talking to me about their beliefs and processes – I find you all incredibly inspiring.

To Asad Hussain, who swooped in to save my skin when my manuscript file corrupted six days before my submission date. You are a technical wizard. Enjoy the whisky!

A special acknowledgement to Treadwell's for keeping me sane when I was lost in the city and to all the wonderful spiritual teachers of Greater Manchester who kept me focused on my path. I also want to give a special thank you to my grandma, who chatted to me every day during lockdown rain or shine and kept believing in me. You are one in a million.

And to Will, the most supportive person I know. You never complain about all the crystals on the windowsill or the rosemary in the bath. Thank you from the bottom of my heart.

(Oh, and thanks to Linnet too.)